Ernest Foster

Heroes of the Indian Empire; or, Storie of Valour and Victory

Ernest Foster

Heroes of the Indian Empire; or, Storie of Valour and Victory

ISBN/EAN: 9783337166847

Printed in Europe, USA, Canada, Australia, Japan

Cover: Foto ©ninafisch / pixelio.de

More available books at **www.hansebooks.com**

HEROES OF THE INDIAN EMPIRE;

OR, STORIES OF VALOUR AND VICTORY.

"THE LITTLE HOSTAGES WERE RECEIVED WITH MUCH DISTINCTION" (p. 81).

HEROES OF THE INDIAN EMPIRE;

OR, STORIES OF VALOUR AND VICTORY.

BY

ERNEST FOSTER,

Author of "Abraham Lincoln;" "Men of Note: their Boyhood and Schooldays," &c.

"—— OUR FORTUNE KEEPS AN UPWARD COURSE,
AND WE ARE GRACED WITH WREATHS OF VICTORY."
King Henry VI., Part III., Act 5, Scene iii.

CASSELL & COMPANY, LIMITED:
LONDON, PARIS, NEW YORK & MELBOURNE.
1886.

PREFACE.

IN the following pages—intended, primarily, for young people—my object has been to sketch the careers of the leading Warriors and Statesmen by whose genius and heroism British rule was established in India; to describe the labours of zealous Missionary-pioneers in that land; and, finally, to tell of some of the men who, when the existence of the Empire was imperilled by the great Sepoy Mutiny, defended it with such valour and success.

No attempt has been made to give full biographies, but I have aimed rather to narrate a series of Stories which, while presenting a view of events in India from the time of Clive downwards, shall, particularly, picture the Heroes themselves and their more striking achievements.

Besides the authorities mentioned in the text, I desire to express indebtedness for historical information to the " History of India," by Mr. Marshman—whose spelling of Indian names I have in the main adopted — and to Mr. Sewell's " Analytical History of India."

E. F.

CONTENTS.

Warriors and Statesmen.

		PAGE
I.	Lord Clive	9
II.	Warren Hastings	42
III.	Lord Cornwallis	69
IV.	Lord Wellesley	84
V.	Eldred Pottinger and Sir Alexander Burnes	100
VI.	Sir Charles Napier	126

Soldiers of the Cross.

I.	William Carey	152
II.	Henry Martyn	169
III.	Alexander Duff	185

Men of the Mutiny.

I.	The Lawrences	202
II.	Sir Henry Havelock and Sir James Outram	223
III.	Colin Campbell, Lord Clyde	242

After the Mutiny 253

LIST OF ILLUSTRATIONS.

　　　　　　　　　　　　　　　　　　　　　　　　PAGE

"The Little Hostages were Received with much Distinction" . . . . } *Frontispiece.*

"Hyder Ali Fled from the Field" 66

"He Seized the Vizier . . . and Dragged him forward to the Breach" 109

"They took the Children up in their Arms" . . 240

HEROES OF THE INDIAN EMPIRE;

OR, STORIES OF VALOUR AND VICTORY.

Warriors and Statesmen.

I.—LORD CLIVE.

"Bob Clive's up the steeple!"

Such was the news that one day, about 150 years ago, passed round Market Drayton.

To say that the good people of the little Shropshire town were surprised would scarcely be true, but that many of them were alarmed was evident from the haste with which they ran to the parish church, to see if what they had been told had really taken place. And sure enough it had; for there, seated astride a stone spout near the summit of the lofty spire, was the small boy whom all the townspeople too well knew as the ringleader in every kind of mischief, and the hero of a hundred escapades.

For what purpose he had scaled the steeple is unknown, though some say that it was to get a certain smooth stone which had lodged there. But whatever the object, there he was, and so far from realising that his position was perilous, or that he was causing anxiety to those assembled below, he showed by his manner that he was quite unconcerned, and, swinging his legs backward and forward, not only refused to make any attempt to descend for some time, but thoroughly enjoyed the situation.

In this exploit we have a typical instance of the adventurous doings of Robert Clive as a lad; and we gain from it an insight into the wayward and reckless disposition which, as will be seen, distinguished the whole of his early life. The eldest of a numerous family, and born on the 29th of September, 1725, in the mansion of a small estate called Styche, a few miles from Market Drayton (where his father practised as an attorney), Robert, during his boyhood, gave little promise of future fame. Mischievous and careless, neglectful of books and study, possessing a fierce temper, he was, indeed, noted only for a wild and quarrelsome disposition.

For certain family reasons, he had, when three years old, been sent away from home to a place called Hope Hall, near Manchester, and put under the charge of a Mr. Bayley, who had married Robert's aunt, and while of a very early age he had given signs of being wilful and passionate, most unusual in one so young. His guardian, indeed, seems to have been somewhat alarmed at the child's conduct; and it is not surprising to find that before long he gave up his charge in despair, and sent him back to his parents.

Next we find him placed at different schools—

at Lostock in Cheshire, at Market Drayton, at the Merchant Taylors' in London, and finally at Hemel Hempstead, in Hertfordshire; but in none did he make progress in study, though in all he appears to have gained the reputation of being an idle, mischievous, and self-willed lad. It was while he was attending the school at Market Drayton that the steeple adventure already referred to occurred; and at about the same period he was engaged in many other daring doings. It is related, for instance, that a favourite amusement was to form as many of the idle boys of the town as he could muster into a kind of brigade. Placing himself at their head as leader, he would then march the little army to various shops, and exact pennies, or apples, or whatever commodity might be convenient, in consideration of which he would promise not to break the windows!

On one occasion, when he met with a point-blank refusal in response to his threats, he and his band set to work to turn a dirty water-course, running near the street, into the shop of the offending tradesman; and they had nearly effected their purpose, when one of the mounds of turf used by them in banking up the water, gave way. But "Bob" was equal to the occasion. Throwing himself down on his chest, he placed his body in the gap through which the water was beginning to pour, and there he remained until the damage had been repaired by his companions.

So passed the early days of Robert Clive; and, as year by year rolled by, not only was the boy a source of annoyance to those on whom he played his pranks, but he was the cause of disappointment and anxiety to his parents and his schoolmasters. Of all his teachers, it is said that one only—Dr. Easton of Lostock—was able to detect, beneath his wild and intractable nature, signs of those qualities which, later on, he was to exhibit so prominently; and the good doctor was wont to prophesy that if fitting opportunity were afforded for their display, it would be found that he possessed talents which "would win for him a name second to few in history."

On what ground this opinion was based cannot be stated, but it was certainly a solitary one, so much so, that by the time the lad was seventeen (when he left school), his parents had begun to lose hope of his being fitted to follow any occupation in which real capacity was needed. It had always been their intention that he, as the eldest son, should study the law with the view of eventually joining his father in the latter's practice at Market Drayton, but—apart from the fact that the boy himself was strongly averse from following such a pursuit—they had abandoned this design, feeling that to make a lawyer of so unpromising a lad would be out of the question. But that Robert could be allowed to remain at home in idleness was, of course, impossible, and it was most necessary, therefore, that steps should be taken to decide as to his future.

And the result was that—wisely recognising what it would have been useless to ignore, that such a nature as Robert's would probably never permit him to settle down to a quiet occupation—they determined that opportunity of a life of adventure should be given to him. So when he was nearly eighteen years old, they procured an appointment for him as a "writer," or clerk, in the service of the East India Company.

At this stage it may be of interest, and it will throw light on some of the valiant and victorious deeds of which the story is to be told in these pages, if we look back for a moment and see how this great Company came into existence, and what its condition was at the time when Robert Clive enrolled himself under its banner.

It was about 250 years previously—in 1498—when the great Portuguese explorer, Vasco da Gama, had succeeded in sailing round the Cape of Good Hope, that direct trading voyages between European countries and India were commenced. Up to that time the commerce of the East had been mainly in the hands of Venetian and Egyptian merchants, who conveyed the bulk of their goods to Europe by way of the Red Sea. Having made the discovery of a direct ocean passage, however, the Portuguese quickly recognised its importance, and the result was that, ere many years had gone by, their merchants had established "factories"—which were store-houses, and not places of manufacture—had secured the most valuable part of the trade with India, and protected by their powerful navy, monopolised it for nearly 100 years.

Towards the end of the sixteenth century, however, other countries, regarding with envy the wealth and influence which the Portuguese had acquired, determined to compete with them. So we find English, Dutch, and French vessels making voyages to the Indian coasts, and, as a consequence, the Portuguese were before long compelled to surrender their monopoly.

Many a story had by this time reached England of the wealth of the vast Empire of India, of the magnificence of its cities, and of the gorgeous splendour by which its ruler, the powerful Mogul Emperor, was surrounded in his Court at Delhi—then one of the largest and handsomest capitals in the world; travellers had also brought home reports that the natives were as willing to trade with the English as with the Portuguese. It is, therefore, not surprising that a resolution was come to, that no longer should the latter nation be permitted to remain in undisputed possession of the privileges they had secured. Thus it was that, after two ill-fated expeditions, which never succeeded in reaching India, the merchants of London assembled on the 22nd of September, 1599, and formed themselves into an association for trading to the East; and in the following year Queen Elizabeth granted to them a charter, under the title of the "East India Company," which conferred the exclusive right to trade with all the countries between the Cape of Good Hope and the Strait of Magellan.

Early in 1601 five armed vessels having been fitted out and laden with goods and money, were despatched to the East, and with this humble expedition commenced the work of the association of merchants, which was destined to become the great military and commercial power that mastered the Empire of India.

It was soon plain that no little opposition would be made to the enterprise in which the English had embarked; for by this time, in addition to the Portuguese, the Dutch were also endeavouring to open up trade; and both nations having succeeded in establishing forts and factories along the Indian coast, took steps to bar the way of interlopers, by equipping fleets to attack their vessels. The consequence was that on some of the English shipping being destroyed in this way by the Dutch and Portuguese, the East India Company caused larger and better-armed vessels to be sent into the Indian Ocean; and when, in 1612, their squadron was challenged by a vastly superior one, off Surat, the commander inflicted on the Portuguese such a decisive defeat, that not only were the English able to land their goods, but the Mogul Emperor Jehangeer, then ruler of the greater part of India, was so favourably impressed with their victory, that he granted them permission to establish factories at Surat, and certain other towns; and there they founded their earliest settlements. Next we find James I. being prevailed upon by the East India Company to despatch a special ambassador, Sir Thomas Roe, to the Court of Delhi, with the gratifying result that still further privileges were obtained by him for the Company.

Then, before very long, occurred one of those little incidents out of which important events so often spring. Dr. Boughton, an English physician attached to the Company's factory at Surat, was visiting the city of Agra, where the Emperor Shah Jehan chanced to be staying; and the favourite daughter of the latter being taken seriously ill, Dr. Boughton was summoned. By his skilful treatment a cure was effected, and such high favour did he then enjoy with the grateful ruler, that he was requested to name his own reward.

"Let my nation trade with yours," was his reply; and the permission, which included leave to establish factories in Bengal, was granted to him. This right he sold to the East India Company, who established a factory at Hooghly; and about twenty-five miles from this spot, some fifty years later (in 1686), was founded the settlement which in course of time became the splendid city of Calcutta, the capital of British India.

Another forward stride was made by the English in 1639, when they obtained leave to settle in a different part of the Empire; and now it was that they erected the factory and fort called Fort St. George, after the patron saint of England, around which grew up the important town of Madras. Rather over twenty years later, when Charles II. married the daughter of the King of Portugal, the fine port of Bombay was given to him as part of the princess's dowry; and not long afterwards it was ceded by his Majesty to the East India Company.

Having thus secured firm foothold in different parts of India, the English rapidly became both powerful and prosperous; but they were by no means satisfied with their progress, and were much irritated by reason of their trading operations being interrupted by the fierce wars then being waged against each other by some of the native princes. They were, however, shrewd enough to understand that though these quarrels did interfere with commerce, yet they could hardly fail to have another effect, which was to gradually weaken the power of the Empire itself; and it was on this prospect that their future hopes centred. India's weakness, arising out of her own internal dissensions was, in fact, to be the Company's opportunity. And so it came about that their former ambition—to be merely a successful band of merchants—began to shape itself anew; and King Charles having already granted to them the important privilege of making peace or war on their own account, there arose before them the vision not only of monopolising all the trade of India, but—grander, and more far-reaching—of even conquering portions of the mighty Empire, through which they were fast scattering themselves.

So, passing on, we find the Company—now designated "The United Company of Merchants of England Trading to the East Indies," from their having joined hands with a rival association started in London—slowly but surely establishing both factories and forts in different parts of India; forming an army, navy, and police; securing from the English Crown supreme control over the persons of all their countrymen in the Empire; in a word, building up an organisation of vast extent and of almost unlimited power.

No easy task was it to accomplish this, for every forward step found them face to face with opposition, and often temporary defeat; but with dogged perseverance they never faltered in their purpose; and as they pressed onwards, as their grip on India grew year by year firmer, so they saw the hold of its sovereign ruler become weaker and weaker through the dismemberment of the Empire, which its internal wars were bringing about. And when, in 1739, the crash came—when Nadir Shah, taking advantage of the Empire's troubles, marched his army from

Persia to Delhi, annihilated the Emperor's troops, fired and sacked his magnificent capital—the East India Company knew that the days of the Mogul rule were numbered; and foreseeing, as they did, that greater disorder than ever was now likely to arise out of the struggles among the native princes, they felt that the time was approaching when they would find fit opportunity for carrying out their daring schemes.

Let us return to the story of Robert Clive, and we shall see how some of their ambitions were realised; how by his genius their arms were carried from victory to victory; and how, from amidst the wreck of empire, even the sceptre of the Great Moguls passed into the hands of the English.

On leaving England, the destination of Robert Clive was Madras, now become the most important of the Company's settlements; and at first, probably through change of scene suiting his restless temperament, it seemed as if he might settle down to his new life. But it was not for long, and his position, for some time after his arrival, proved anything but agreeable to him. It seems, indeed, to have been most distasteful, for he found his office duties uncongenial, his pay was so small that he ran into debt, while the place at which he lodged was uncomfortable, and the gentleman to whom his letters of introduction were addressed had left India before he landed. We can scarcely wonder, therefore, that he felt unhappy and dissatisfied in the strange land to which he had come, and that the same dislike to regular occupation which he had exhibited at school should show itself now. In spite of his waywardness, he seems, however, to have had great affection for those whom he had left at home—for his mother, especially, he had ever the most tender affection—and in one of his earliest letters he thus expresses himself:—" I have not enjoyed one happy day since I left my native country. . . . I must confess, at intervals when I think of my dear native England, it affects me in a very remarkable manner. . . . If I should be so far blest as to revisit my own country . . . all I could hope or desire would be presented before me in one view."

Chafing under what he looked upon as the hardships of his new career, the old impatience of control which we have seen in his earlier days was now equally marked. One day, when he had allowed himself to be irritated by some duty which he was called upon to perform, he so grossly insulted one of his superior officers that he was commanded by the Governor of the settlement to apologise. Forced to obey, he did so, though most reluctantly; but he did not forget the humiliation, as he deemed it, for when, desirous to remove all recollection of the unpleasantness, the injured official a few days afterwards invited young Clive to dinner, he received from him a most decided refusal.

"No, sir," was the scornful answer; "the Governor desired me to apologise, and I have done so; but he did not command me to dine with you!"

On two occasions at this period Robert Clive tried to take his life, but each time the pistol which the rash youth put to his head failed to go off; and it is said that on the second attempt, after finding that the weapon was properly loaded, he received the impression that Providence had prevented the mad act from being accomplished, and that he was destined for some important career in life.

Amid this unpromising behaviour, it is a little surprising to discover that he should have begun to find solace in study. The Governor of Madras possessed a good library; and Clive, having permission to use it, devoted much of his leisure to hard reading, and thus acquired considerable knowledge of books—almost all he ever possessed—as well as of the native languages of India.

After the lapse of some two years spent in this way, an event happened which opened up the path that led Robert Clive to fame. For many years previously the French had been trying hard to establish themselves in India; and their efforts had been so far attended with success, that *their* East India Company, by which an important settlement had been established at Pondicherry, was now regarded by the English as a formidable rival. Both nationalities had, however, hitherto lived on peaceful terms, quite content that their energies should be confined to the extension of trade. But in 1746 the policy of the two companies underwent a great change; for each having now become jealous of the other's increasing influence and prosperity, was determined to be supreme in India; and the fact that England was fighting with France in Europe formed an excellent pretext for entering upon the struggle. Accordingly, the war spread from Europe to India, and soon the English and French fleets—the former sent out to protect the Company's settlements, the latter to attack them—met in the Indian Ocean. The English squadron was not half so strong as the French one, but it was better manned, and in the hands of a capable commander it would probably have succeeded in driving off the enemy. As it was, however, before the action between the two fleets was decided, the English admiral, on the plea that one of his ships needed repairs, suddenly sailed away, and the French commander, Labourdonnais, being thus left free, hurried to Madras, and called upon the town and fort of St. George to surrender.

Then it was that Robert Clive for the first time experienced actual warfare. Though Madras was the most important of the English settlements, it was not a large place, and the defence it could offer was very weak. The garrison did not number more than 200 in all, for the Company had not as yet enlisted many sepoys (as the native soldiers were called) into their service; and when, therefore, on the Governor parleying with him, it was found that Labourdonnais, whose force numbered eleven ships manned by 3,700 men, had commenced to attack the place, it was deemed prudent to capitulate in order to spare it the horrors of bombardment. So the inhabitants, with the garrison, became prisoners of war, though they were subsequently granted liberty on giving their word of honour not to attempt to escape, and Labourdonnais promised that Madras should be restored to the Company on payment of a fixed ransom.

But a difficulty arose. Dupleix, the Governor of the French East India Company, and head of the settlement at Pondicherry, had, as already intimated, resolved that the English should be overthrown in India; so, on the plea that so long as they were in possession of Madras, Pondicherry could not be expected to flourish, he refused to acknowledge the right of Labourdonnais to make terms. Declaring that the latter had exceeded his powers, and that he, as Governor of Pondicherry, was in supreme command in India, he insisted on the treaty with the English being broken, and issued an order that Madras should be destroyed.

Such disgraceful conduct was naturally regarded by the English as a grave breach of faith, but, utterly helpless to alter matters, they had to abide by the decision, though they considered that their engagements with Labourdonnais being thereby cancelled, they were at liberty to escape if they could. Accordingly, Robert Clive, disguised as a native, fled by night to Fort St. David, a small English settlement subordinate to Madras. Some of his comrades were less fortunate, the Governor and many of the principal inhabitants being made prisoners by order of Dupleix, carried off in triumph to Pondicherry, and there exhibited to a mob numbering many thousands of natives.

It was while at Fort St. David that Robert Clive exchanged the pen for the sword; and having, at the age of twenty-one, obtained an ensign's commission, he now entered on the career for which of all others he was fitted. He soon showed that the discipline to which he had been subjected since his arrival in Madras was yielding good fruit; and the excellent qualities he possessed—such as obedience, attention to military duties, deference to seniors—at once gained him the esteem of his superiors.

He gave proof, too, of the personal courage for

which he was ever distinguished. On a certain occasion he was one of a small party of officers playing cards, and two of the number won money from the others by cheating. These winners were well-known duellists, and it is said that all the losers, except Clive, paid their money without protest, but he flatly refused to do so, and charged the players with knavery. He was thereupon challenged by one of them to fight, and after the positions of the combatants had been fixed, and Clive, who had first fire, had missed his aim, his adversary, stepping up to him, and putting his pistol to his head, bade him ask for his life. Clive complied, but the scoundrel now insisted that he should pay the amount he had lost, and withdraw his charges.

"And if I refuse?" asked Clive.

"Then I fire," was the answer.

"Fire, and be hanged!" was the reply. "I say you *did* cheat, nor will I ever pay you."

The bully, struck with Clive's boldness, simply called him a madman, and threw away his pistol.

Madras having been captured, Dupleix, in furtherance of his plans for the expulsion of the English, resolved to send an expedition to Fort St. David, which had now become the Company's chief settlement. He did so, but without result, for it was gallantly and successfully defended by its little garrison, of whom Clive formed one; and on a second attempt, though he had now secured the co-operation of one of the native princes, he also failed. A third attempt was made, but fortunately by this time an English squadron had arrived off the coast, and a large reinforcement of troops being landed, the

French were obliged to retire, and preparations were made to retaliate upon them by laying siege to Pondicherry itself.

The attempt to capture this place was destined to fail, owing mainly to the obstinacy of the English naval commander, Admiral Boscawen, who, though he understood little of military tactics, and would not accept advice, insisted on conducting the operations himself. It was, however, a gallant undertaking, and it is of special interest to us because Robert Clive had now the first real opportunity of exhibiting his pluck. The besieging army consisted of nearly 4,000 men, the largest number of Europeans which had yet assembled in India, and the conduct of Robert, who, of course, served in a subordinate capacity, won from his superiors, especially from his chief, Major Stringer Lawrence, the warmest praise.

From the fact of young Clive having only recently emerged from civilian life, there seems to have been a tendency on the part of a few of his military companions to make a butt of him; but it was only for a little while. It happened, one day, while hotly engaged during the siege, that the ammunition for the battery where he was posted fell short, and his anxiety to obtain a fresh supply led him, instead of despatching a sergeant or corporal, to run himself for it. Of this circumstance a brother officer took advantage, in order to attempt to cast a slur upon his character, by asserting that it was fear, not zeal, which led him to leave his post at such a moment. The remark was repeated to Clive, who forthwith went to the person who made it to insist on either acknowledgment or disavowal of the slander. Some attempt at withdrawal of the words was made, but it did not satisfy Clive, and a challenge followed. It is said that as they were retiring to settle the dispute, his opponent, becoming irritated by some circumstance or remark, struck him. Thereupon Clive drew his sword, and would have proceeded to punish him, had the two not been separated by persons who witnessed the occurrence. A court of inquiry was held, and the officer who had defamed Clive was ordered to ask his pardon in front of the battalion to which they belonged. The Court, however, having taken no notice of the blow, Clive next demanded satisfaction for that insult too. But this was refused, whereupon he waved his cane over the head of his antagonist, and publicly told him that he was too contemptible a coward to be even thrashed. The day after this transaction the man whom he had thus disgraced resigned his commission.

The siege of Pondicherry lasted fifty days, at the end of which period it was decided to abandon it. Blunder after blunder had been made by Admiral Boscawen; nearly 1,000 men had been lost; the prospects of capturing the place had become remoter every day; so the ships of the squadron set their sails, while the troops marched back ingloriously to Fort St. David. This failure might, under ordinary circumstances, have had serious consequences, for the French, now left in undisturbed possession of their settlement, soon published throughout the Empire the news of the English retreat; and it is probable that their success might have secured for them such alliances with native princes as would have enabled them to gain real ascendency in India. Fortunately, however, at this crisis, news was received of the cessation of war between England and France in Europe; and as it was stipulated by the home governments that any settlements abroad which had been conquered were to be given back to their original owners, Madras, much to the disgust of the ambitious Dupleix, was restored to the Company, and the progress of French influence was checked.

Peace having been thus arranged, it seemed at first as if young Clive would find that his military duties were at an end; but though he returned for a short time to the desk, his services were soon needed in the field. For there now arose fresh quarrels between the French and English East India Companies, both of which, with a view to their own eventual aggrandisement, had begun to take up sides with rival native princes, and so had caused disagreement amongst themselves. Without attempting to give details of these new difficulties, it will suffice to say that the result was that the French were victorious for some months; that good fortune attended their operations wherever carried on; and that their crafty commander, Dupleix, had extorted from the native princes, whom he either assisted or conquered, such privileges and power as to make him the real master of Southern India. The condition of the English meanwhile had become most lamentable. They had in vain endeavoured to stay the career of the French; nearly every step taken by them had only tended to expose their own feebleness and to further the cause of Dupleix; and now, as their failure was so apparent, even the natives began to look upon them with contempt.

A grave crisis had therefore arrived, during which England's influence in India lay trembling in the balance; and of all the officers of the East India Company there was but one—"an obscure English youth" of twenty-five—capable of turning the tide of disaster. This was Robert Clive.

The French, in concert with Chunda Sahib, whom they had helped to become Nabob of the Carnatic (territory in the south-east of India), was at this moment besieging Trichinopoly, the sole remaining city of importance, which Chunda's great rival, Mahomet Ali, yet possessed. The garrison was hard pressed, and though the English, who favoured the cause of Mahomet Ali, had sent a small force to its aid, it was clear that the day of surrender was at hand; in which event there was nothing to prevent the French from driving the English out of India.

Robert Clive realised the perilous condition of affairs, and by his natural military genius was prepared to deal with it. Finding how matters stood at Trichinopoly—for he had accompanied the small expedition thither — he, on returning to Madras, immediately represented to his superiors that only by some sudden and dashing blow could a catastrophe be averted. He proposed, therefore, that an expedition should be sent to Arcot, Chunda Sahib's capital —a town of 100,000 inhabitants—the result of which would be that a considerable portion of the Nabob's army would be drawn off for its defence from Trichinopoly. The authorities—well knowing the young officer's ability—approved of his plan, and entrusted him with the conduct of the enterprise, which was to be carried out with a force of only 500 men.

In August, 1751, Robert Clive—now holding the rank of captain—arrived within ten miles of Arcot. A fearful storm was raging—"thunder, lightning, and rain, more terrific than is usual even in India, seemed to render further advance impracticable;" but, nothing daunted, the little force pushed on, and after marching through the streets amid thousands of astonished natives, entered the fort without opposition.

But although Clive was permitted by the garrison, numbering 1,500 men, who left in dismay at his approach, to take possession in this easy manner, it was not likely that he would be allowed to remain in peace; so he made preparations for defence accordingly. Within a short time the soldiers who had fled from the fort, accompanied by many others, returned; and news of the doings of the English having been carried to Trichinopoly, Chunda Sahib, as Clive had calculated, immediately despatched a large force, under the command of his son, to the rescue of his capital, the French also lending assistance; so that ere long no fewer than 10,000 troops besieged it. For fifty days the siege was maintained, though the provisions in the town became more and more scanty; and during the whole time Clive nobly continued the defence "with a firmness, vigilance, and ability which," as Macaulay says, "would have done honour to the oldest marshal in Europe."

Having failed to retake the fort, the commander of the besieging army offered large bribes to Clive to surrender, but they were scornfully rejected. Then in a rage he sent word that if his proposals were not accepted he would instantly storm the fort, and put every man to the sword; on which Clive defied him, by retorting "that his army was a rabble, and that he would do well to think twice before he sent such poltroons into a breach defended by English soldiers."

At length the threat was carried out, and the besiegers commenced the assault; but after a struggle lasting eighteen hours, during which Clive was in the thick of the fight, directing the movements of his men, the attacking troops were driven back with such heavy losses that they retreated from the city, leaving behind their weapons of war.

The news of this splendid victory was received with joy in Madras, whither—after pursuing his fast-retreating foes, who were overtaken and scattered in all directions—Clive ere long returned; and the fame of the young commander was soon established throughout the Empire. His valour and genius won for him from the natives the name of *Sabat Jung*, or the Daring in War, while—most important result of all—the effect of his success on the waning fortunes of the English was most striking. Instead of being looked upon as they had previously been, with contempt, Clive, by his doings at Arcot, caused his countrymen to be regarded with respect and admiration; and one immediate consequence was that native chiefs, who up to this time had been, in a sense, merely looking on, waiting to see which of the two rival companies was likely to prove the stronger, now came forward with their forces to join hands with the English. Thus the Madras authorities, with about 30,000 soldiers at their disposal, were enabled to follow up the advantage which Clive had gained for them. And so it was that an expedition—which Clive accompanied as second in command to Major

Stringer Lawrence — having been despatched to Trichinopoly, the remnant of Chunda Sahib's army, and the forces of his French allies, were overthrown; the Nabob himself was killed; and after re-taking the city, the conquering army marched through all the neighbouring country until, by the time they returned to Madras, victory after victory had been gained both over the French and the natives; and while the influence of their rivals was thus nearly destroyed, that of the English was firmly established.

Soon after these events—in 1753—Robert Clive, whose health had become impaired by the climate, as well as by sufferings during his campaigns, returned on leave to his native country, and he was heartily welcomed, both in his own home and by the English people, to whose name he had added such lustre in the East.

On his arrival he was received with great distinction by George II.; public receptions were given to him in different parts of the country, while honours and rewards were showered upon him by the Directors of the East India Company. The latter, in thanking him for his services, wished to bestow on him a diamond-hilted sword, but this token of gratitude he with graceful delicacy told them he could not accept, unless a similar gift were presented to his old chief, Major Stringer Lawrence.

It is said that his parents could not quite comprehend how it was that their "naughty, idle Bobby" had become so famous. His father, particularly, was at first very incredulous when the news of his doings arrived from India, but little by little he began to be convinced that, "after all, the booby had *some* sense," as he expressed it, and he became at length proud and fond of him.

Clive remained in England until 1755, when, having been appointed Governor of Fort St. David, and presented by the King with the commission of a lieutenant-colonel, he returned to India, and within two months of his arrival he was again required to fight.

A young and cruel prince, named Suraj-ood-dowlah, the Nabob of Bengal, who hated the English, had been much enraged because they had concealed a fugitive from him, and he determined to attack their settlement at Calcutta. This he did, and not only was the town, which was ill prepared for defence, captured, but nearly 150 of the English fell into his hands.

The infamous brutality with which these poor fellows were treated seems too awful to relate. We are told that after being brought before the prince, they were left to the mercy of his soldiers, and forced by them in the night into a cell used as a guard-room known as the "Black Hole." This was so small—only about twenty feet square—that it would have been cruel to confine even one person in it, yet no fewer than 146 persons were driven by the soldiers into the place at the sword's point, and the door was immediately closed upon them. When the horrible chamber was opened on the following morning, only twenty-three of the prisoners were found to be alive; the rest had perished from the suffocating atmosphere. In this cruel way, though the survivors were allowed to depart, were the English expelled from Bengal.

The news of the terrible event soon spread, and loud was the cry for vengeance. Shortly afterwards Robert Clive was entrusted with 2,500 men, and started for Bengal. The ruler of this province in the meantime had no idea that his territory was to be so quickly attacked—indeed, he is said to have been so ignorant that he believed there were not 10,000 men in all Europe; and great was his surprise when he learned that not only had Calcutta been recaptured by the English, but that the latter with their comparatively small force were quite prepared to fight him.

Clive was soon encamped near Calcutta, and the Nabob hearing of this, marched an army against him consisting of 40,000 men. With his usual success, however, Clive compelled even this vast host to offer "terms of accommodation," which produced a peace advantageous to the Company; and when he found that the enemy had been looking for assistance from the French, against whom the English were again at war, he attacked the important settlement of Chandernagore, belonging to the former, and took that also. It was after the capture of this place that Clive is said to have remarked, "We cannot stop here;" and events soon showed how true the prophecy was.

And thus was avenged the massacre in the "Black Hole" of Calcutta.

But grand as was this achievement, it was soon to be eclipsed by a victory more brilliant than any which had yet been won. Scarcely had peace been made with Suraj-ood dowlah, than there were signs that he intended to break the treaty into which he had entered, and to surprise Clive by falling upon him with his whole army. Meanwhile, however, some of the Nabob's own officers, disgusted with their master's bad and oppressive government, formed a plot to dethrone him ; and to Clive's astonishment, he received a secret letter from Meer Jaffier, the commander-in-chief of the Nabob's army, offering to desert and come over to the English, if they would enable him to become ruler of Bengal! In this communication, after betraying his master's intentions to attack the English, Meer Jaffier stated that his own plan was to wait until the day of battle arrived, when, after pretending to lead the Nabob's army, he would suddenly take sides with Clive, accompanied by at least one half of his men.

To the terms of this daring proposal Clive—excusing himself on the ground that "there could be neither peace nor security while such a monster as the Nabob lived"—consented; and so the bargain was made. But among the conspirators was a powerful banker of Calcutta named Omichund, and he, being jealous because Meer Jaffier had been promised such a great reward, threatened to reveal the whole plot to the Nabob unless a large sum—equal to £300,000—was paid as the price of his assistance and secrecy. The native plotters were at their wits' end on receiving this astounding demand, but it was not so with Clive. He knew with whom he was dealing, and declaring that "art and policy were warrantable to defeat the plans of such a villain," he resolved to meet fraud by fraud. So—though Clive was guilty of forging Admiral Watson's name, which was required in the document—a fictitious treaty was drawn up on red paper, in which Omichund's demand was

C

agreed to, while the real treaty, on white paper authenticated by the seals of the confederates, and the only one produced when the time came for its provisions to be carried into execution, contained no mention of the agreement with the banker of Calcutta.

All being in readiness for the coming battle, Clive started—in June, 1757—from Chandernagore, where he had remained after its capture from the French, and at the head of only 3,000 troops, of whom 2,100 were natives, marched towards a place called Plassy, near which the army of the Nabob, numbering no fewer than 50,000 men, lay encamped. It was a most perilous situation in which Clive and his brave followers were placing themselves; for apart from his force being so insignificant compared with the Nabob's, Clive had reason to suspect that after all Meer Jaffier might be deceiving him; and as they neared their goal, even the stout heart of the Hero of Arcot might well have quailed at the prospect before him. Only for a few moments, however, was any hesitation shown, and this was when, overtaken by a furious storm, a council of war was held—in which Clive voted with the majority—which decided on postponing the advance. But hardly had the decision been come to, when Clive, after retiring to think, reversed it, and on the evening of the 22nd of June his small band took up their position in a grove of mango-trees near Plassy, close to the Nabob's camp. Clive, we are told, was "unable to sleep, and heard through the whole night the sounds of drums and cymbals from the Nabob's vast camp. . . . Nor was the rest of Suraj-ood-dowlah more peaceful. His mind at once weak and stormy, was distracted by wild and horrible apprehensions. Appalled by the greatness and nearness of the crisis, distrusting his captains, dreading every one who approached him, dreading to be left alone, he sat gloomily in his tent, haunted, a Greek poet would have said, by the furies of those who had cursed him with their last breath in the 'Black Hole.'"

And now morning dawned on the plain of Plassy, as the two armies met. Opposed to the English—led by their "Heaven-born general," as Pitt afterwards designated him—was a force twenty times as numerous—and as yet Meer Jaffier had made no sign; but so telling was the resistance offered by Clive, and so great the damage caused by his artillery and bayonet charges, that by midday disorder reigned throughout the Nabob's camp; and within a few hours Suraj-ood-dowlah, panic-stricken, fled on a fleet camel, while his mighty hosts, with the exception of the wing under the leadership of Meer Jaffier, who now came forward to join the victors, immediately followed in direst confusion.

Within a few days, Suraj-ood-dowlah, deserted, and a fugitive, was assassinated; and in fulfilment of his promise, Clive carried out his bargain with Meer Jaffier by installing him on the throne of his late master, while Omichund found out, when too late, how completely he had been outwitted. And thus was overthrown the tyrant who, hating the English, had opposed them at every stage; and thus, by a master-stroke, did Robert Clive raise the fortunes of his countrymen, by making a dependent of their own ruler of Bengal.

Vast riches were now showered by Meer Jaffier

upon the East India Company and upon Clive, in acknowledgment of the aid given in placing him upon his throne. No less a sum than £800,000 was sent to Calcutta for the former, while Clive himself, in addition to a special gift of £160,000 from the grateful Nabob, found the treasury of Moorshedabad, then the capital of Bengal, thrown open, and liberty given to him to help himself. He received between £200,000 and £300,000; and it was in reference to this circumstance that some years later, when called to account in the British Parliament for his rapacity, he indignantly replied—"When I recollect entering the treasury, with heaps of gold and silver to the right hand and to the left, and these crowned with jewels, I stand astonished at my own moderation."

Clive was now—in 1758—appointed by the East India Company the first Governor of all their possessions in Bengal; and his power is described as having been boundless and far exceeding even that which Dupleix had wielded in Southern India. The new Nabob is said to have stood in "slavish awe" of him, and Europeans and natives were alike at his feet.

But events marched rapidly; and there arose a new difficulty with which Clive was called upon to cope. Shah Alum, a son of the so-called Emperor of Delhi—the real power of whose dynasty had, as we have seen, been long since destroyed—had secured the adhesion to his cause of a number of influential native princes, and of the Nabob of the province of Oude in particular; and, with an army of 40,000 men, he had determined to overthrow Meer Jaffier, and secure the sovereignty of Bengal. The latter ruler trembling for his crown, proposed disorder through the dishonesty and corrupt practices of its servants, high and low; and Lord Clive was looked upon as the only man capable of restoring them to order. How this disorganisation had arisen may be briefly stated. No sooner had Clive left for England in 1760, than the East India Company's officials determined to enrich themselves at any cost. They therefore commenced by dethroning the Nabob of Bengal; and by setting up his son-in-law in his place, they received as their reward no less a sum than twenty lacs of rupees (equal to about £200,000), in addition to three rich districts in the province. Hardly had this ruler been thus raised to power, than, anxious to be independent of the English, he got together a large army, and obtaining the assistance of the Nabob of Oude, as well as such co-operation as the nominal Emperor of Delhi could render, a war began. The combined armies were, however, signally defeated, and the result of the war was that the Nabob of Oude surrendered to the English, which left them masters of a large additional territory in India, and the Emperor himself sought protection in their camp. Meer Jaffier had, in the meantime, been reinstated on the throne, by which act the Company's officials again secured enormous sums from his treasury as their reward; and on his death, in 1765, they proceeded to make his son Nabob, but only on condition of another payment of twenty lacs of rupees being guaranteed to them.

It was at this juncture that Lord Clive arrived back in Calcutta; and he is said to have declared that "there were not five men of principle to be found" in the Company's service, while the name of England, through the oppression and the extortions of the officials, had become hated throughout the Empire. He quickly perceived that such a condition of affairs could end only in overturning the structure which he had been instrumental in erecting in India; and he vowed that he would destroy "these great and growing evils which had sprung up, or perish in the attempt."

He kept his word. In spite of the opposition and intrigues of the corrupt officials, whom he found in no way disposed to abandon a course of conduct which had proved so profitable to them, he began the work of reform with a firm hand, and never flinched from the task until every one of his opponents had yielded to his iron will.

And now followed the crowning achievement of the great hero's career—an achievement by which the East India Company was to secure the virtual sovereignty of a wide extent of territory. Having established his authority in Calcutta, Lord Clive's first act was to propose to the Emperor of Delhi—who though now a fugitive, and under English protection, was yet the titular ruler of the Empire—that he should officially transfer to the East India Company the government of the three important provinces of Bengal, Behar, and Orissa; and he offered in return to make a large annual payment from the revenues of these countries, not only to the Emperor, but to the Nabob, who was still to retain the title and semblance of authority. And the poor helpless Emperor consented, nor, indeed, had he power to act otherwise.

So on the memorable 12th of August, 1765, this bold bargain was completed in the city of Benares. For a throne, we learn that two dining-tables were put together in Clive's tent, with a chair on them, and covered with embroidery; and amid such simple surroundings, the descendant and heir of the mighty Mogul Emperor took his seat, and transferred the government of twenty-five millions of people, and a yearly revenue of three crores (equal to about £3,000,000), to Lord Clive, as the representative of the East India Company.

And thus was founded that British sovereignty which ere long was to spread from north to south, and from east to west.

Lord Clive's real life-work was now accomplished, and after a residence of twenty-one months in India, he returned in shattered health to his native land in 1767. In spite of all that he had achieved, however—in spite of the reforms which, during his last term of office, he had introduced into the Company's service; in spite of his own upright conduct during a most trying period—he found his reception in England very different from what he had every right to expect. Enemies who had been jealous of his successes as a soldier, relatives of officials in India whose career of oppression and corruption he had stayed—these, and many others, banded themselves against him.

And such was the influence of these persons, that within a few years they had actually succeeded in inducing Parliament to call him to account for some of his proceedings in India long previously, when it was alleged that he had abused his authority.

The inquiry was, therefore, held, and the whole history of Lord Clive's doings in the East was reviewed; but, though certain transactions, notably those connected with the treaty with Meer Jaffier and the deception of Omichund, were shown to have been discreditable, yet Parliament refused to cast blame upon him, and even passed a resolution that he had rendered great and meritorious services to his country.

The fact that such an inquiry should have been held at all was, however, more than the great soldier could endure. He thought that, after what he had done for his country, he had been treated not only ungenerously but most unjustly; his proud spirit, notwithstanding his honourable acquittal, could not brook the insult; and, brooding over his wrongs, he ended his glorious career by his own hand on the 22nd of November, 1774.

II.—WARREN HASTINGS.

At the time when Robert Clive, neglecting his lessons, was fast gaining reputation for mischievousness and wilfulness, a little boy seven years his junior was attending the village school of Churchill, in Oxfordshire, eagerly gathering in all the knowledge he could. Save that he thus "took to learning kindly," as his old playmates used to say, there was nothing about the lad—not even in his dress or appearance—to indicate that he was different from the rustic children of the village. Yet though these were his companions as well in play as in school, the child was in no way one of themselves; and not only was he of gentle birth, but in capacity and in many other respects he was far removed from them. It was indeed solely through dire misfortune that he had found a place in their midst.

The little lad was Warren Hastings. Born on the 6th of December, 1732, he had been left motherless when a few days old; and his father, going abroad very soon after, gave the charge of the baby boy and his sister to their grandfather, the rector of Daylesford, a poor clergyman, who by this time had ruined himself through unsuccessful lawsuits. Ere long, the grandfather, unable to maintain possession of the Daylesford living, and compelled to leave it, had settled as a curate at Churchill. And it was under such unfavourable conditions that Warren Hastings entered on life.

Ancient and illustrious was the race from which Warren was descended. As far back as King Alfred's days could be traced their line of ancestors famous in many a brave struggle; and at the time of England's great Civil War the family was both "wealthy and highly considered." Then it was that the zeal and loyalty of the head of the house involved the estate in ruin. For John Hastings, a gallant cavalier, aided King Charles I. in the field, and raised money for him by selling lands and plate; and never afterwards were the owners of Daylesford able to revive its glories. Indeed, the day came when, too poor to keep up the estate, the family sold it to a London merchant, and all that they retained in their possession was the parish rectory, which the last Hastings of

Daylesford presented to his son—Warren's grandfather.

Early in young Warren's career he dreamed ambitious dreams, such as seldom come to children. From his grandfather he had begun to hear of the departed greatness of the Hastings family. He was told stories of the wealth and the loyalty and the brave deeds of his ancestors; and when he had realised that all these were of the past—that even the last remnant of the Daylesford possessions had gone into the hands of strangers—the effect upon the lad seems to have been remarkable. He would now often betake himself to the bank of a stream near the village, where he would lie down and muse on bygone times; and one bright summer day, when seven years old, he formed a scheme which, says Macaulay, "through all the turns of his eventful career was never abandoned." He would, he resolved, recover the estate which had belonged to his fathers. "When under a tropical sun he ruled 50,000,000 of Asiatics, his hopes amidst all the cares of war, finance, and legislation still pointed to Daylesford. And when his long public life, so singularly chequered with good and evil, with glory and obloquy, had at length closed for ever, it was to Daylesford that he retired to die."

When about eight Warren was gladdened by the news that an uncle, Mr. Howard Hastings, a Government official in London, intended to take him under his charge so that he might be well educated; and it is easy to understand that the boy turned his face towards the metropolis most willingly. Arrived there, he was placed in a school at Newington, where he remained two years, but though well taught, he is said to have been half-starved, and he afterwards believed that his short stature was caused by the lack of food at this period. Better days followed. His uncle was enabled when he was ten to remove him to the famous Westminster School; and there under the care of Dr. Nichols young Hastings gave promise of high repute as a scholar. He soon distinguished himself, too, in athletics, especially in rowing and swimming; and he became much liked by his companions, and formed friendships which lasted through life.

Now came a bitter disappointment. The boy had been at Westminster about six years—a period singularly pleasant—and having by ability and perseverance gained the first place on the list of King's Scholars admitted to the foundation in that year, he was looking forward to entering the University of Oxford. At this juncture his kind uncle died; and the course of his whole career was changed. The care of Warren immediately passed to a distant relative named Chiswick, and this gentleman, who had no regard for the lad, and was evidently anxious to get rid of him, decided that he should leave Westminster. Dr. Nichols pleaded hard that his clever pupil might continue his studies—even volunteering to defray the expense of sending him to Oxford; but to no purpose. Mr. Chiswick, it appears, had influence with the East India Company; he saw in their service an opportunity of relieving himself of his charge; so Warren Hastings was removed from Westminster, and having been placed for a while under a private tutor to study book-keeping and accounts he, like Robert Clive, became a "writer" and sailed for India. This was in January, 1750.

Warren Hastings's earliest experiences in the Company's service were at Calcutta, where he worked in the Secretary's office. Little is known of his doings then, save that in spite of the small pay he received and of the temptations that surrounded him, his character as a capable, steady young fellow stood high; and it seems probable that during this time he spent his leisure in studying native languages. At the end of two years he was sent up the country to the Company's factory at Cossimbazar, near Moorshedabad, where his duties consisted in the main of superintending the exportation of silk and other goods to the English market. There he remained for a few years, giving much satisfaction to his superiors by careful attention to his work; and there it was that important events happened by which his whole future was affected.

At this period Suraj-ood-dowlah—whom we have already met—succeeded to the throne of Bengal; and after his attack on the Company's settlement at Calcutta, during which the awful "Black Hole" tragedy was enacted, this cruel prince proceeded to destroy the other English factories in the province. On Cossimbazar being seized, Hastings became a prisoner, and would probably have so remained but for the influence of a neighbouring Dutch factor who secured his release. After a while he fled to an island on the river Hooghly, to which certain English fugitives from Calcutta had already betaken themselves; and it was while there that the force which, under Robert Clive, was to avenge the "Black Hole" massacre arrived. Hastings immediately volunteered his services; and in the attack on Calcutta which followed he took his place in the ranks and carried a musket.

It was not, however, as a soldier that he was to distinguish himself. In certain negotiations with Suraj-ood-dowlah, with which he had been entrusted by the commander, Hastings had already displayed marked diplomatic skill; and Clive was not slow to perceive that he was eminently fitted to render valuable service in a civil capacity. When, therefore —in 1757—after the battle of Plassy, Meer Jaffier was raised to the throne of Bengal in place of Suraj-ood-dowlah, Warren Hastings was appointed to fill the high office of Resident Agent of the Company at the court of the new Nabob.

Hastings performed the duties of this post until 1761, during which time, though he had ample opportunity of enriching himself after the manner of other officials similarly placed, he gained enviable reputation for honourable conduct; and he then became a Member of the Council at Calcutta. (At this time, each of the three Presidencies—Bengal, Madras, and Bombay—had its own Governor, who was assisted by a Council.) His acceptance of this important post took place during the period when Clive was visiting England—the period when the greed for wealth on the part of certain unscrupulous officers of the Company led them to abuse their power, and to commit acts of "grinding oppression," which have been stigmatised as forming "the most revolting page in our Indian history." Against this conduct Hastings vehemently protested, but he was one only against many; and though his efforts were unceasing, his resistance was unavailing in preventing the train of evils which went on accumulating until Clive's return.

Three years thus passed; and then Hastings returned to England, where he settled down to quiet pursuits, devoting himself especially to study of Oriental literature. He was in possession of only a moderate fortune, and, owing to generous gifts to relatives and to unfortunate investments, even this he gradually lost; and when after a stay of four years in his native country his thoughts again turned to India, the Directors of the Company gladly acceded to his request for employment by appointing him second Member of the Council at Madras.

On resuming duty Hastings soon showed that he meant to work with the same zeal which he had already exhibited; and finding great need of reform in an important financial department of the Indian service, he determined to effect it. He applied himself to the task; and having performed it, his superiors were so pleased with what he had done that they appointed him in 1772 to the responsible office of Governor of Bengal.

It was no path of roses which lay before him; indeed, as events proved, difficulties loomed ahead which, had they been foreseen, might well have deterred even a resolute man like himself from encountering them. Clive had left India, as we have seen, in 1767; but from that year the administration of the country had gradually fallen into a state of almost hopeless confusion, while, in addition, a terrible famine had overtaken Bengal, by which it is estimated that one-third of the people were destroyed. Under the system of Government established there by Clive, on its transfer by the Emperor, much abuse of power had again grown up after his departure. It had arisen mainly from the Nabob having been permitted to retain his outward semblance of authority, and from a native official who was permitted to reside at the Court of Moorshedabad, the capital, being allowed to control the collection of the revenue on behalf of the English. This arrangement had resulted in the people suffering great oppression at the hands of the collectors, who not only fleeced them in the name of the "puppet Nabob," but intercepted the revenues belonging to the Company. Thus, while the latter was defrauded of income, its power was also weakened by the discontent which such treatment of the people engendered.

The Directors of the Company had determined that this condition of affairs should come to an end; and to Hastings was entrusted the task of carrying out their orders. His first act was to remove from office the Native Minister, Mahomet Reza Khans, then he placed the collection of the revenues in the hands of responsible officials of the Company; and at the same time he changed the seat of the Government from Moorshedabad to Calcutta—which became henceforth the capital of Bengal. Other changes also were made, among them, the introduction of courts of justice in which Englishmen instead of natives had supreme power; and having in this way deprived the Nabob (who, however, as already stated, was still to be nominally the ruler and to receive a large yearly allowance) of the only vestige of authority remaining, Hastings effectually destroyed the double system of government which Clive had set up. In its stead he secured for the Company the real sovereignty of Bengal.

The government of the province was thus placed upon a sound foundation, and order restored; but beyond the borders of Bengal a fresh cloud was gathering; and ere long events happened which, with all their mitigating circumstances, cast a stain on the fame of Hastings.

Truth to tell, the Governor was at this time in a dilemma. His treasury, from various causes, was empty, and though the new system of government gave promise of better financial results in future, the Company was for the present in debt. Accordingly, mail after mail from England brought fresh demands from the Directors for remittances. How was the money to be obtained? Already, at the time he dissolved the double system of government, Hastings had, by orders from home, cut down to one half the allowance promised by Clive to the Nabob—an act which was a gross breach of faith. He now determined to go a step farther. When the Emperor transferred the provinces of Bengal, Behar, and Orissa to the English, the Company agreed to pay him, in return, a sum equal to about £300,000 a year; they also made over to him the districts of Corah and Allahabad. Seizing as an excuse the fact that a few years previously the Emperor had been engaged in transactions with the Mahrattas—a warlike race of mountaineers inhabiting a portion of West Central India—who were hostile to the English, and had thus forfeited his claims, Hastings declared that henceforth no more tribute should be paid to him; in addition to which he despatched troops to take possession of the two ceded districts. But in seizing these he had but one object—to sell them; and knowing that their situation was such that they would be highly prized by the Nabob of Oude, he made overtures to that ruler, with the result that half a million sterling was paid for the stolen territories, which found its way into the Company's coffers!

Nor did Hastings's discreditable transactions end here. He now entered into another shameful compact. The Nabob of Oude had long coveted the fertile territory of Rohilcund, in the north-west of Hindostan; and on the ground that the Rohillas, as the inhabitants were called, refused to pay a sum, equal to about £450,000, which they owed to him for assisting them to defend their country, he offered to the Company a like amount, together with a large subsidy for the pay of its troops, if it would lend a force to aid him in seizing Rohilcund. This base proposal was accepted by Hastings; and thus, in order that the Company's treasury might be replenished, and the greed of the Nabob satisfied, was the fate of a valorous and industrious people sealed.

We are told that when the Rohillas heard of the treaty which the English had made with the Nabob, their brave chieftain implored that his country might be spared, and offered to pay the sum that was owing; but the Nabob, bent on war, only increased his demand to five times its original amount; on hearing which, the Rohillas, to a man, declared that they "would die sooner than submit to such extortion." Thereupon, the allied troops marched forward, and ere long the country was swept with fire and sword. While the decisive battle was being fought, the Nabob, it is recorded, remained beyond the reach of danger, but as soon as he found that the unhappy Rohillas had been beaten, he sent his troops to plunder the camp. Well might the English commander exclaim—"We have the honour of the day, but these banditti the profit of it!"

All this time, while the East India Company had been acquiring more and more power—first through the instrumentality of Clive and next of Hastings —the people of England had been regarding its progress with watchful eyes; and by 1773, the matter having been discussed in Parliament, it had been decreed that considerable changes should be made in the mode of government. The law then passed, known as the "Regulating Act," provided that a new Council of four appointed by the Crown should be sent out from home; and that the officials comprising this body should—jointly with the Governor of Bengal, who was henceforth to be the Governor-General of India—have authority over all the English possessions in the Empire. At the same time, a Supreme Court of Judicature, comprising a Chief Justice and three other judges, was to be established in Calcutta, and entrusted with jurisdiction of like extent. The object of this great change was to curtail the immense authority which the Company had acquired, and to prevent it from engaging in transactions at variance with the views of the British Government.

Warren Hastings, however, did not regard the coming of these English officials with equanimity, more especially as he had but a poor opinion of some of the Councillors who had been selected, while he knew that more than one was determined to thwart the Company at every possible turn. And open warfare between them and the Governor-General soon began.

A grievance against Hastings seems to have been formed on the very day of their arrival at Calcutta, in October, 1774. The Councillors expected a salute of twenty-one guns—the number reserved for the Governor-General alone—but only seventeen were fired. This, with the knowledge they possessed that they were regarded by Hastings as interlopers, put them into ill-humour; then they found no guard of honour awaiting them, as they had expected, which made them more sulky; while, to crown all, one member in particular, Philip Francis, chose to be dissatisfied with a certain portion of the attire worn by Hastings when he met them. In a letter to a friend written at the time, this gentleman actually gave vent to his feelings by saying that, "Surely Mr. Hastings could have put on a ruffled shirt!" As illustrating the amazing ignorance of India shown by some of these new-comers, too, it is related by Marshman the historian, that on the same occasion, as the judges stepped on shore, one of them noticing the bare legs and feet of the natives, remarked to a colleague: "Our court, brother, was certainly not established before it was needed. I trust we shall not have been six months in the country before these victims of oppression are comfortably provided with shoes and stockings!"

Such behaviour as that of the Councillors boded ill for the future relations between the Governor-General and themselves; nor was it long before the latter began to prove very disagreeable, and put into force the authority with which they were armed. On the day after their arrival they assembled, so that the commission which set forth their powers might be read; and when a few days later they again met, in order that Hastings might lay before them a statement of his proceedings in Bengal during his governorship, it was plain that a fierce storm was brewing.

No sooner had the Governor-General referred to his dealings with the Nabob of Oude and the war with the Rohillas, than he was called upon to produce all the correspondence which had passed between himself and the Nabob's court—thus implying that they suspected that the transaction had been entered into in order that he might enrich himself. The suspicion was groundless; for disgraceful as his bargain with the Nabob had been, it was made wholly and solely for the Company's benefit. So Hastings flatly refused the demand. He stated that the correspondence included confidential communications, and while ready to show the other portions of them, he declared that "no power on earth could authorise him to give up the letters themselves."

The Governor-General was supported by only one member of the Council, and the result was that he, being outvoted, the majority were enabled to wrest all power out of his hands. Thereupon they proceeded, in spite of his remonstrances, to intermeddle in affairs in different parts of India; and it is not surprising that their ignorance of the country soon led them to create confusion in Bengal and elsewhere. Meanwhile—for Hastings continued to sit at the head of the Council board—they never missed an opportunity of wounding the President's pride, and of setting him at defiance.

Among other indignities which the Councillors heaped upon him was an inquiry into the Rohilla war, in which some of his own officers were compelled to give evidence, and by which they hoped to ruin him. Failing in this, such was their eagerness to convict him, that they even stooped to accept the services which a certain notorious Hindoo informer—an inveterate hater of Hastings—offered. "An Indian Government," says Macaulay, "has only to let it be understood that it wishes a man to be ruined, and in twenty-four hours it will be furnished with grave charges, supported by depositions so full and circumstantial that any person unaccustomed to Asiatic mendacity would regard them as decisive." This was the case now. Hastings was known to have been stripped of real power, and to have had taken from him even the valuable patronage which he had possessed; and the natives, realising this, had already followed their natural inclination, to side with the strong rather than with the weak, by currying favour with the majority of the Council. This was done by concocting stories containing charges against the Governor-General, which were most readily listened to.

Now, foremost among the natives who came forward at this juncture was one Nunkoomar, a man with a long-standing grudge against the Governor-General—an unblushing scoundrel who had been regarded by both Clive and Hastings as "the worst man they knew in India." Some years previously, at the time when Hastings removed Mahomet Reza Khan from his office as Native Minister at Moorshedabad, Nunkoomar had quite hoped that by the exercise of his wonted craftiness *he* would get the vacant post; but when he found that, instead, its duties were henceforth to be entrusted to Englishmen, his rage knew no bounds; nor had he ever forgiven Hastings. So on the arrival of the new officials he, knowing how hostile they were to the Governor-General, set to work to gain their favour; and having so far succeeded, he came forward with most serious charges against Hastings. In particular, he went so far as to accuse him of having accepted for his own use the large sum of £35,000 in connection with the dismissal of Mahomet Reza Khan. The Councillors were only too ready to believe Nunkoomar; and they decided that he should appear before them to substantiate his charges. But this crowning indignity Hastings would not endure; and declaring that the Board had no power to sit in judgment upon him, and refusing to be insulted by being confronted with such a blackguard as Nunkoomar, he hastily left the Council chamber. The Hindoo was then brought in, and his statements were not merely listened to, but—accepting as evidence a letter afterwards found to be forged, which he produced—it was declared that the charges were made out, and the sum alleged to have been appropriated by Hastings was ordered to be forthwith repaid into the Company's treasury. Needless to say, the Governor-General flatly refused to obey the order; but—especially as other grave charges were now being similarly " proved "—it is easy to understand that the position of Hastings came to be very unpleasant.

It was only for a time. While Nunkoomar was enjoying his revenge, and flattering himself that his score against the Governor-General would soon be paid off by the latter's ignominious dismissal; while the Councillors—of whom at least one was fondly hoping to supplant Hastings as Governor-General—were revelling in their persecution of him, a plan was being formed which was to upset all their calculations. Aware of the authority with which the new English judges of the Supreme Court had been invested, and knowing that these gentlemen did not share the animosity of the Councillors, Hastings turned to them. The result was that in a little while he brought an action for conspiracy against Nunkoomar and others who had preferred charges against him; and after a trial lasting many days the prisoners, though released on bail, were ordered to be again brought up. This was not all. The people of Calcutta were astounded one morning to hear that Nunkoomar had been suddenly arrested on a fresh charge—that of forgery—and by order of the Supreme Court thrown into the common gaol as a felon! Six years before, it was alleged, he had counterfeited a bond; and the prosecutor—a native merchant—probably considered that an opportune moment had now come for bringing the culprit to justice.

The rage of the Councillors on hearing what had happened rose to boiling-point, and they at once demanded the release of Nunkoomar on bail, and endeavoured also to overawe the judges. All was of no avail, however, and after a prolonged trial the wretched Hindoo, having been sentenced to death, was hanged.

From this event, though his difficulties with the majority of the Council had not ended, may be said to date the recovery of Hastings's authority. For the fate of the man who had been his principal accuser, and the inability of Nunkoomar's friends in the Council to save him, created a profound impression, and effectually silenced every native who had dared to utter a word against the Governor-General. Henceforth Hastings was a man to be feared.

Passing over the minor events that followed, concerning which it will suffice to remark that after continued difficulties with the hostile Councillors, and with the Directors of the Company in London, the Governor-General had in due course become reinstated in power, and all opposition to him had been crushed, we come next to a time of great trial for the English power in India—a time when Warren Hastings, put on his mettle, proved to his countrymen the rare qualities of statesmanship with which he was gifted.

Secure in his position, he now felt that the period had come when the hold upon India which the Company had obtained should be more firmly secured and further extended. With his wonted sagacity, he plainly perceived that the power of the English, now covering a large portion of the north of the Empire, must either increase or decrease, for there was no probability of it long remaining unchallenged by native rulers; and he began to form plans accordingly.

At this time, in addition to many smaller States,

there were three detached countries of India, each ruled by a powerful prince, awaiting opportunity to overwhelm the British, namely, that of the Mahrattas, a strong confederation of scattered principalities; Mysore, of which Hyder Ali was king; and the Deccan, of which Mahomet Ali was Nizam. It was to checkmate the designs of these formidable princes that Hastings bent all his energies.

Now it happened that already the Company's authorities at Bombay had given offence to the Mahrattas, by affording protection to one Raghoba, who, having assassinated his nephew, had fled from their country; and at this crisis news came to the Governor-General that the French—between whom and the English war had again broken out in Europe—had concluded an alliance with the Mahrattas hostile to the Company. In face of this new danger, Hastings resolved to strike a decisive blow. Forthwith, therefore, every French factory in Bengal was seized by him; directions were sent to Madras to occupy Pondicherry; and then an army was ordered to proceed from Calcutta to Bombay to march against the Mahrattas.

But how to transport the troops to their destination was the difficulty, for there were neither transports enough to carry them, nor men-of-war to convoy them. Hastings hit upon a bold plan, one that had, we are told, never yet presented itself to the mind of any Englishman in India. He decided to march the army right across the country, and thus not only achieve his end, but show to the potentates of the interior what the might of the Company really was!

So this expedition, consisting of over 7,000 troops,

accompanied by 30,000 camp-followers, was despatched in 1778; and, in spite of not a few unlooked for obstacles, its commander, carrying everything before him and spreading the " military renown of the English through regions where no European flag had ever been seen," pushed on until he reached the coast, and after a while inflicted a decisive defeat on the Mahratta army 40,000 strong. And this victory being followed by the capture of Gwalior, a most important fortress belonging to Sindia, one of their great chiefs, the difficulty with the Mahrattas was effectually disposed of.

Meanwhile a far more formidable danger had arisen. Some thirty years previously Hyder Ali, a Mahometan soldier of humble position, had begun to take a prominent part in the wars of Southern India. Though unable even to read or write, he was a man of singular energy, and combined all the qualities of the soldier and the statesman. Among those who on the fall of the Mogul Empire had rushed forward to take part in the scramble for independent power, Hyder had been one of the foremost; and so successful had he been in carrying out his plans, that little by little he had built up a prosperous kingdom —that of Mysore, of which he had become the sovereign. He was now an old man, but full of spirit and vigour, and having by this time surrounded himself with an army of tremendous strength, his power was such as to be a standing menace to his neighbours. To the English, Hyder bore no goodwill. Like other native rulers, he had naturally looked upon them as interlopers, and viewed their progress in India with jealous anger; and the upshot was that when, in 1778, war broke out with the French and the English, he declared in favour of the former. Matters were then brought to a climax by the reckless conduct of the Company's authorities at Madras, who, regardless of consequences, just then despatched an expedition, by way of Mysore, against a French settlement at Mahé, which so enraged Hyder that he determined on immediate action. So, having completed his preparations and secured the aid of French officers, he on a sudden—in July, 1780—burst into the Carnatic at the head of 90,000 men; and, having laid the country waste, marched towards Madras.

The incapable Governor of Madras had already blundered in provoking Hyder; he now committed a worse blunder. The army at his disposal numbered nearly 8,000 men, in two divisions, separated at a considerable distance. First, however, there was delay in taking the field, for we are told that not till the inhabitants of Madras had at night seen "the eastern sky reddened by a vast semicircle of blazing villages," was any attempt made to resist Hyder's advance; and next the unaccountable error of allowing the English army to be divided into two forces (the one under Sir Hector Monro, the other under Colonel Baillie) was made. The consequences were disastrous. Baillie, with his 2,500 men, while trying to effect a junction with Monro, was intercepted by Tippoo Sahib, son of Hyder, and unable to advance, Baillie begged Monro to join him with his whole force. Instead of doing so, only 1,100 were sent; and hardly had they arrived and proceeded on their march before Hyder himself brought up his force, and in the darkness of the following night surrounded Baillie and his men with his whole army. Tremendous as were the odds against them, the pluck of the English did not desert them, and they fought like true heroes—fought, indeed, until their numbers were reduced to 300; and even then they demanded to be once more led against the enemy. But their bravery did not avail them, poor fellows, for when unwilling to sacrifice their lives, Colonel Baillie went forward to ask for quarter, Hyder's soldiers rushed upon them, and one-half of the small force was butchered in cold blood, while the remainder, made prisoners, were doomed to horrible captivity for some years.

One of the unfortunate victims of Hyder's cruelty on this day was a brave young officer—afterwards famous in the annals of India as Sir David Baird. He was among those who had been taken prisoners; and though suffering severely from wounds received in battle, he had been thrown into a cell with his companions. One morning, we are told, the gaoler entered, bringing with him some fetters, each weighing nine pounds, with which to secure his captives. The unfortunate men were quite helpless; so one by one they could only yield to their fate. When, however, Baird's turn came, and it was seen how ill he had become from his wounds, one of his comrades, Lieutenant Lucas, begged that fetters should not be put on him. The gaoler replied that he had his orders, which were that each prisoner should be placed in chains. "Then," said the noble Lucas, "put a double pair on me, and spare Captain Baird;" and the man, familiar as he was with scenes of misery and cruelty, was so struck by this self-sacrifice, that he brought the matter under the notice of his superiors, with the result that Captain Baird was permitted to remain unfettered.

In the meantime, while the army of Colonel Baillie was being annihilated, Sir Hector Monro, though only two miles off and within earshot of the cannonade, instead of hastening to his countrymen's assistance, had thrown away his guns into a great tank, or pond, destroyed his stores, and fled in dismay to Madras!

By this calamity, which took place within three weeks from the commencement of the war, the British Empire in Southern India was brought to the brink of ruin; for only a few fortified places now remained in the Company's hands; the prestige of the Company was destroyed; while to make matters worse, it was reported that a great French expedition was expected on the coast to recover Pondicherry and co-operate with Hyder Ali.

Then it was, as Macaulay tells us, " that the fertile genius and serene courage of Hastings achieved their most signal triumph. A swift ship, flying before the south-west monsoon, brought the evil tidings in few days to Calcutta. In twenty-four hours the Governor-General had framed a complete plan adapted to the altered state of affairs. The struggle with Hyder was a struggle for life and death." The first step taken by the Governor-General was to place the control of affairs at Madras in competent hands; and this was effected by appointing Sir Eyre Coote, a veteran who, four-and-twenty years previously, had distinguished himself at Plassy, to replace the incapable Governor, and to undertake the direction of the new military expedition which was to be despatched against Hyder. Next he proceeded to form an alliance with his former enemies, the Mahrattas—by which masterly stroke a portion of Hyder's own territory would be menaced; and then every soldier who could be spared from Bengal was despatched to Madras. Within a short time, all these preparations having been completed, Sir Eyre Coote took the field; and then was begun the work of avenging the disaster which had overtaken Colonel Baillie.

Hyder Ali had now under his command about 80,000 men, and at the time when Coote started, his forces were engaged in besieging various garrisons defended by British officers. One of these places, called Wandewash, to which Coote first marched, had been the scene of a deed of daring on the part of a young officer, so remarkable that mention of it cannot be omitted. When, some little time before Sir Eyre began his march, it became known that this garrison was about to surrender to Hyder, the native officer in command was suspected of having betrayed it; so an Englishman, Lieutenant Flint, was despatched, with only 100 soldiers, to get possession. On his approach he was warned that the guns of the fort would be turned on him if he did not retire; but in spite of this he went up to the gates, saying that he had a letter from the Nabob, which he must deliver into the hands of the commandant himself, and for this purpose begged permission to enter with a few men. It was refused, but the officer consented to receive the letter in the space between the door and the inner barrier. Attended by only four Sepoys, Flint entered, and found the commandant surrounded by more than thirty swordsmen as his personal guard, while 100 troops were also drawn up.

On arriving, Flint at once said he had no letter from the Nabob, but offered, instead, the order of Sir Eyre Coote to take possession. This the officer only treated with contempt, and bade Flint be gone without delay. . On this, we are told, "Flint seized him by the throat and threatened him with instant death if he raised a hand for rescue, while the four Sepoys levelled their weapons at his heart. At that moment the rest of the little detachment rushed in, and Wandewash became ours on the very day it was to have surrendered to Hyder. Overawed by the resolute courage of this hardy young Briton, the Nabob's garrison agreed to serve under his orders, and he at once took every means to defend it." For more than a fortnight the little garrison held out bravely; and then, when the enemy were working their way into the place, Flint repulsed them by a sortie; after which, on hearing news of the approach of Sir Eyre Coote, they abandoned the siege, though Flint had expended his very last cartridge.

The place was thus secured, and such a profound impression did its capture and defence produce on Hyder, that he withdrew his army from the neighbourhood. Coote, however, followed him, and after considerable delay the two armies—one ten times the strength of the other—met at Porto Novo, near Cuddalore. It was a tremendous risk for the English, but Coote did not flinch. On the morning of that day "the fiery veteran launched his 8,000 men against the myriads of Mysore, with a skill and resolute courage that nothing could long withstand."

E

And after several hours of hard fighting, Hyder Ali fled from the field, having lost 10,000 of his followers, while Coote's force was weakened by only 300 men.

One incident of this eventful day is of great interest. During the battle, the gallant 73rd Highlanders were on the right of the first line leading all the attacks; and it is recorded that Sir Eyre Coote's attention was particularly attracted by one of the pipers, who invariably struck up a stirring pibroch when the noise of the musket firing was greater than usual. So pleased was he with the man's ardour that he galloped up to him and exclaimed—

"Well done, my brave fellow! You shall have a set of silver pipes for this."

Nor was the promise forgotten.

From this blow Hyder Ali never recovered; for though later on in the year he again tried conclusions with the English, he still met with defeat; and it was in despairing bitterness that, finding his efforts unavailing, he remarked: "The defeat of many Baillies will not crush them. I may ruin their resources by land, but I cannot dry up the sea, and I must be exhausted by a war in which I gain nothing by fighting." Still, the difficulties of the English had not ended, for in the following year Hyder Ali having died, his son Tippoo succeeded him, and he having obtained the co-operation of France, continued the war with vigour. And not till 1784, when peace —destined, however, as we shall see, to last only a few years—was made, did hostilities cease.

It was a most dangerous crisis through which India had passed; but though the ship of State had been thus carefully piloted, the work of Hastings was

"HYDER ALI FLED FROM THE FIELD" (p. 66).

not yet done. We must, however, content ourselves with a brief glance at one only of the remaining scenes in his career as Governor-General.

Foremost among these was an event which arose out of financial difficulties caused by the war. The expenses had risen to such a height that there seemed no possibility of meeting them, and the Governor-General had to seek fresh sources of supplies. Having exhausted all other means, he therefore determined to exact a large sum from Cheyt Sing, the Rajah of Benares. This personage had been under the Company's protection for some time, conditionally on paying an annual tribute; but latterly he had evaded the demand for it. So Hastings, called upon him to pay a heavy fine in addition to the arrears. Cheyt Sing refused, and Hastings thereupon went in person to Benares and put him under arrest. But this proceeding led to an insurrection in the city, and the two companies of Sepoys who had accompanied the Governor-General were massacred; he himself, with only fifty of his men, was shut up in a building around which the angry populace gathered in thousands; while the Rajah escaped by letting himself down into the Ganges, and rowing to the other side to join his own people.

Though placed in this perilous situation, Hastings exhibited the greatest coolness; and, further, he hit upon an ingenious device for summoning aid. Among his men were some native soldiers, who undertook to make their way through the crowd on the other side of the water, and proceed to the English cantonments. It is customary in India for the natives to wear large earrings, but when they travel the ring is taken out for safety, and in place of it a small quill or a roll of paper is inserted in the hole to prevent it from closing. So Hastings placed in the ears of the messengers letters rolled up in the smallest possible compass, by which means he sent details of what had happened to the English officers. And in due course an army marched against Cheyt Sing, and, his forces being routed, he was deposed, and his territory was added to the English possessions.

On account of this attack on Cheyt Sing, as well as of a subsequent transaction by which he induced the ruler of Oude to deprive his mother, the Begum (or princess), of her riches, a strong feeling ere long grew up against Hastings both in India and in England, and knowing as he did that all he had done had been for the benefit of the Company, and not to serve his private interests, he felt aggrieved and indignant. And declining to submit to the treatment he was receiving on every side, he resigned his post and returned to his native land.

By this time (1785) affairs in India had been brought to a state of tranquillity, and the beneficial results of his masterly administration had become manifest. For, apart from the system of government having been placed on a sound basis, not only had the power of the English in the East been by his genius and daring saved from utter destruction, but the invading armies of their enemies had been driven back; the French had been prevented from recovering their foothold; vast additions had been made to the Company's territories; the confidence of native populations, who now began to enjoy security, was gained; and the might and valour of the British were feared throughout the land.

But on reaching England no laurels awaited the great statesman. Instead he found, just as Clive had found, only with greater bitterness, that he was to be hounded down and called to account for not a few of the acts which he had committed as Governor-General. To make the story short, hardly had he landed, ere he was summoned before the House of Lords, and impeached for over twenty charges of wrong-doing; and with such relentlessness did his enemies persevere in their efforts to convict him, that not till nine long years had passed did his trial end, when he was completely acquitted. Even then, though nearly ruined in fortune through the expenses of his defence, no honours and no recompense—save an annuity from the East India Company—were his; and all that now remained to Warren Hastings was to seek the repose of which his troubled spirit stood in such need.

To Daylesford, therefore—to the ancestral home which, in fulfilment of his childhood's dream, had become his—he retired; and here, on the 22nd of August, 1818, after two-and-twenty years spent in peaceful country pursuits, Warren Hastings was laid to rest.

III.—LORD CORNWALLIS.

STRANGE as it may seem, while Warren Hastings, who had saved India in her darkest hour, was subjected to a long and cruel persecution, the General who had surrendered with all his troops to the Americans, at York Town, in Virginia, was appointed to fill the former's place! Yet probably no better Governor-General could have been chosen; for by his achievements as a soldier, and by the wisdom and judgment he showed in work of reform, he gave proof of being well fitted to carry on the great work begun by Clive and Hastings.

Of the events in the earlier portion of Lord Cornwallis's life, brief mention will suffice. Descended from an old family long resident in Suffolk, he was born on the last day of 1738, and little is known of his early days except that, having been educated at Eton, he entered the army when eighteen. After this he obtained permission to travel on the Continent, where he began a course of study at the famous military academy at Turin; but war breaking out ere long, he joined the English camp in Westphalia, and served as aide-de-camp to the Marquess of Granby in the great campaign which followed. He became Earl Cornwallis on the death of his father in 1762; next, in 1766, was made a colonel; then, in 1770, was appointed Constable of the Tower of London; and in 1776, though opposed to the war with America, proceeded to that country as local Lieutenant-General. There he commanded the British forces in South Carolina, and succeeded in winning important victories against superior forces in 1780 and 1781; but in the latter year, having been blockaded at York Town, by the American army and the French fleet, he was compelled, as has been said, after an obstinate defence, to capitulate.

As might have been expected, this disaster to the English arms produced much dissatisfaction at home, and many were disposed to censure the unlucky General; but there were extenuating circumstances connected with the surrender, and beyond a heated discussion as to whether he was blamable, no adverse action was taken. Indeed, Lord Cornwallis, who was a man of sterling principle and high soldierly qualities, continued to retain the confidence of the Government, and the high favour of the King.

During the next few years, Lord Cornwallis was disinclined to accept any fresh appointment, though pressed to do so. He was again and again sounded as to his willingness to fill some responsible post, and it was especially felt that in no part of the world would his services be of greater value than in India. At one time he was offered the chief command of the British army there, but feeling that the restricted conditions under which this post was then held would be such as to make it intolerable, he refused it. Then the Governor-Generalship was suggested, but he said that to accept this would prevent him from being as serviceable to his country as he would be if he followed his own profession of a soldier elsewhere. So for a while matters remained as they were.

By the year 1786, however, after Warren Hastings had returned to England, the Governor-Generalship (the duties of which had been temporarily performed by Sir John Macpherson) having become vacant, it was necessary not only to fill up the post, but to appoint to it a man of high character and of well-tried capacity.* Lord Cornwallis was again invited to accept

* Rather more than a year previously an important measure known as Pitt's India Bill had been passed in Parliament, by which much of the East India Company's power of government was transferred to the

the high office; and at last feeling it to be his duty to do so, though, as he expressed it, "much against his will and with grief of heart," he consented, on condition that larger powers were vested in him than had been provided for in the India Bill. He wished, he said, "to hold in his own hands both the supreme civil and the supreme military authority; and seeing that if thwarted, as Hastings had been, by a jealous opposition in the Council, he would have no real power of any kind, he declared it to be an essential condition of his acceptance of the office that he should be empowered, on great occasions, to act on his own responsibility, against the votes of the majority of the Council." These conditions were agreed to, and in 1786 he embarked for India as Governor-General and Commander-in-Chief.

Notwithstanding all that Warren Hastings had done in introducing method and order into the internal management of Indian affairs, there was still much room for improvement, and on landing Lord Cornwallis lost no time in acquainting himself with the real condition of matters. He soon found that many abuses existed by which officials of the Company and others were enabled to enrich themselves at the expense of the natives, as well as by other means, and he set to work with great vigour to correct these.

Crown. This Bill provided for the establishment in London of a Board of Control who were, among their other functions, to "check, superintend, and control all the acts, operations, and concerns" connected with the civil and military administration and revenues of India; while the appointment of the highest officers there was to be subject to the veto of the Home Government. The Company were, however, to be allowed to retain the entire management of their business affairs, as well as their patronage, and their "trappings of dignity."

"He hunted out frauds of every kind," and whenever he found opportunity to introduce new regulations tending to purify the Indian service, and to make the English rule more acceptable to the natives, he availed himself of it. Indeed, without attempting to enumerate the various reforms for which India is indebted to him, it may be said that from the time when Lord Cornwallis commenced to hold the reins, the administrative system was raised to a high standard which had never before been reached, and which has been maintained ever since.

It was in work of this kind that Lord Cornwallis spent the first three years of his new career; and during this time there was to a great extent a cessation of those hostilities with native powers which had been so frequent in the days of Clive and Hastings. So uneventful, indeed, was this period, that to a man like Cornwallis, much of whose life had been passed amid the excitement of the camp, it must have been somewhat dull. In a letter written in 1789 to his son, who was at Eton, the Governor-General said: "My life in Calcutta is perfect clockwork. I get on horseback just as the dawn of day begins to appear, ride on the same road, and the same distance; pass the whole forenoon after my return from riding in doing business, and almost the same exactly before sunset; then write or read over letters or papers for two hours, sit down at nine with two or three officers or my family to some fruit and a biscuit, and so to bed soon after the clock strikes ten."

But this was only the lull before the storm; and soon the sound of trumpets and the call to battle were again heard. The same Tippoo Sahib, calling himself Sultan of Mysore, with whom it will be remembered peace had been made in 1784, was now the cause of a great war in which the strength of the English was to be severely tried.

From his father, Hyder Ali, Tippoo had inherited bitter hatred of the English; and, cruel as the former had been, his son was even more cruel. What his character was may be judged from his name "Tippoo," signifying tiger, and from his repeated saying that "he would rather live two days like a tiger than 200 years like a sheep." His savage nature, too, was well illustrated by an ingenious machine-toy, still to be seen in London, which belonged to him, and which was found in his palace. It was called a "Tiger-organ," and in it was represented in gold and jewels a tiger standing over a prostrate man, whose face and uniform indicated an English soldier. The figures were moved by mechanism, and the music of the instrument, produced by turning a handle, represented the screams of the luckless victim, with the accompanying growls of the wild beast. The footstool of his throne—now preserved in Windsor Castle—was also in the form of a tiger's head made of gold, with eyes and teeth of crystal.

Ever since peace was made, Tippoo had behaved with the utmost arrogance towards the English, and again and again openly vowed that he would yet drive them out of the Empire. He had, however, been wise enough to wait a while, not only with the view of finding a suitable pretext, but in order to husband his resources. Now, after a lapse of about five years, he felt that the moment for action had arrived. At this time Tippoo became greatly exasperated by reason of certain alliances with native rulers into which Lord Cornwallis proposed to enter; and feeling that these were hostile to himself, he resolved on war.

On the coast of Malabar there was a principality called Travancore, which had for some years been under the protection of the English, and by whose rajah, or ruler, the latter were in honour bound to stand. Tippoo had long coveted this territory, and seizing as an excuse the fact that the rajah refused to give up two towns which he had bought, but which the Sultan of Mysore asserted were his, he assembled an army and suddenly marched to Travancore. He was, however, repulsed by the brave ruler with a loss of 2,000 men.

Such an attack upon an ally was of course tantamount to a declaration of war against the English themselves. Alliances were immediately offered to the Nizam (the ruler of the Deccan), as well as to the Mahrattas, which their hatred of Tippoo led them to eagerly accept; and it was agreed between the three allies that whatever conquests were effected should be equally divided.

At first the English forces were entrusted to the command of General Medows, but skilfully though his movements were directed, success did not attend this officer; so Lord Cornwallis determined to assume command in person.

The war then commenced in real earnest, and we are told that the native as well as the British troops "burned with impatience to take their revenge for the atrocious and brutal degradation to which their brothers-in-arms had been subjected during the last war, and even after the conclusion of it." Pushing on with all speed, Lord Cornwallis first made for Bangalore, and after feeble resistance this important stronghold was captured; whereupon Tippoo, in dismay, fell back towards Seringapatam, his capital, some seventy miles distant. A delay now took place, owing to the wavering conduct of the allies of the English, who, as in instances before referred to, had again lingered in the background till they saw which way the fortune of war was turning. But as soon as he was able, Lord Cornwallis resolved to follow up the advantage he had gained, by penetrating to the very heart of Tippoo's dominions, and ere long the allied armies arrived in sight of Seringapatam, defended by Tippoo himself at the head of a powerful host.

At first it seemed as though victory were assured; for when, on Tippoo sallying forth to attack the invaders, a great battle took place, not only were the latter successful, but the enemy was put to flight and sought refuge in Seringapatam.

But a disappointment was in store. For several weeks the allied forces had suffered much privation from scarcity of food. Now it was found that the stores were exhausted, and, worse still, that owing to the swelling of the river surrounding Tippoo's capital, and the interception of food supplies by the enemy's light horsemen, they were nearly reduced to starvation. To attempt to storm the place was, therefore, out of the question; and bitter though the mortification, only one course remained open—to retire homewards as rapidly as possible. So the dreary retreat commenced; but before British territory was reached many a brave fellow had dropped by the way, and the march is described as having been one of the most melancholy occurrences in Indian history.

Still, notwithstanding such a serious check in his plans, Lord Cornwallis was not discouraged, as we shall see.

In the meantime Tippoo, in rage against the English, had been trying hard to gain allies outside the Empire. His vanity and religious fanaticism had led him to regard himself as a chosen servant of Mahomet, " and predestined to root out the infidels from India," and to this end he had sent envoys to Constantinople to endeavour to induce the Sultan to assist him ; but these persons all perished of the plague during the journey. Next he despatched a mission to Louis XVI., begging for the aid of 6,000 of his best troops, and undertaking with such help to crush the English. The envoy seems to have met with a favourable reception from Louis' ministers, and it was at one time thought that the expedition would be sent. But the King, more cautious than his counsellors, would not consent.

An amusing incident is recorded in connection with this mission to France. By his envoy Tippoo had sent a number of presents to King Louis and his Queen, but he had been rather niggardly in his choice of them. The portion sent to the King consisted, we are told, "of some gold gauze, some crimson silk stuff flowered with gold, some Persian linen, partly plain and partly printed, an aigrette [or ornament] of bad diamonds, flat, yellow, and ill-set, with a clasp of the same kind ; while the Queen's consisted of only three bottles partially filled with essences, a box of perfumed powder-balls, some scented matches, and nothing more!"

When this mean collection of Oriental gifts was presented, his Majesty is said to have exclaimed, laughing, "What can I do with all this trumpery? It seems only fit to dress dolls! But you have little girls who may be pleased with such—give it all to them."

"But the diamonds, sire?" urged the official.

"Oh, they are truly fine," said the King, in a jeering tone. "Perhaps you would like them placed among the jewels of the crown? But you may take them too, and wear them in your hat if you like!"

Eventually, it is said, the Queen would accept only a bottle of otto of roses, and King Louis some of the fine linen which had been sent.

After his retreat to Madras, Lord Cornwallis commenced preparations for the second attempt on Tippoo's capital; and having organised a strong army, he, after certain preliminary operations, took the field with 22,000 men and 86 guns—a force which is said to have been so imposing in appearance that it led Tippoo to exclaim—

"It is not what I see of the resources of the English that I dread, as what I do not see!"

On the 5th of February, 1792, having been joined by his allies, the Nizam and the Mahrattas, the whole force had reached a position from which the minarets and embattled walls of Seringapatam were visible. Tippoo's army, numbering 56,000 men, was already encamped in a strong position, and protected by three lines of defence, in which were no fewer than

300 guns, and around them was "a hedge of thorny plants, absolutely impervious to man or beast."

No time was lost by Lord Cornwallis; and it was a bold movement which he had determined upon. On the morning after arrival orders were issued that a general attack should be made by night; and nine o'clock that evening was fixed for beginning operations. No cannon were to accompany the force, nor were tents to be struck; the plan of the General being to take Tippoo by surprise, and, if possible, capture his camp and the works he was constructing without firing a shot. Lord Cornwallis was to accompany the troops in personal command of the central division—a proceeding which gave rise to not a little comment on the part of the generals of the native allies, who it is said were lost in astonishment when they heard that the Governor-General and Commander-in-Chief intended to go with a fighting party "like an ordinary captain."

Night came: the signal was given in silence; by the soft light of the moon every plan was rapidly carried out; and soon the invaders were in the centre of the sleeping enemy's camp. Here the force was divided into three columns; and then the real work of the night commenced, and was ere long accomplished. When daylight appeared—though not till after hard fighting, in which Lord Cornwallis bore a prominent part—Tippoo's field-works were captured, and a large force established close to the city of Seringapatam; while the Sultan "who had seen, first with credulity and then with dismay, a long line of English footmen advancing under the silence of the night into the very heart of the camp, had shut himself in his fort." Desperate fighting now took place. But vain were the efforts of the enemy to dislodge the allies from the positions they had gained; and, before evening, besides losing 80 of his cannon, 4,000 of the Sultan's troops were killed or wounded, 10,000 fled or were made prisoners, while the remainder were glad to seek shelter within the fortress. The English casualties did not exceed 550. Fortunately, too, for Lord Cornwallis, he was now joined by an additional force under General Robert Abercromby, who had pushed on from Bombay with 6,000 Highlanders and Sepoys.

It was next determined to lay siege to Seringapatam, and preparations were accordingly made; but by this time Tippoo, alarmed and disheartened by his disasters, and feeling that to effectually cope with such a force as now surrounded his capital was impossible, showed signs of submission.

Rage still filled his cruel heart, however; and, savage that he was, he now hit upon an expedient by which he thought his troubles might be easily ended. Believing, as was natural for such a man to believe, that if only the Commander-in-Chief were removed the English and their allies would lose heart and retire, Tippoo resolved that an attempt to assassinate Lord Cornwallis should be made. So he summoned some of his followers, and having pointed out how great would be the glory of ridding themselves of the invaders by such a simple deed, he induced them to undertake the foul commission; on which, attired in a fashion which might easily cause them to be mistaken for some of the native allies' troops, they made their way to the English camp.

But in his anxiety to ensure, as he thought, the success of his plan, he drugged the men almost to the point of madness. The result was that they behaved in such a wild and reckless manner that their movements betrayed them; and a party of Sepoys having turned out, they fled in terror from the encampment.

After this occurrence the Sultan, feeling that he was outdone, sent messengers to Lord Cornwallis, offering to submit, and suing for peace. His request was granted, though on very severe terms, namely:—
(1) That Tippoo should cede one-half of his dominions to the allied powers; (2) That he should pay three crores and 30 lacs of rupees (about £3,300,000); (3) That he must release all prisoners of war; and (4) That his two sons should be delivered into British protection as hostages for the due performance of the treaty.

Hard as these conditions must have been to the haughty Sultan, he agreed to them; and on the 26th of February the young hostages, each mounted on a richly caparisoned elephant, and attended by an imposing escort, left the fortress and proceeded to the camp of Lord Cornwallis.

The scene that followed is described as having been most impressive and touching. As the procession left the archway the guns of the citadel roared forth a salute; then followed several rounds from the British cannon; and when their destination was reached, the little hostages were received with much distinction, and Lord Cornwallis, having embraced them, took the hand of each, and led the way to his tent. The elder of the two, Abdul Kalik, was only

F

about ten years old, while the younger, Mooza-ud-Deen, was about eight; and it must have been an interesting sight to see these little fellows, attired in robes of white muslin, with red turbans richly adorned with pearls, standing amidst the grim warriors around them.

The two boys were formally surrendered by an important officer of Tippoo's Court, who, when Lord Cornwallis had placed one on each side of him, said—

"These children were this morning the sons of my master, the Sultan. Their situation is now changed, and they must look to your lordship as their father."

On which the Governor-General replied that they should have every kindness and attention; and it is said that he spoke so gently and cheerfully to them that he at once gained their confidence. Then presents were exchanged, Lord Cornwallis giving each prince a gold watch, and, in addition, a pair of pistols to the elder one; while they, in return, presented him with a valuable sword; after which they were conducted to a specially prepared tent, attended by a guard of honour.

Thus was the war, one of the most important since Plassy, ended; thus was added to the possessions of the English one-third of the territory which had been exacted from the Sultan—the native allies receiving the remaining two-thirds; and thus were the designs against the British rule in India, which Tippoo had fondly hoped he might carry out, frustrated.

The great task which he had set himself completed, Lord Cornwallis now disappears from the scene, though not until after he had instituted further changes in the Indian administration, all tending to reform the Company's service as well as to improve the relations of the English with neighbouring rulers, and to conciliate the native populations subject to them; and, created a Marquess by George III. in recognition of his achievements, he started for England in 1793.

It was not, however, to a life of ease that he returned; for his country, beset by troubles at home and abroad, stood in need of all her sons—especially of such a gallant leader as Lord Cornwallis. He was now, therefore, employed in various important capacities, notably as Lord-Lieutenant and Commander-in-Chief in Ireland—from 1798 to 1801—where he succeeded in crushing the Rebellion of that period; until, in 1805, he was again summoned to India. But it was only for a brief period that he was there; for, in feeble health on arrival, he rapidly became worse, and within three months, while on his way to the Upper Provinces to carry out certain fresh plans for the welfare of the Empire, he died on the 5th of October, at Ghazeepore, near Benares.

What Lord Cornwallis's brilliant qualities as a warrior were we have seen. What he accomplished as a humane and upright ruler alike testified to his ability and to his zealous endeavour to do his duty. One of his biographers, Sir John Kaye, has well said that he was "the first great Indian ruler who can properly be regarded as an administrator. Up to the time of his arrival, the English in India had been engaged in a great struggle for existence. Clive had conquered the richest province of India. Hastings had reduced it to something like order. But it was not until Cornwallis carried to that country the large-minded liberality of a benevolent English statesman that our administrative efforts took shape and consistency." And, referring to the corruption which had previously prevailed in the land, the same writer says: " Lord Cornwallis sounded its death-knell. And from that time the great company of merchants which governed India was served by a succession of soldiers and civilians unsurpassed in rectitude of life by any whose names are recorded in the muster-roll of the world."

IV.—LORD WELLESLEY.

IT was at a critical period in the history of British rule in India that the subject of this sketch was appointed Governor-General, and it was fortunate for his country as well as for the East India Company that the helm of State passed into such skilful hands. His brilliantly successful administration is the more remarkable because at the time of entering upon it he was a comparatively untried man, and, moreover, during the years he held office his energies were taxed in solving most intricate problems.

The elder brother of the great Duke of Wellington, Richard Colley Wellesley, the future Governor-General—who became Lord Mornington on the death of his father, and was subsequently created Marquess Wellesley—had from childhood showed signs of remarkable ability. At Eton, where, at the age of twelve, he was sent in 1772, he highly distinguished himself, and at Christ Church, Oxford, where he proceeded in 1778, his fame as a scholar also stood high. Early in life he showed decided taste for the study of Asiatic history; and when, in 1782, he became a member of Parliament, his statesmanlike qualities attracted much attention. For some years he continued to apply himself specially to Indian matters, and such repute did he gain that in 1793 he was appointed one of the members of the Board of Control. After four years' experience in this capacity, during which period he had, of course, peculiar opportunities of obtaining comprehensive knowledge of Oriental affairs, he was selected as the most fitting man to rule India.

On his arrival in Calcutta in May, 1798, Lord Wellesley (as he may be called in anticipation of the title afterwards conferred on him) found that the condition of affairs was most serious, and that the British rule had become hedged round with formidable dangers. The causes were not far to seek. To begin with, fresh difficulties had arisen with Tippoo Sahib. Notwithstanding the treaty of peace which Lord Cornwallis had dictated to him in 1792, this prince, though humbled at the time, had never ceased to cherish feelings of hatred against the English, and, his spirit rankling under the heavy losses sustained, he had ever since thirsted for revenge. To this end he had carefully improved his resources, and awaited fitting opportunity for taking action. This opportunity he thought had at last been afforded through Great Britain and France being again at war, and it was within three weeks of Lord Wellesley reaching

India that he received the astounding intelligence that Tippoo had publicly sent to the Mauritius proposing to the French an offensive and defensive alliance, with the object of expelling the English—which having been accomplished, the country was to be divided between them. And the result had been that in response to his request a small body of men had already been sent to Seringapatam to enter the service of the Sultan.

The second problem which demanded solution by Lord Wellesley was in connection with the attitude of the Nizam, with whom, and with the Mahrattas, it will be remembered, an alliance had been entered into a few years before by Lord Cornwallis. Unfortunately, Lord Wellesley's predecessor had withdrawn from this compact at a time when the Nizam was engaged in a quarrel with the Mahrattas, and the consequence had been that, angry at what he considered his desertion by the English, he had not only dismissed the British officers who had been in his service, but had, in their stead, sought and obtained French officers. These—though meanwhile he had been grievously defeated by the Mahrattas—he had continued to retain. But the French, taking advantage of the Nizam's weakness, had after a while begun to acquire such influence in his territory, that it not only seemed probable that their authority would ere long be paramount in the Deccan, but it was plain that already the English power was seriously jeopardised by their presence. Thus, apart from the Nizam's unfriendly feelings, Lord Wellesley had to reckon with a fresh danger—a danger now intensified through the overtures which Tippoo Sahib had made to the French in the Mauritius.

There was a third difficulty with which Lord Wellesley had to cope, though it was not, as we shall see, for some little time that it proved really serious. In another part of India, the Mahratta chieftain Sindia had become very powerful. Some years previously his uncle, whom he had succeeded, had acquired the right of demanding *chout*, or tribute, over a large area of territory, including such important places as Delhi and Agra, and, moreover, had exacted from the deposed Mogul Emperor such special dignities and authority, that he had risen to much greatness. And at the period of Lord Wellesley's arrival in India, not only did Sindia—who even had possession of the person of the Emperor at Delhi—enjoy immense influence and authority, but he, too, had secured the services of the French, by whom his well-equipped army of 40,000 men was, to a large extent, officered.

Nor were these all Lord Wellesley's anxieties. The situation was rendered the more perplexing by the fact that Bonaparte, who had recently invaded Egypt, was believed to contemplate an attack on the English possessions in India; while, to make matters worse, much discontent prevailed among the Company's officers at Calcutta, and the treasury was absolutely empty.

So it will be seen that the English were more or less threatened on nearly every side—mainly, too, through the instrumentality of their bitter enemies, the French; and the task which lay before Lord Wellesley, and with which he was so boldly and splendidly to grapple, was indeed no easy one.

Quick to perceive that to effectually cope with the dangers now rapidly spreading, a daring blow must be struck in the directions most threatened, the Governor-General resolved to lose no time in anticipating Tippoo Sahib's hostile movements by marching an army on his capital. Before he could hope to be successful in this, however, it was necessary to take decisive action, so as not merely to change the attitude of the Nizam, but even to gain over his alliance. So, ignoring the fact that his predecessor, when asked for it at a critical moment, a few years previously, had refused aid to the ruler of the Deccan, Lord Wellesley now called upon the latter to give *his* assistance in accordance with the agreement which had been made by him with Lord Cornwallis; offering at the same time to substitute English officers in place of the French then in his service, as well as to protect his dominions from all unjust demands that might be made upon them. It was a bold proposition, but, fortunately, circumstances were favourable to its acceptance. For it happened that the French officers in the Deccan had by this time proved themselves so arrogant and overbearing towards the Nizam, and he had become so alarmed at the influence and authority they had acquired, that he was not indisposed to be rid of them. So Lord Wellesley's offer was accepted—on condition that the English held themselves responsible for removing the Frenchmen.

Lord Wellesley carried out his design, and the success of this his first great act as Governor-General testifies alike to his courage and his capacity for understanding the real needs of the moment. Mustering a suitable force, he caused it to be marched to Hyderabad, the capital of the Deccan; and on proclamation having been issued by the Nizam dismissing the Frenchmen, the British troops were suddenly placed in a position which commanded the camp of the latter; and by skilful manœuvring they disarmed all the regiments without a single life being lost. The French, having then been paid off, were ordered out of the country; and, their influence in the Nizam's dominions having been destroyed, the English were reinstated.

Having by this prompt and remarkable move enabled the Nizam—now quite ready to do so—to co-operate with the English, no time was lost in preparing for the campaign in Mysore; and the energy with which Lord Wellesley set to work is characteristic of every achievement with which his name is linked. On his sending orders to Madras to assemble the army, the authorities were, it is said, "thunderstruck with his venturous project," and raised not a few objections to it on the ground both of the lack of money in the Company's coffers, and the unequal strength of the English compared with Tippoo's forces. But Lord Wellesley, when once determined on a given line of action, was not to be daunted by such obstacles, and in reply to the communication received from Madras, he peremptorily commanded that the army should be put in order without delay; while he wrote in severest terms to "those who presumed to thwart him and arrogated to themselves the power of governing the Empire committed to his charge." Recognising, however, the impossibility of conducting the campaign without funds, he himself subscribed a large sum of money towards the tremendous expenses of the war; and his example was speedily followed by Europeans and wealthy natives. Meanwhile, he had sent letters to Tippoo calling upon him to explain his intrigues; and the evasive reply of that treacherous ruler having made it evident that the reports of his designs against the English were true, and that, moreover, he was engaged in soliciting still further aid from the French, Lord Wellesley gave orders that the troops should take the field forthwith.

At length, in February, 1799, the allied armies, numbering about 40,000 men, including the Nizam's contingent of nearly 20,000—which was under the command of Colonel Arthur Wellesley (afterwards Duke of Wellington), who had arrived in India about two years before his brother, the Governor-General —began their advance, starting from different points; and within two months the whole force effected a junction within sight of Tippoo's capital.

The march had been an eventful one, and attended with many dangers; for the progress of the troops had been made difficult by the loss of many of their cattle on the way, while Tippoo with all his men had unexpectedly intercepted the column which had started from Bombay, and attempted to destroy it before it could join the main army. Fortunately, the gallant little force had been able to effectually resist the Mysoreans, who, after six hours' hard fighting, fled in confusion with heavy losses.

The Sultan had next mustered up courage to fight the force which had marched from Madras, and at a place called Malavelly a furious battle had been fought.

Tippoo had arranged what he conceived to be a clever plan of preliminary attack by concealing in the jungle a force of 300 horsemen, who, having been infuriated with drugs, were ordered, first, to await the approach of the English, then to break suddenly through their right wing, on which the Sultan was to dash with his cavalry into the gap, and throw its whole weight on the invaders. Luckily this scheme was discovered before it could be put into execution, and when the 300 men burst out of their hiding-place, the English general, having anticipated the attack, was ready to give them a warm reception; so the ruse failed. Tippoo's men were so discouraged by this failure that many of them retreated, and the other English wing, under the command of Colonel Arthur Wellesley, who now for the first time drew sword on Indian soil, commenced an attack by which the whole Mysorean host was routed, with the loss of 2,000 men and their six standards, the British casualties numbering only about sixty.

After this discomfiture, Tippoo lost no time in seeking refuge, with the remainder of his followers, in his stronghold at Seringapatam; and feeling certain that the invaders would follow him, he laid the country waste, leaving neither food nor forage along the route. But his plans were frustrated by the English general, who, instead of taking the road in question, chose one in an opposite direction, along which he could not only proceed without difficulty, but obtain the requisite supplies for his army, and, which was equally important, effect a junction with the army from Bombay.

This movement was successful; and we are told

that when Tippoo, who to his astonishment found himself confronted by the whole English force just as he himself was approaching the capital, realised how he had been outwitted, his rage and despair knew no bounds.

Calling together his chief officers, he exclaimed, with tears in his eyes—

"We have arrived at our last stage. What is your determination?"

And with one accord they declared, as each man laid his hand on his sword, that they would make one last desperate attempt to save their capital; "or," said they, "we will die with you!"

And now the English began to surround the walls of Seringapatam, and with the recollection which many of the troops had of Tippoo's barbarities towards companions-in-arms who had fallen into his hands, it is not difficult to understand with what alacrity officers and men proceeded with their preparations to besiege the tyrant's fortress.

After the lapse of a month, during which the city had been closely invested, a breach was found to be practicable, and the storming immediately commenced under the leadership of General David Baird, who, it will be remembered, had some years previously, after being taken prisoner by Hyder Ali, been thrown into one of the dungeons of this very fortress.

Precisely at one in the afternoon, we are told, the tall and noble-looking figure of this officer was seen to issue from the trenches in view of both forces. Mounting a parapet and brandishing his sword, he exclaimed to his men—

"Come on, my brave fellows. Come, follow me, and prove yourselves worthy the name of British soldiers!"

Then with ringing cheers the English dashed into the fortress, manned by a garrison nearly 20,000 strong, with nearly 300 cannon. A furious struggle ensued, but though the defenders fought well and valiantly, they were no match for their antagonists, and within seven minutes the British standard was waving on the battlements.

During the fight so many young officers who carried the English colours were shot down, even in that short time, that at last they were borne by a sergeant of a Bombay regiment, a Scotsman named Graham. Rushing forward, and mounting the summit of the breach, he took off his hat, and with three cheers shouted—

"Success to Lieutenant Graham!"—referring to his getting a commission if he survived. Then, planting the colours on the ruined wall, he shouted, "Hang 'em—I'll show 'em the British flag!" but at that moment the brave fellow was shot dead by the enemy.

The Mysoreans were now driven from their stronghold, and the struggle was continued in the streets. It is described as having been terrible, and, though lasting only an hour, thousands of Tippoo's troops fell before the victorious English.

And Tippoo Sahib—where was he? At first he could not be found, and when after their victory the British took possession of his palace, it was believed that he was still alive. But it was not so. In the heat of the attack he had rushed towards the breach, and side by side with his men had fought with great bravery, until at length he had fallen, severely wounded by their musket-balls. As he lay at the point of death, an English soldier seized his belt, which was richly jewelled, and attempted to pull it off; but the dying Sultan, who still had a sword in his hand, made a final cut with it, and, though wounded, the man thereupon shot him through the brain and killed him. It was not till late in the evening that his dead body was discovered and recognised; and on the following day it was buried with military honours in the great mausoleum of his father, Hyder Ali.

So, owing to the bad faith and perfidious conduct of its sovereign, was finally subdued the kingdom which for nearly thirty years had been the powerful and dangerous rival of the English.

By the ordinary rules of war, it was now open to the Governor-General to divide the conquered territory between the English and the Nizam; but for various reasons Lord Wellesley felt that this course was not desirable, and he determined to restore a large portion of Tippoo's dominions to a descendant of the ancient Hindoo dynasty, which had been overthrown by Hyder Ali. The heir was a boy five years old, then living in poverty and obscurity; and this child having been sought out was, amid much pomp, placed on the throne of his ancestors, with a revenue of fifty lacs of rupees (about £500,000) a year, while the administration of the country, which was to be under British protection, was entrusted to Colonel Arthur Wellesley. The rest of Mysore was divided among the allies, and the spoils of Seringapatam, comprising jewels of the value of one million pounds sterling, besides much other valuable treasure, were shared by the victorious troops. Of these the sum of £100,000 was offered by the Directors of the East India Company to Lord Wellesley; but, declining to be enriched with prize-money, he refused it, though afterwards he was voted, and accepted, an annuity of £5,000 a year. It was for this splendid victory that, in the same year, he was created Marquess Wellesley.

The effect of the Governor-General's bold doings was soon apparent. That within little more than twelve months it should have been possible to accomplish so much—to destroy French and to substitute English influence in the Deccan; to overthrow Tippoo, and to place another ruler on his throne under English protection—all this created astonishment, "struck terror into the hearts of the native princes, and exalted the prestige of the Company's Government." So profound was the impression produced by the conquest of Mysore—not alone the overthrow and death of Tippoo, but Lord Wellesley's wise and just policy in restoring to the throne a descendant of its ancient ruler—that the Governor-General was able ere long to enter into treaties with various ruling princes of India which were of the greatest advantage to the British. Into the particulars of these arrangements we need not enter; it will, however, convey some idea of their extent to say that within a very short time such valuable territories as those belonging to the Nabob of the Carnatic, the Nabob of Oude, the Rajah of Tanjore, and others, were placed under the civil and military administration of the Company—these rulers enjoying merely a pension, an empty title of sovereignty, and the management of internal affairs And by the year 1802 the only rival power of importance left was that of the Mahrattas, who by this time were divided into five different parties (including Sindia, already referred to) not on friendly terms with one another.

The Governor-General had been desirous to enter into the same kind of relations with the Mahrattas which he had established with the native rulers just mentioned, and he had already approached the Peshwa, nominally their "supreme governor,"—whose authority, however, was ignored by other chieftains, particularly by Sindia and by Holkar. But, so far, his overtures had been in vain. It happened, however, towards the end of 1802, that war broke out between the Peshwa and Sindia and Holkar, the result of which was that the first named was glad to seek refuge in British territory. This was Lord Wellesley's opportunity. Again pressing upon the Peshwa the offer of an alliance, by the terms of which he was to be reestablished at the head of the Mahratta nation, while he in return was to place himself under British protection, the vanquished prince reluctantly yielded; and on the last day of the year the treaty with him—"considered by many as sealing the fate of India"—was signed at Bassein.

The completion of this compact produced the utmost consternation amongst some of the other Mahratta chieftains. Sindia, in particular, was alarmed; and regarding the entrance of a foreign power into their dominion as a serious menace and a gross indignity to their name, he determined to prevent the English from making further encroachments, and to inflict a crushing blow upon them. So the signal was given for action.

Lord Wellesley entered on this formidable struggle with his usual spirit. Dividing the army into two portions, he instructed his brother, General Arthur Wellesley, to march to Poona, the Mahratta capital—to drive out the force then in possession, and to reinstate the Peshwa; while, simultaneously, General Gerard (afterwards Lord) Lake was to go northward to attack Sindia's army (then officered, as already stated, mainly by Frenchmen). These operations were triumphantly carried out; and the campaign presented a series of brilliant achievements from beginning to end. General Wellesley having established British power in the Mahratta dominions, and with imposing ceremony re-enthroned the Peshwa at Poona, then led forth his army against the enemy; and his first step—the capture of the strong fortress of Ahmednuggur—having been accomplished, he, on the 21st of September, 1803, formed a plan by which, he starting in one direction and Colonel Stephenson, his second in command, in another, he hoped his whole force would be enabled to make the attack.

But on the morning of the 23rd, General Wellesley, with only 4,500 men, suddenly came upon an encampment of 50,000 Mahrattas, with 100 guns, commanded by Sindia, and evidently awaiting the British. This was at Assaye. Regardless of the overwhelming numbers arrayed against him, Wellesley resolved to give them battle, and ordered his men to advance in line with bayonets fixed. This was done, and the brave fellows charged right up to the muzzles of the Mahratta guns, from which a deadly fire poured forth. But Sindia's army, with all its strength, was no match for the English, who pushed their way on and on until at length they forced the Mahrattas to flee in disorder. The loss of the latter amounted to no fewer than 12,000 men, together with their guns and camp belongings, while that of the British was one-third of their number: and the victory—followed up by others also successful—has been described as one of the most complete which ever crowned the Company's arms in India.

Meanwhile General Lake, marching northwards, had fought with like courage and determination, and been fortunate enough to complete the discomfiture of Sindia. Advancing on Delhi with 10,000 men, he had not only overthrown the enemy's troops and their French officers, but had captured the cities of Delhi and Agra, and released the aged Emperor, then held, as already stated, in captivity, and placed him under British protection. Following up these successes, he had fought a great battle at Laswaree, where the scattered Mahratta forces had assembled to make another desperate stand against the British; and here, too, he had been victorious.

This final blow completely shattered for a time the power of the enemy; and, though Lord Wellesley, before his term of office expired, had some further trouble with Holkar and other of the Mahratta chieftains, and after he left India much hard fighting became necessary before they were finally subjugated, yet the immediate effect of his operations was to enable the Company to assume the sovereignty of the whole territory north of the Jumna, besides securing some provinces beyond that river, as well as various concessions, all tending to the extension of their influence and authority.

Lord Wellesley remained in India for about a year after these events. During his Governor-Generalship he had ruled with a masterly hand, and wrought great deeds. Surrounded on arrival by most formidable difficulties, he had overcome them one by one. He had destroyed French influence, and substituted that of the English; he had overthrown Tippoo Sahib, and made Mysore dependent on the Company; he had conquered the Mahrattas, scattered Sindia's hosts, and taken possession of his dominions. He had, besides, secured the virtual sovereignty of other large territories in various directions; he had introduced numerous reforms into civil affairs, and had established the famous institution at Calcutta called Fort William College, for training young civilians for the Company's service; while so successfully had he managed the Company's finances, that its yearly revenue had been raised by him from seven to over fifteen millions sterling, "with advantage to commerce, and without injustice to the inhabitants."

But notwithstanding all that he achieved, his vigorous and aggressive policy had come to be regarded with disfavour by the home authorities, and in 1805, alarmed by the magnitude and costliness of his military enterprises, as well as offended because they considered he was acting contrary to their wishes, Lord Wellesley was recalled, and, in imitation of the course pursued towards Clive and Hastings, an attempt was made to impeach him in Parliament for "high crimes and misdemeanours."

This, however, signally failed, and though Lord Wellesley was subjected at the time to severe censure, yet some years before his death, which took place on the 26th of September, 1842, after serving his country in various high offices at home and abroad, he had the satisfaction of being assured by the Directors of the Company, who at the same time voted him a grant of £20,000, that "in their judgment he had been animated throughout his administration by an ardent zeal to promote the well-being of India, and to uphold the interest and honour of the British Empire."

V.—ELDRED POTTINGER AND SIR ALEXANDER BURNES.

ELDRED POTTINGER had a love for gunpowder from his earliest days, and during the whole of his boyhood nothing seems to have given him more delight than to take part in pretended warlike projects. When a mere child he succeeded in nearly blowing up himself and his little brother; and on another occasion, after constructing some mimic fortifications, he had a narrow escape from serious injury. For, having with a number of heavy stones built up his structure on a garden wall, the entire fabric collapsed, and only just missed falling on two persons seated below.

Apart from his inclination towards such exploits, the boy seems to have been of a naturally studious disposition, and by the time he was fourteen he had, under a private tutor, made considerable progress in his education. It was during that year, 1825, that he chose his future profession. His uncle, Colonel Pottinger, brother of his father (an Irish gentleman belonging to County Down), had many years before gone to India, and at this period was a person of consequence there. Young Eldred had, of course, frequently heard of his relative and his doings, and delighting as he did in every kind of adventure, it is not surprising that his own thoughts should have turned towards the East. And the result was that in the year named he entered the Company's military seminary at Addiscombe.

Eldred Pottinger appears to have quickly become a favourite here. He secured a good place in his class by his industry, and he gained the goodwill of his comrades alike by his manliness, pluck, and truthfulness. He had not cast off his old childish habits, however; nor had his liking for gunpowder diminished. It was soon after arriving at Addiscombe that he invented an ingenious implement of war in the form of a bomb-shell; but, unluckily, he broke the rules by firing it from a mortar in the college grounds. This was a serious offence, which well-nigh brought about his expulsion; but it seems to have been eventually passed over; and from this time he devoted himself so steadily to his studies that within two years he passed his examination successfully, and came out as a cadet of artillery.

Young Pottinger now embarked for India, and as his uncle held his post in the Bombay Presidency, he decided to begin his duties in that portion of the

Empire. Joining the head-quarters of his regiment there, he entered with enthusiasm into the many details he was called upon to learn, and he showed singular aptitude for acquiring knowledge of his profession, and especially also for mastering native languages.

Making rapid progress, he was ere long appointed to a post in the Political (or Diplomatic) Department; but it can easily be understood that to an ambitious young soldier like Pottinger quiet employment of this kind would not be so congenial as active service; and that he should at this time have found his mode of life somewhat irksome was not unnatural.

But it was only for a time; and before long opportunity was afforded by which the desire of his heart was gratified. Events were taking place in countries beyond the north-western borders of India which caused affairs there to be very unsettled; and it was considered important that the Government should be, in particular, accurately informed about what was happening in Afghanistan. The services of an officer, at once brave and trustworthy, who was willing to undertake this mission were therefore needed. When Lieutenant Pottinger heard of this he eagerly volunteered; and much to his delight the offer was accepted.

So—in 1837—he started on his dangerous errand, accompanied by only a few followers, and disguised as a native horse-dealer, so as to conceal his nationality, as well as, of course, the real object of his journey. As far as the city of Cabul the young subaltern met with few obstacles; but arrived there, he deemed it well to change his disguise into that of a Mahometan *Syud*, or holy man, believing it would enable him the more easily to reach his goal, namely, the fortified city of Herat—known as the "Key of India," from the circumstance that all the roads leading to the Empire converge within its territory. He had not long left Cabul—from which city he had, indeed, escaped with some difficulty—before a series of adventures befell him.

First, he had to run the gauntlet of more than one passing traveller, who cast suspicious glances at him, and asked awkward questions. Next a more formidable difficulty presented itself. He had arrived at the country of Yakoob Beg, a notorious native chief, who made a rule of levying blackmail upon all travellers, and sometimes even sold strangers into slavery. Hardly had they reached his territory when Pottinger and his companions were imprisoned in Yakoob Beg's fort; and while here they were subjected to so much cross-examination as to the religion they professed, as well as many other matters, that their position was most uncomfortable. At one time, through the mistakes they made when answering questions, it seemed probable that their disguises would be detected; but, as it happened, they were eventually able, by dint of ready wit and presence of mind, to persuade Yakoob Beg to let them depart. And, having previously presented him with a detonating gun, they went on their way after eight days' imprisonment.

But hardly had they started, congratulating themselves on their escape, when a body of men followed at their heels, calling on them to return. Compelled to obey, they did so, trembling for the result; but it was soon plain why their presence was required. As they approached the chief, there was a shot, then a loud shout of triumph; upon which Yakoob Beg, in answer to Pottinger's "Peace be with you!" replied—

"You may go now. I don't want you. I only sent for you to make the gun go off, and it has gone off!"

Pottinger and his companions now journeyed on, and reached their goal by the middle of August. Arrived there, peril again attended them; and once more they were nearly carried off into slavery. Happening to wander unarmed outside the fortifications, they were seized by a party of slaveholders, but fortunately the presence of mind of Pottinger—who declared that aid was on its way to them—had the effect of inducing their captors to release them.

At this time Herat was ruled by Shah Kamran, the rest of Afghanistan being subject to Dost Mahomet; and the "Key of India" was about to become the scene of important events. Four years before, the Shah of Persia had looked with covetous eyes upon this place, though when he had gone so far as to attack it he had been completely routed. He had now again mustered up courage; and at the very time when Eldred Pottinger entered the city the Persians, encouraged and assisted by Russia, were preparing to besiege it, with the object, it was believed, of leading up to an invasion of India.

Pottinger took up his abode in Herat, retaining his Mahometan garb; and when, in September, Shah Kamran, with his Vizier, Yar Mahomet, who had been absent on a campaign, returned, he begged for an interview with the latter, who received him graciously, and accepted a brace of pistols from him. Then he paid a visit to Kamran, who was also friendly; and, under his protection, he was able to throw off his disguise, and be free from molestation.

It was shortly after this that news arrived of the advance of the Persian force, numbering 40,000; and the prospect that opened up to Pottinger, though full of unknown perils, could hardly fail to have been a pleasing one. He knew that so long as Herat remained in the hands of its Shah Kamran no danger threatened India; but he knew, on the other hand, that if once it passed into the hands of the Persians and Russians, the result would, in all likelihood, be injurious to the British. He longed, too, to gratify his strong warlike tastes; why, then, should he not volunteer his services to aid Shah Kamran in defending Herat? He did so; his offer was gladly accepted; and when the Heratees soon afterwards found their city surrounded by Persians, and it seemed clear to them that they must give in, it was to Eldred Pottinger that they turned in despair to save them.

Apart from his natural courage and ability, Pottinger's training as a soldier now stood him in good stead, and from this time forward he became the central figure in the defence of Herat. Day by day he laboured incessantly in organising the troops of Shah Kamran, as well as in strengthening the fortifications of the city; and Christmas arrived while yet the Persians had not been able to effect an entrance. By this time Shah Kamran had begun to get somewhat alarmed, fearing that he might be starved into submission; he therefore determined to despatch an envoy to the Persian camp, in order to ascertain whether terms of peace could be arranged. But no Heratee would venture on such an errand; so it was to Pottinger that he had at last to turn, and to him the mission was entrusted. But on reaching the Persian camp, it was evident that nothing short of unconditional surrender would satisfy the Shah, who gave vent to his anger on hearing that Kamran had merely sent to treat for peace on terms favourable to himself; so after an interview, lasting about three-quarters of an hour, the envoy was dismissed and returned to Herat.

The Persians ere long, feeling that the powerful resistance of the Heratees was mainly attributable to the Englishman, made an attempt to induce Shah Kamran to get rid of him, but in this they failed; and six months passed, and the Heratees still held out gallantly. During this time Pottinger had not a few narrow escapes. One day, for instance, a shell was thrown into the house next to where he lived, but though others around were killed, he was untouched; and on another occasion, when the walls on which he was standing fell, and the musket shots showered around him, he was uninjured. He seemed to bear a charmed life, for though constantly in danger, he was ever shielded from harm.

The time now approached when the resources of the young Englishman were to be taxed to the utmost, and when he was to show to the astonished Heratees what it was possible for one resolute man to accomplish. In June, 1838, the Persians, finding their siege operations unavailing, resolved to make a desperate attempt to storm the city. "The Heratees," says Sir John Kaye, "were almost at their last gasp. Yar Mahomet (the Vizier) was beginning to despond, and his followers were almost in a state of prostration. Food was scarce; money was scarce. There was a lack of everything but of the stubborn courage which continued to sustain the solitary Englishman."

On the 25th of the month a fierce attack was made on Herat. Though suddenly determined upon, signs had not been wanting of what was coming; yet Yar Mahomet, unwilling to take the warning which Pottinger had given, had remained quietly at his quarters; and the Heratees had, therefore, been led to believe that no special danger was impending. Indeed, even after the commencement of the attack, when a lull occurred in the firing, the majority of the garrison, in ignorance of what was occurring, lay down to sleep; and it was only when another terrible cannonade showed them the real condition of affairs that they were sufficiently alarmed to rush to their posts. Then they found that the defensive works were being assaulted from five different points.

Herat's hour of peril had come; and it was well for the city that its garrison had not to trust for guidance to such a weak and helpless man as the Vizier, its nominal commander. From four of the five points the Persians were gallantly repulsed by the Heratees; but at the fifth a serious breach had been made in the defences; and following the example set by the Vizier, the courage of the men began to fail during the long and terrible struggle that ensued. It was at this crisis that Eldred Pottinger was the means of turning what, but for him, would have been disastrous failure into splendid victory.

The defenders had been falling one by one; the stormers had followed up the advantage they had gained; and the moment came when the breach was nearly carried. Both Pottinger and the Vizier instantly realised the gravity of the situation;—but what happened? While Pottinger was equal to the occasion, the Vizier was lamentably unequal; while the Englishman sprang forward to dash on to the breach and infuse new courage into the wavering defenders, the poor affrighted Heratee lost heart and sat himself down! Such conduct at such a time was simply ruinous, as Pottinger well knew; nor was there a moment to lose in deciding what was to be done. So he rushed to the Vizier's side, and in indignant tones urged him to advance to the breach, or, if not, to send his son to help him to encourage the men. At first there was no response, and again and again he called on him. After a time the Vizier yielded, and, going forward, ordered his troops to fight. But in a very little while his courage gave way, and, returning to the place where he had been sitting, he once more resigned himself to despair. The garrison now began to retreat; seeing which the Vizier, at Pottinger's bidding, roused himself and returned; then he lost heart again.

This was more than could be endured; and when, for the third time, the young artilleryman called on the Heratee and found that words of entreaty and words of reproach were alike thrown away, he adopted other means. Pointing to the disorganised

"HE SEIZED THE VIZIER . . . AND DRAGGED HIM FORWARD TO THE BREACH" (*p.* 109).

and fast-retreating soldiers, and taunting him with his cowardice, he seized the Vizier firmly by the arm and dragged him forward to the breach; then he ordered him to join him in leading on the garrison. The effect was magical. With Pottinger at his side Yar Mahomet went to the front, urging on his men, and the resistance to the Persians was renewed with furious energy. Then came a moment when it appeared as if, after all, the enemy would be victorious; and hesitancy showed itself in the Heratee ranks. Seeing this the Vizier, thoroughly aroused, seized a large staff, and "rushed like a madman upon the hindmost of the party and drove them under a shower of heavy blows." The Heratees were by this time in such a position that if they would they could not fall back; so on they rushed, and within a few minutes they had, by leaping over a parapet, burst down upon the stormers.

The scale was turned; the victory was won. Seized with a panic at this sudden movement the Persians, abandoning their position, fled in dismay, leaving 1,700 men killed and wounded. And so the city of Herat was saved, and whatever designs the Persians and the Russians may have formed for advancing towards India were completely frustrated. It was a remarkable achievement, but it would never have been accomplished but for Eldred Pottinger's heroism.

For some little time after this the enemy, though foiled in their attempt to capture the "Key of India," did not remove their camp; nor were the Heratees free from danger. The Persians tried for a while to blockade the city, with intent to starve it into submission; but after a while—though the inhabitants suffered from want of food, and had to endure many trials, in all of which Pottinger shared—they returned to their own country, their departure having been finally hastened by the announcement that the British Government had sent an armed naval squadron to the Persian Gulf to commence hostilities in their own country.

Though the storm had thus blown over, Pottinger did not leave Herat immediately, but for some months gave his advice and assistance to Shah Kamran in restoring order in the city. In the meantime, events were happening elsewhere, destined to affect his subsequent career, to which reference must be made.

As already stated, the whole of Afghanistan, with the exception of Herat, was subject to Dost Mahomet. In the year 1836, the dominions of this prince had become in a disturbed condition, owing not only to the threatening attitude of Persia and Russia, but also to a war which had been waged by Runjeet Sing, the powerful ruler of the Punjab, who had wrested the important town of Peshawur from him. Dost Mahomet was very anxious, therefore, to secure the alliance of the English. The Governor-General, Lord Auckland, feeling that the intrigues of Persia and Russia were, in reality, directed against India, was, on his part, not unwilling to cultivate friendly relations with the Afghan sovereign; and accordingly, in 1837, he had despatched a trusty officer, Captain Alexander Burnes, to Cabul, with the object of discussing the matter. But before telling the story of this mission and of its disastrous consequences, let us glance for a moment at the adventurous career of the young officer to whom it was confided.

Alexander Burnes was born at Montrose in the year 1805. His father was a man of considerable local importance, and it was to this circumstance that the choice of the profession adopted by his son was attributable. For at this time a distinguished Indian official, Mr. Joseph Hume, represented Montrose in Parliament; and to him Mr. Burnes, one of his strongest supporters in the borough, knew that he could look to secure an advantageous start in life for some of his children. So it had come about that Alexander Burnes was destined for the East India Company's service.

Nothing remarkable, and nothing indicative of the love of travel and adventure which subsequently showed itself, is recorded concerning Burnes' early days. "He was," says his biographer, "a clever, in some respects a precocious, boy, and had learnt as much in the way both of classics and mathematics as most promising striplings of his age." He was well grounded, too, in ordinary subjects, and, in common with other plucky boys, he was at all times ready to take his own part, whether by words or blows. Altogether, indeed, "though not to be accounted a prodigy, he was a youth of high spirit and good promise, and had in him some of the stuff of which heroes are made."

So passed his boyhood, and it was when he was nearly sixteen that he went to London "in a Dundee smack," and after studying under an Oriental professor, his name was entered for a cadetship of infantry, and he sailed for Bombay soon afterwards.

Arrived in India, Burnes devoted himself steadily to the study of his profession, and worked hard, too, in mastering Eastern languages, especially Hindustani and Persian; and by 1823, when only eighteen, he had progressed so rapidly that he was made interpreter, and in the same year was offered the adjutancy of the 1st Extra Battalion then stationed at Surat. He seems to have been greatly excited by this promotion, and he announced his success to his friends at home in these terms: "Behold," said he, "your son Alexander, the most fortunate man on earth for his years! Behold him—Lieutenant and Adjutant Burnes, with an allowance of 500 to 600 rupees (£50 to £60) per month!"

Then followed other appointments of greater importance—Burnes in the meantime continuing to apply himself assiduously and successfully to the study of native languages and of military duties, until by 1830 he had gained such high reputation as a capable and shrewd officer, that he was selected by the Government of India to undertake a somewhat hazardous and delicate mission. This was to proceed to Lahore, the capital of the Punjab, in order to present to its ruler, Runjeet Sing, a number of horses, together with other gifts from the King of England; and at the same time—this being the real object of the mission—he was to acquaint himself with the territories through which he passed, and, having "spied the nakedness of the land," to report thereon to the authorities. He was also to inspect the countries on the Lower Indus, and to be the bearer of presents to the Ameers, or rulers, of the province of Sinde.

The undertaking was eminently suited to Burnes' tastes; for, like young Eldred Pottinger, he had now become to some extent tired of inactivity, and his ambition was to travel, to explore, and to win a name amid more stirring scenes than those in which he had so far spent his life. The journey was full of danger at almost every step, for in those days scarcely anything was known to Europeans of the territories through which he was to pass, and he had to force his way through "numberless briery obstructions and difficulties;" in addition to which the Ameers of Sinde, suspecting his design, at one time drove him forcibly out of their country, and at another starved him out. Yet he contrived to accomplish the object of his mission, and on his return was most warmly complimented by the Governor-General for what he had done.

Now followed a still more perilous enterprise. Suspicions of Russia's designs on India were prevalent, as we have seen, at this period; and as Burnes was aware that the Governor-General was anxious to acquire information about the countries bordering on the river Oxus and the Caspian Sea, and also to learn whether the advance of a hostile army was practicable through those regions, he boldly volunteered to proceed thither and report on the subject. His offer was eagerly accepted; so once more—now disguised as a native—he started into unknown lands, accompanied this time by three companions.

Full of interest as this journey is, it cannot be dwelt upon here; still, some idea of its extent may be formed when we learn that after leaving Delhi—in January, 1832—the intrepid young officer and his friends travelled on, by way of the Punjab, to Cabul; thence, after crossing the great Hindoo Koosh Mountains, to the city of Bokhara; then across the Turkoman Desert to Merv and the shores of the Caspian; and thence to Teheran, the capital of Persia. From this city they moved down to the Persian Gulf, where they embarked for Bombay, and afterwards made their way to Calcutta. It was a remarkable tour; and not only was it successful from beginning to end, but it had a result highly satisfactory to Burnes. When he returned and placed his report before the Governor-General, accompanying the letter with certain recommendations as to the policy which should be pursued towards the states in which he had sojourned, he was, to his agreeable surprise, ordered to proceed to England to lay before the Government the information he had acquired. And needless to say, he lost no time in embarking.

Arrived in his own country, he found that his fame had preceded him; and his doings in Central Asia secured for him a reception for which he could scarcely have been prepared. From the time of his landing he was everywhere received with distinction, and from the King downwards "the magnates of the land were contending for the privilege of a little conversation with 'Bokhara Burnes.'" In a letter which he wrote at the time he said: "All, all are kind to me.... 'There's the traveller,' 'There's Mr. Burnes,' 'There's the Indian Burnes,' and what not do I hear.... I am killed with honours and kindness;" and throughout his stay in England, where he remained till 1835, when he returned to Bombay, he was the hero of the day.

This, then, was the man to whom, in 1837, the

Governor-General determined to entrust the mission to Cabul; and well would it have been if the advice soon afterwards tendered by Burnes had been followed.

Arriving in Cabul, he found matters in a serious condition. Dost Mahomet was anxious to assume a position of independence towards Russia and Persia; he was eager also to have assistance to check the advance of Runjeet Sing; so an unusual opportunity was offered to the English to enter into an alliance with him if only they could agree to his terms —which were that, in return for his friendship, his country should be protected by them from attack from any quarter. Burnes perceived at once that the proposition was in every way a fair one, especially as the English desired to establish close relations with Afghanistan; and knowing, as he did, that at the very time while he was in Cabul, emissaries from Russia were trying to induce Dost Mahomet to ally himself with their country, he strongly urged the Governor-General to enter into the arrangement.

But, unfortunately, by this time Lord Auckland had lent a willing ear to "alarming stories of deep-laid plots and subtle intrigues emanating from the Cabinet of St. Petersburg, and of the widespread corruption that was to be wrought by Russian gold;" and he had been advised by high official personages in Calcutta that it was essential that the Government of India should have not merely a friendly prince on the Afghan throne, but that the ruler of that country should be at once "a tool and a puppet in their hands," in order that their will, and their will only, might be carried out.

So, disregarding the safe and sound advice of

Captain Burnes, the Governor-General resolved that Dost Mahomet should be dethroned, and that Shah Soojah, who had once ruled in Afghanistan, but who had been banished, and was now under English protection, should be restored in his stead. And ere long a proclamation of war was issued; a great army of 20,000 men was organised; and towards the end of 1838 the expedition, which was to enforce the Governor-General's decree, started for Cabul. Burnes—who had some time before returned from Afghanistan, and had, in consideration of his services, been made a knight with the rank of Lieutenant-Colonel—accompanied the force as assistant to Mr. (afterwards Sir) William Macnaghten, the newly-appointed Envoy to Shah Soojah.

After enduring many privations, and defeating the forces of the enemy that barred its progress on the road, the army, which was accompanied by many thousands of camp-followers, appeared on the 6th of August, 1839, before the walls of Cabul; and within two days, Dost Mahomet having fled, and the British having taken possession of his capital, Shah Soojah, "gorgeous in a regal apparel, resplendent with jewels, and mounted on a white charger, whose equipments sparkled with Asiatic gold," was replaced on the throne, from which he had been driven thirty years before.

Matters now seemed tranquil in Afghanistan; and the Government of India congratulating itself on the success, so far, of their bold doings, and on the establishment of what it was believed would prove an effectual barrier against schemes of aggression on the north-west borders of India, determined that the greater portion of the army should be recalled; and only 8,000 troops, Europeans and Sepoys, were left in Cabul to support the newly-restored sovereign.

Some time passed by, during which Sir Alexander Burnes continued to perform his civil functions at the Court of Cabul, and there were yet no outward signs of the evil days at hand. But the natives objected to Shah Soojah, while the presence of his foreign supporters was more obnoxious still; and after a while, in spite of the fact that Dost Mahomet had surrendered in person to Sir William Macnaghten, there were ominous rumours of coming revolt. Moreover, it became well known that in the person of Akbar Khan (son of Dost Mahomet) the English had a sworn enemy.

At length the long-threatened storm arose; then it spread from place to place; until, on the 2nd of November, 1841, it suddenly burst with furious force upon the city of Cabul. Up to this time the British authorities had disregarded the warnings of impending dangers which had been given to them; indeed, so satisfied had they been with the condition of affairs, that it was felt that Sir William Macnaghten could be spared, and he was about to quit Cabul for Bombay, leaving Sir Alexander Burnes as his successor; and even when on the night before the outbreak (the 1st), native messengers arrived at the house of the latter, stating that an insurrection was imminent, he did not believe them. Then they begged him to retire to the British camp, or to have a guard sent to protect him; but not only did he refuse—saying, that it would seem as though he were afraid—but so little heed did he pay to their words that he lay down to rest as usual.

It was Alexander Burnes' last night on earth; his over-confidence cost him his life. At daybreak the streets of Cabul were in possession of the rebels; and we are told that first one and then another person called to tell him of what was taking place. Still he slept on, nor would he consent to arise and dress himself till the arrival of Shah Soojah's Vizier made it necessary to receive him. Then it was too late. By that time the insurgents had, with loud yells, gathered round his house. Burnes was implored by the Vizier to escape, but he would not quit his post, and all that he did was to send to Macnaghten for assistance, and to address the mob, "now angry, excited, wild as savage beasts," from his window. But they would not listen—they were thirsting for the Englishman's blood, and nothing could turn them from their fell purpose. They next began to fire, and one of Burnes' companions dropped by his side; and then he found that his stables were being burned. Again he appealed to the crowd, and this time offered large sums if they would spare his life. Hearing this they called on him to come down into the garden, as if to make terms, and at last, when an offer to protect him was made by one of their number, who swore that he should be conducted to a place of safety, Burnes, feeling that this was his only chance of escape, yielded. Alas! no sooner had he reached the garden, and found himself in the midst of the insurgents, than the scoundrel who had decoyed him gave a signal, and within a few seconds the hapless officer was hacked to pieces! And so, at the early age of thirty-six, perished brave Alexander Burnes.

Disaster followed disaster as the insurrection went on. At length came the crisis. In vain the British had tried to resist the enemy's attacks, in vain they had looked for aid from an army of their countrymen known to be in another part of Afghanistan;—all had been to no purpose, and by this time their supplies were cut off, and they were face to face with starvation. Just at this juncture, and when preparations were being made for a retreat to India, Akbar Khan arrived; and, sending a messenger proposing that the British should remain till the following spring on certain conditions, he invited Sir William Macnaghten and his leading officers to a conference. It was a cruel trap. The envoy and a companion, with a small body-guard, proceeded to the place of meeting; but hardly had they arrived when the treacherous prince giving a sign, the escort was surrounded, and while the latter was seized from behind, Akbar, grasping Sir William Macnaghten by the right hand, drew a pistol and shot him through the heart!

It was immediately after this tragic event that Eldred (now Major) Pottinger, who had recently reached Cabul, again came upon the scene to take prominent part in Afghan affairs. Pottinger had remained in Herat till 1839, when he had returned to India to report to the Governor-General on the various matters which had come under his observation; and it need not be said that his achievements at Herat had secured him a splendid reception. Sir John Kaye says that on his joining the camp of the

Governor-General, Lord Auckland was delighted with his gallant conduct and with the information with which he was laden; and he relates an amusing incident which occurred on the day when he was invited to join the Government circle at dinner. While the guests were assembling, a shy-looking stranger—an "Afghan native," apparently—was seen standing alone, against one of the poles of the tent. Some of the officials thought he had no right to be there, especially as they were about to do honour to the man whose courage at Herat stood in such marked contrast to that of the Afghans, and advised that he should be bidden to depart. But while they were discussing who should send him away, the Governor-General entered with his sister, the Hon. Miss Eden, on his arm, and leading her to the reserved-looking "stranger," said, "Let me present you to Eldred Pottinger, the Hero of Herat!"

The important events in Afghanistan already referred to were now taking place; and at such a time the services of a man like Pottinger were invaluable. After remaining in Calcutta for a short while, he was appointed to act as Political Agent in the Kohistan country (north of Cabul); and accompanied by a small staff of officers and a native escort, he took up his quarters in the fortress of Lughmanee. For a time all went well with him; but when the Afghans raised the standard of revolt against Shah Soojah and the English, his castle was one of the first places attacked. Ere long he was so hemmed in by the surging hordes that surrounded the fortress that no chance of escape seemed possible; but his old courage sustained him, and under cover of darkness he and his companions contrived one night to escape to a place two miles off, where a regiment of Shah Soojah's troops was stationed. Here he took command of the guns, and kept the enemy at bay for some time. But at last, the supplies of food and water cut off, death stared them in the face; so they resolved to fight their way to Cabul. The attempt was made; but with terrible result. Of the brave little garrison that sallied forth from the castle of Lughmanee, four only—one of them Pottinger, badly wounded—reached the city.

On the death of Sir William Macnaghten, the British authorities in Cabul seemed distracted and paralysed. The commander of the troops, General Elphinstone, suffering from ill-health, was incapable of acting, nor was he willing to allow others to act; and such was the supineness of the military chiefs generally, that no effort was even made to avenge the murder of the envoy. Meanwhile, the whole British force, and those dependent on it for protection—including the wives and children of officers who had joined them in Cabul, and many thousands of camp-followers—were at the point of starvation. It was now that all in the British camp turned to Major Pottinger—by this time recovered from his wounds; and he it was who was relied upon to help his countrymen in their dire extremity. But matters had gone too far, and not even the Hero of Herat could stem the tide of ill-fortune; nor was his noble example of avail in face of the despair to which the authorities had resigned themselves. When, a few days after Macnaghten's death, a council of war was held, and the majority of the officers in command decided to surrender the city, and to agree to most humiliating terms, provided that the Afghans granted the British safe conduct through their country, he strongly urged that the condition "should be rejected with scorn and defiance." But his protests were in vain. And so a treaty, "dictated," says Marshman, "in a spirit of arrogance, received in a spirit of humility, and violated without a blush," was entered into with Akbar Khan, by which it was agreed to leave behind all the guns but six, to surrender all the treasure, to give up three officers as hostages, and to pay a considerable sum in bills drawn upon India. In return, Akbar Khan undertook to conduct the army to Jellalabad, then held by General Sale, on the Afghan side of the Khyber Pass, and rather more than eighty miles from Cabul.

It was on the 6th of January, 1842, that the ill-fated retreat towards India began; and on that memorable morning, the army—by this time reduced to about 4,500 fighting men—with 11,000 camp-followers, besides the wives and children of officers, including Lady Macnaghten and Lady Sale, left Cabul. The snow lay deep on the ground, the cold was intense; and so difficult was it to travel that by the end of the second day only ten miles had been covered. On that evening a halt was made on some high ground at the entrance of the Khoord-Cabul Pass, "where the great mass of men, women, and children, horses, ponies, and camels, lay down to find a winding-sheet in the snow, there being neither shelter, nor firewood, nor food." On the next morning the army began to enter the terrible Pass (which runs for a distance of five miles between precipitous mountain ranges, so narrow and so closed in on either side, that the sun scarcely ever penetrates there); and then Akbar Khan appeared with a troop of cavalry, and offered to escort the British to the frontier if three more hostages were given up—this time for the surrender of certain British outposts in other parts of the country. Pottinger, who was one of the three, now became Akbar's captive. Then the march was resumed; but scarcely had the retreating army advanced into the dreadful defile than there was poured down upon it by the treacherous enemy from the heights above such a deadly fire that 3,000 persons almost immediately perished; and "it was in this scene of carnage that delicate English ladies, some with infants in their arms, had to run the gauntlet of bullets amid a heavy fall of snow." Then another morning dawned; and once more the black-hearted Akbar appeared—now with an offer to take charge of the ladies and children, and convey them to India—but really to make prisoners of them. And, rather than subject them to further horrors on the march, these were given up; and, accompanied by eight officers, they were taken to the enemy's camp.

Next followed Akbar's crowning atrocity—one that has scarcely a parallel. As the remainder of the army—now a disorganised rabble—pushed on, the natives again showered down their cruel bullets; and when the end of the Pass was reached only 500 or 600 of all the vast host that had started survived. Still the ferocity of the natives was unabated, and though when they rushed upon them with their knives the fugitives made a brave stand, it was to no purpose, for ahead of them there lay another Pass, which was already blocked up by bloodthirsty Afghans. It was at this spot that after a direful struggle, in which the English fought with desperate valour, the rest of the Cabul army was annihilated. For though about fifty men contrived to escape, they were ere long shot down, and (excepting those in captivity) out of the 15,500 who had marched forth from Cabul, one only—the sole remnant of an army—was left to tell the story! This was Dr. Brydon, who, on the 13th of January, was seen from the ramparts of Jellalabad, seated on a half-starved pony, exhausted by famine, making his way to the city gates.

Such was the terrible catastrophe that followed the ill-advised resolution of the Government of India to ignore the advice of Alexander Burnes, and to restore Shah Soojah to the throne of Afghanistan.

And how fared it with Eldred Pottinger? Carried off into captivity by Akbar Khan, he was destined to remain a prisoner for some time; and not till the avenging army, under General (afterwards Sir) George Pollock, which, in the following September, was to wipe out the disgrace to the British name, had accomplished its work, did he regain his liberty. A few days after the massacre, he was, with the other prisoners, numbering sixty men, women, and children, conveyed first to a fortress in the interior of Afghanistan; then they were taken back to another stronghold at Tezeen, a few miles from Cabul; and next, when Akbar Khan found that the British were marching victoriously towards the capital, he suddenly ordered them to be "hurried over the barren wastes and steep ascents of the Hindoo Koosh mountains, many thousand feet above the level of the sea," to Bameean, intending to give them as presents to the chiefs of that wild region.

Their privations during this time were great, but they were endured by all with heroic fortitude from first to last. That their sufferings were not more severe seems attributable to a large extent to the personal courage displayed by Eldred Pottinger on more than one occasion; and it was to a daring stroke on his part, too, that the captives were at length indebted for their release. While in the fortress of Bameean they were placed under the charge of one Saleh Mahomet. Soon after their arrival Pottinger found that this man was open to a bribe. He, therefore, induced him, by promising a large sum of money, to release all the prisoners, and to secure the allegiance to Pottinger of some of the neighbouring chieftains. This done, he proceeded to depose the Governor of the place, and, having hoisted a "flag of defiance," he called upon the inhabitants to make their submission. This bold move was completely successful, and preparations were made for defending the fort. Just then a horseman galloped up with news that Akbar Khan had been defeated by General Pollock near Cabul; and by a fortunate combination of events the captives were enabled to quit their prison. Amid great peril they then ventured on flight towards Cabul, and, fortunately, on the way thither they were met by Sir Richmond Shakespear, who, with 600 men, had been despatched to their relief. On the 20th of September they were at length restored to freedom and to their anxious fellow-countrymen at Cabul; and the joy and thankfulness of all on this happy day of reunion can be better imagined than described.

By this time the Army of Retribution had, by a series of successful battles, completely vanquished the enemy; and the honour of the British name having been thus retrieved, General Pollock's force marched back triumphantly to India, whither Eldred Pottinger accompanied it. And so the curtain falls upon the tragic drama enacted in Afghanistan.

Of Eldred Pottinger little remains to be said. Already his days were numbered. Returning to Calcutta he enjoyed some well-earned rest; and after a while he determined to visit his uncle, Sir Henry Pottinger, then at the head of the British Mission in China. But during his stay in Hong-Kong, the young artilleryman was seized by fever; and on the 15th of November, 1843, a career at once brilliant, truly heroic, and of highest promise, was brought to a sudden close.

VI.—SIR CHARLES NAPIER.

"Ready, aye, ready"—the motto of his family—well sums up the career of Sir Charles Napier. From first to last he acted up to this motto—from the day when, a boy of twelve, he girded on his sword, to the day when, full of years and honours, he sheathed it for ever.

Whitehall, London, where he was born on the 10th of August, 1782, was the earliest home of Charles James Napier; and he was the eldest of a family of eight children, three of whom became known in the Peninsular war as "Wellington's Colonels."

Both his parents were of distinguished lineage: his father, Colonel the Hon. George Napier, being descended from John Napier of Merchiston, the inventor of Logarithms, and from the great Montrose, while his mother was daughter of the second Duke of Richmond. Of the latter, who was in every way a remarkable woman, we are told that "to the end of her long life she inspired the deepest love and veneration in her children . . . . and in the affections of Charles, her first-born, she filled, perhaps, larger space than his deeply affectionate nature gave to any other."

When Charles was three years old his father removed to Celbridge, a small town about ten miles from Dublin; and here the future warrior grew up amidst surroundings in every way calculated to awaken in him love of activity and adventure. While still very young his delight was to listen to ancient and stirring Irish legends, told to him by Lauchlin Moore, his father's man-servant, and his English nurse, Susan Frost, was "a woman of wonderful strong natural sense," and "just fitted to fashion a child of high aspirations into a hero."

Charles was, moreover, at this period a constant companion of his father, from whom he received his early education, and he was thus enabled to become familiar, very early, with all that pertained to military life. Nor was the bent of his mind long in showing itself. By the time he was ten, though described as being demure and thoughtful, he had become passionately fond of military history and biography; and his brother, Sir William Napier, tells us that at this period when deep in Plutarch's Lives he "rejoiced to find he was short-sighted, because his chosen author said Philip, Sertorius, and Hannibal were one-eyed, and Alexander's eyes were of different colour!"

He seemed, even in childhood, never to have been lacking in pluck, and a story is told illustrative of this. One day "a wandering showman, a wild-looking creature, short of stature but huge of limb, with thick matted hair and beard, and a thundering voice," was exhibiting his powers; and after a while he balanced a ladder on his chin and called upon a little sweep standing by to mount and sit on the top. The boy shrank in fear and trembling from the man, and Charles Napier was asked by his father if he would like to venture. For a moment he was silent, as if gathering up courage; then he suddenly looked up, saying, "Yes," and was borne aloft amidst the applause of the lookers-on.

Charles Napier's home-life came to an end when he was twelve years old. He was determined to be a soldier; and after the custom of those days his father obtained for him a commission; so he became an Ensign in the 33rd Regiment. The little officer now accompanied Colonel Napier to the camp at a place called Netley, to which the latter had just been appointed; then, on this camp breaking up, he exchanged to the 4th Regiment, though instead of joining it, he returned to Celbridge, where he attended the grammar-school for a little while. Here his brother states "he was noted for a gentle but grave demeanour, as if he felt that he was an officer, not a schoolboy;" and it is hardly surprising to learn that he organised his companions into a volunteer corps, and that they willingly acknowledged him as leader.

But stirring times were at hand; for in 1798 the Rebellion broke out in Ireland, and the country was in a blaze. Young Napier therefore left school to take part in the terrible Civil War which had begun. Many families now took refuge in Dublin, but Colonel Napier refused to do so, and, instead, fortified his house in Celbridge, armed his five sons, and awaited the coming of the rebels. No attack was, however, made, and after a while he removed to Castletown, where he commanded a body of Militia. An amusing incident occurred here. It was the custom of Colonel Napier to scour the country,—Charles being always at his side; and one very dark night the troop came suddenly upon an armed body of men. Both sides halted, and a fight seemed imminent; but the colonel, suspecting the truth, gave a loud military order as a test. It was immediately recognised, and it turned out that the supposed "enemy" were in reality the Cork Militia. At this moment the moon shone out, and showed Charles Napier, with his fusil (or small musket), charging bayonets against Tim Sullivan, the biggest man of the Cork Militia, while a moment later Tim, looking down with astonishment at his small foe, had caught him up in his arms and kissed him!

Young Napier remained in Ireland four years, during which time he assisted in putting down the Rebellion as well as a subsequent insurrection in 1803; and in the latter year he became captain. After a while he joined the camp at Shorncliffe; and here, under Sir John Moore, he made rapid progress in the study of his profession. Then—in 1808—came the time when he was called upon to take part in campaigning on a grander scale than he had yet dreamed of. The war in the Peninsula had broken out, and Charles Napier—now major—was ordered to Lisbon, where, in the absence of the colonel, he took command of the 50th Regiment under Sir John Moore.

We cannot follow the young officer through his varied experiences in this war, but one notable incident which stands out amidst many others may be briefly mentioned. At the memorable retreat on Corunna, the brave Moore had received his death-wound; the firing of the Frenchmen had had such deadly effect that the 50th Regiment were giving way to the overwhelming forces arrayed against them; and at one period of the battle, when Napier had called on some of his men to follow him, all had been shot down around him. He was about to attempt to rejoin the regiment when he came upon a wounded man, and while in the act of helping him he was struck by a musket ball, which broke the small bone of his leg. He now felt obliged to leave the man, and, limping along with the help of his sword, he met four soldiers, who declared that they were all cut off, as the French were upon them. Forgetting his pain, Napier at once shouted to them, "Follow me, and we will cut through them;" and on they dashed. But hardly had he uttered the words when a cowardly Italian, one of the enemy, ran a bayonet in his back, threw him on his face, and prepared for a second thrust. Before the latter was made, Napier regained his feet, and then a fierce struggle commenced, during which he contrived to secure his assailant's weapon. Meanwhile, the four soldiers had been killed.

Others now rushed on Napier, struck him with their firearms and bruised him; then a tall, dark man came up and dealt him a powerful blow on the head with a sabre; but the gallant major still fought for life, though half-fainting, and clung to the musket with all the strength left to him. At length the Italian was in the act of giving him a final blow, which would in all probability have been fatal, when a noble-hearted French drummer rushed up in indignation, rescued Napier, and had him conveyed to a place of safety. Covered with wounds, some of them very serious, the major was now, of course, a prisoner of war; but as no tidings were heard of him, he was believed by his friends to have been among the slain. Though mourning for him as dead, however, they persuaded the Government to ascertain his fate, and the circumstances of his release are of interest, as showing the generous disposition of the French commander, Marshal Ney. A frigate one day appeared off the coast, and Ney was soon after informed by an aide-de-camp that an officer had landed with a flag of truce to inquire whether Major Napier was living.

"Tell him yes," said Ney, "and that he is well. Let him be seen."

The aide-de-camp, we are told, then looked expressively at the marshal, without moving, and said, "He has an aged mother, a widow, and blind."

"Has he? Let him go, then, and tell her himself that he has arrived," was the response.

We next find Charles Napier, for a time, in England on parole not to serve again till exchanged.

Then in 1811, after the Government had effected an exchange, he returned to Spain, where he distinguished himself in a great number of actions, and had his jaw broken and his eye injured, besides having two horses shot under him; and, after that, the daring warrior—by this time lieutenant-colonel—again found himself, for a while, in his own country. He next took part in some operations during the second American War, and, though on returning to Europe he was too late to fight at Waterloo, he accompanied the victorious army to Paris.

Hard and continuous study in perfecting himself in the details of his profession now engaged his attention up to 1819, when he proceeded to the Ionian Islands, and soon after became Governor of Cephalonia. Here he remained until 1830, his administration having been carried on with much benefit to the inhabitants. Then after a lapse of eleven years—the greater portion spent in peaceable pursuits, and the rest in the North of England, where he was in charge of a military district during the Chartist Riots—he was ordered to India to take command of the Bombay Army. He was now Major-General Sir Charles Napier, having been promoted as well as knighted for his splendid services in the Peninsula.

At the end of 1841, when Sir Charles arrived in Bombay, the British power in India had received a shock which shook it to its foundations. By his dethronement of Dost Mahomet, the Governor-General had brought disgrace as well as disaster upon his country; and though, as we have seen, the day of retribution came and British honour was vindicated, the effect of the reverses at Cabul had soon extended beyond the confines of Afghanistan. One immediate result of these direful events was to cause the Ameers of Sinde, emboldened by the misfortunes of the British, to assume towards the latter an attitude which seemed in every way unfriendly; and as the year 1842 went on, this spirit of hostility became so marked that at length the Governor-General declared his intention of inflicting such punishment on any Ameer who should, on inquiry, be proved guilty, as would effectually deter all others from like behaviour.*

A grave emergency therefore arose; instant action was necessary; and there was no man in India so well fitted to cope with the difficulty as Sir Charles Napier. Accordingly, he was ordered to proceed with a body of troops to Sinde, to investigate the charges that had been made against the Ameers; and on the 25th September he appeared in Hyderabad, its capital. Sir Charles was a man of strong feelings; and there is no doubt that he was violently prejudiced against the chiefs, into whose conduct he was to inquire; and in the end, though all the charges except three were at once dismissed, he reported unfavourably about them to the Governor-General, declaring that the Ameers had grossly violated their engagements with the British. It was therefore determined that a new treaty, which was disadvantageous to the Ameers, and provided for the cession of territory to

---

* The province of Sinde, which bordered on the River Indus, was at this time divided into principalities, governed by their own Ameers. In 1839 these chieftains had become allies of the British by virtue of treaties entered into with them, and for a time had behaved, on the whole, faithfully and loyally.

the British, should be imposed upon them; and this was presented. It was, however, met with alternative remonstrances and promises of submission—all being in reality pretexts for delay. Meanwhile Sir Charles commenced to occupy the districts in Upper Sinde, and made careful preparations to meet every contingency. That the treaty should be enforced, and the Ameers be compelled to discontinue their intrigues against the British, he was resolutely determined; and if they would not agree to his demands without force, then force should be used by him. "Danger from their warfare," he wrote, "I can see none. I can beat all the princes of Sinde."

While this delay in the negotiations was taking place, the suspicious behaviour of some of the Ameers had the effect of precipitating matters. The office of Rais, or Lord Paramount, of Upper Sinde, was held by Meer Roostum, then eighty-five years old, and the sons of the latter wished the "Turban," which was its symbol, instead of descending to Ali Moorad, his brother, who was entitled to it, to be bestowed on one of themselves. Ali Moorad, in his anxiety to secure it, thereupon set to work, first to ingratiate himself with Sir Charles Napier, of whom he hoped to make use, and next to poison his mind against Meer Roostum, by alleging that the latter was conspiring against the British. He so far succeeded, that when Roostum, terrified by the violence shown by his sons in the matter, made an offer to enter the British camp, Sir Charles refused to see him, and further advised him to seek the protection of his brother. Arriving at the latter's fortress, Ali Moorad compelled him to write a letter stating that he had voluntarily resigned the "Turban" and his possessions to him; and information to that effect was sent to Sir Charles, who, however, suspecting that it had been obtained by force, sent word that he intended to see Roostum in person. Thereupon Ali Moorad, knowing that if the interview took place his schemes would be laid bare, awoke his brother at midnight, and telling him that he was to be arrested on the next morning, persuaded him to fly. We are told by Marshman, the historian, that hearing this, "the bewildered old chief rode off in haste to the camp of his relatives, twelve miles distant, and Sir Charles immediately issued a proclamation to the Ameers and the people of Sinde, charging Meer Roostum with having insulted and defied the British Government, and announcing that he was resolved to maintain Ali Moorad" as the Rais. So convinced was Sir Charles that Roostum was guilty, and that Ali Moorad was truthful, that although the old chief sent his minister to assure him that the letter had been written under compulsion, and that Ali Moorad had advised him to escape, he only returned an arrogant reply. He determined, moreover, that he would start on an expedition to a fortress in the desert of Upper Sinde, called Emamgurh, where Roostum's sons were believed to have collected a large hostile force, with the object, as he stated, of showing the chiefs that "neither their deserts nor their negotiations could intercept the British Army." By this time he knew that a large army had been raised in another part of Sinde, which was believed to be meditating a descent on the British encampment; and his hope was that in taking Emamgurh he would not only be able to disconcert that force as well as the one assembled in the desert, but as it was the one place of refuge regarded by the Ameers as inaccessible to the enemy, he would prove to them the greatness of the British power and the uselessness of further opposition to his demands.

"Emamgurh is," he wrote, "their fighting cock, and before three weeks pass my hope is to take off his spurs."

The undertaking on which Sir Charles was bent was beset with great peril. To begin with, he was unaware of the exact situation of Emamgurh, for no European had hitherto approached it, and all that was known was that it was in the heart of the desert of Sinde, about a hundred miles from Hyderabad. Next, to reach this mysterious place it would be necessary to march through a wild, almost trackless, country; while, greatest danger of all, none knew whether or not a hostile force, sufficiently strong to cut off the retreat, or even to annihilate the British force, might not be encountered on the road. These very difficulties seemed to possess a charm for Sir Charles; so preparations were made, and in January, 1843, with only 550 men—200 native cavalry, and 350 European infantry mounted on camels, two on each animal—he plunged into the desert.

Day by day the gallant little force now pushed on, "sometimes finding water, sometimes not, but always cheery and resolute," and a week passed without any sign of the stronghold being discovered. But by this time it was not far off, and after the eighth day a shout was heard, and before them was their goal.

Sir Charles now met with a strange surprise.

Emamgurh was reached, but—it was deserted! On the top, the cannon were found freshly primed, and on every hand were signs that the place had been recently occupied, but not a man of the garrison remained; all, numbering 2,000 men, had marched out a few hours previously, leaving behind their ammunition and stores. Emamgurh was, therefore, occupied by Sir Charles; and so the fortress, hitherto regarded by the Ameers as impregnable, fell into his hands without the loss of a single soldier. The principal object of the expedition having thus been accomplished, but one more step remained to be taken. This was the destruction of the stronghold in order to prevent it from being again used as a place in which the Ameers could find refuge; it was accordingly blown up with 10,000 pounds of gunpowder.

After this exploit, Sir Charles returned to the British camp without molestation, and believing that the effect of his dashing march would be to overawe the Ameers, he called upon them to meet the British Resident, Major Outram, to discuss and sign the treaty. They consented, and at a conference at Hyderabad their seals were at length affixed to the documents.

But, as was soon proved, the acceptance of the treaty was far from being a settlement of the matter; it was on the contrary, the signal for most alarming events. Hardly was it sealed before there were murmurs and commotions throughout the city; and it was plain that mischief was brewing. Assembled in and around Hyderabad were now seen thousands of Beloochee warriors, to whose chiefs (who were feudatories of the Ameers) had belonged the land which had already been taken possession of by the British; and the reason of their appearance was soon evident.

Exasperated at the loss of their territory, as well as at the dethronement of the aged Meer Roostum by Ali Moorad, with Sir Charles Napier's approval, they had resolved to attack the British. Every hour the excitement in Hyderabad grew greater, and ere long messages were received by Major Outram from the Ameers, pointing out that as no pledges had been given that the grievances of the Beloochees would be redressed, the chiefs and tribesmen were determined to fight, nor could the Ameers any longer restrain them.

The spirit of disaffection spread rapidly. On the 14th of February, two days after the signature of the treaty, insults were offered and stones thrown at Major Outram and his attendants, and it is said that a plot having been already laid to murder him, he would have been seized by the angry Beloochees had not the Ameers' guards conveyed him in safety to the British Residency. Next day matters came to a climax. On that morning no fewer than 8,000 men, with six guns, marched down to the Residency and opened fire upon it. To encounter this force Major Outram had only 100 men! Nothing daunted, he and his little force made a gallant stand, and for four hours kept the infuriated Beloochees at bay. Their ammunition running short, they were then obliged to abandon the Residency; and thereupon they effected a skilfully arranged retreat to an armed steamer 500 yards away, by which they were enabled to proceed to the British camp.

The attack on the Residency rendered an appeal

to arms inevitable. And now followed those splendid deeds of valour which were to cause the name of Sir Charles to be for ever famous in the annals of war. It was plain that the Ameers had been acting a double part, and that they had not only been making vast military preparations, but had signed the treaty simply to gain time. Sir Charles resolved on immediate action; and knowing that the Beloochees were still gathering in great numbers in and around the capital, he marched thither.

It was on the 16th of February that, having arrived within sixteen miles of Hyderabad, he received intelligence that the enemy were entrenching themselves about ten miles away, and during that night he advanced towards them. At nine o'clock on the next morning at Meeanee, six miles from the capital, the little British force, numbering only 2,600 men of all arms, stood face to face with the Beloochee army 35,000 strong.

No change of plan was attempted even when the tremendous strength of their antagonists was realised by the British; it had been resolved by their General—" the fiery scion of an old fighting race "—to attack them, and the resolution was to be carried out. So the British line of battle was formed, and then the daring order to advance having been given, the gallant troops marched forward under heavy fire from the enemy's guns. The struggle that ensued was a deadly one, and for nearly three hours the Beloochees, fighting with desperate energy, disputed every inch of the ground; but under the masterful generalship of Sir Charles British pluck triumphed; and after a sharp hand-to-hand combat, "a gallant charge of their cavalry decided the day, and being followed up by a steady advance of the infantry with fixed bayonets, the enemy gave way and fled in disorder."

One stirring incident which took place at the commencement of the struggle, and which mainly contributed to its successful result, may be mentioned. When the British advanced to the attack—at which time many of the Beloochees were hidden behind their fortifications—the General suddenly perceived a wall with only one opening, not very wide, behind which swarmed numbers of the enemy. He saw that they intended to rush out through this opening; so with the inspiration of genius he instantly detached eighty men of the 22nd Regiment, and told their officer, Captain Tew, that he was to block that gap—to die in it if necessary. And obeying the order the brave captain did die; and after he had fallen his men still filled up the opening, and thus no fewer than 6,000 men were paralysed by the skilful disposition of 80!

Sir Charles himself had as usual not a few narrow escapes during the fray. Not only had he maimed his hand, the pain of which was so great that he could scarcely hold his horse's reins, but at one critical period of the battle he was so placed that he was compelled to ride between the fire of two opposing lines not twenty yards apart. "I expected death," he afterwards wrote, "as much from our men as from the enemy, and I was much singed by our fire—my whiskers twice or thrice so, and my face peppered by fellows who, in their fear, fired high over all heads but mine, and nearly scattered my brains." Once he saw a chief advancing towards him with long strides. "My hand having been broken," he said, "I could not cope with such a customer, but half held my reins with great torture, designing to give Red Rover (his horse) a chuck that should put his head between me and the coming blow. The Beloochee was only four paces from me, when Lieutenant Marston, on foot, passed my right side and received the swordsman's blow on his shoulder-strap." At another time he was "alone for several minutes in the midst of the enemy. They stalked round him with raised shields and scowling eyes; but, apparently affected by some superstitious feeling, none lifted sword against him, and he emerged unharmed."

Thus was the battle won, though with loss to the conquerors of 250 killed and wounded, while that of the enemy was computed to be between six and eight thousand. Some years afterwards, when presenting new colours to the 22nd, Sir Charles Napier, addressing the regiment, thus spoke of this terrible struggle:—"Men of Meeanee," he said, "you must remember with exultation and with pride what a view burst upon your sight when, under a heavy fire, you reached the bank of the river, and a hurl of shields and capped and turbaned Sindian heads and flashing scimitars, high brandished in the air, spread as a sea before you, and 35,000 valiant warriors of Beloochistan threatened you with destruction! Then the hostile armies closed and clashed together, and desperate combats thickened along the line! The superb 9th Cavalry of Bengal, and the renowned Sinde Horse— the dark chivalry of India—burst as a thunder-storm cloud charging into the bed of the torrent, driving the foe before them! At that moment a terrible cry arose on the right. It was the dreadful British shout of battle. It began with the 22nd, and was re-echoed from right to left, from regiment to regiment along the line. Lines of levelled bayonets now gleamed, charging through the smoke, and the well-fought field of Meeanee was your own. . . . Young soldiers of the 22nd, when future battles arise, and the strife grows heavy and strong, remember the deeds that were done by these old soldiers of Meeanee. It was they who covered their colours with laurels, it was they who won the legends which these standards bear emblazoned in golden letters on the silk. Remember these things, and move shoulder to shoulder with the day."

Following this great victory came the submission of six of the Ameers; and on the 20th of February the British flag was floating over the tower of Hyderabad.

But the war was not yet over. On the morning after the battle it became known that one of the most powerful of the Ameers—Shere Mahomet—known as the "Lion of Meerpoor," was only a few miles off with 10,000 men. He had purposely abstained from taking part in the fighting at Meeanee, having intended—so confident was he that the British would be beaten—to wait till the final struggle was over, and then march on to the field and share in the honours of victory with the other Ameers. At first Sir Charles Napier determined to strike a blow at the Lion before he had time to recover from his astonishment at the events at Meeanee; but he afterwards decided to form an entrenched camp on the bank of the Indus, and await attack. By this move he felt he would be able to choose his own battle-ground, and would also be in a better position to receive the reinforcements which he knew were on their way. The plan was in every way successful. The Lion finding he was not attacked began to gather up courage, believing that Sir Charles was afraid. Then he drew nearer and nearer to the British camp, and at length, when only twelve miles off, his confidence in himself was so great, that he sent a message to the General stating that he would allow him to quit the country if he would liberate the Ameers and restore what he had taken! (Previously a boast had been made that Sir Charles and his men should be "Cabuled," as it was phrased.)

It so happened that just as this insolent offer was delivered the evening gun was fired in the British camp.

"There," said Sir Charles to the Lion's messenger, "do you hear that?"

"Yes."

"Well," he added, significantly, "*that* is your answer!"

Sir Charles still continued to play his waiting game, and now the Lion, waxing bolder and bolder, began to assume the offensive with not a little vigour. But his downfall was at hand. Some reinforcements had by this time reached the British camp; and on the morning of the 23rd of March Sir Charles was sitting at breakfast with his staff, when he suddenly exclaimed—

"Now my luck would be great if I could get my other reinforcements . . . but it cannot be. They will not be here for a week; and I will not let the Lion bully me any more. I will fight him to-morrow."

Hardly had he said this when an officer called out, "There are boats coming up the river!"

Then another shouted—"There are more boats—a fleet coming down the river!"

The glad news was true; and on that evening a striking scene occurred. The reinforcements had been landed; and so as to accustom the new-comers to their posts and duty, the whole force was drawn up in front of the camp. Just as the line was formed there arrived messengers from the Lion, who delivered a final summons to surrender. Sir Charles Napier's answer was a simple one. "Silently he led them along the front, and then told them to report what they had seen. . . . In two hours more he was in the saddle again, and marching straight upon the enemy."

The General had now about 5,000 men under his command, and at the head of these he pushed on towards a village called Dubba, where the enemy, whose accumulated forces consisted of 26,000 men, were strongly entrenched. At nine o'clock, the British, eager for the coming fray, arrived at their goal, and Sir Charles ordered an instant attack; on which all their guns, nineteen in number, opened on the enemy, and the struggle began in grim earnest. It lasted only three hours; but during that period most fearful slaughter took place. In many respects it was a tougher fight than the previous one; but under the inspiring leadership of Sir Charles—whose "clear, high-pitched cry of war had at Meeanee sent the same fiery soldiers to the charge"—his valiant followers were enabled to carry everything before them; and after inflicting a loss of 5,000 men on the enemy, their own casualties being only 270, the British won a complete and decisive victory.

So the Lion, who had fled from the battle-field, was overthrown, and though this chieftain made one more stand against his enemies, and had to be utterly routed before he gave in and fled for ever, Sinde was conquered, and has since remained a British province. "We have taught the Beloochee," said Sir Charles Napier, "that neither his sun, nor his deserts, nor his jungles, nor his nullahs (watercourses), can stop us. He will never face us more."

War was now at an end; and the Ameers who had been taken prisoners were removed to Calcutta, and eventually pensioned off—Ali Moorad, who, Sir Charles considered, had remained faithful, receiving an increase of territory. Then the rich harvest of prize money reaped from the war was distributed to the troops, including a sum equal to £70,000 (seven lacs), which fell to the share of the General; and the latter having being appointed first Governor of Sinde proceeded to pacify and reorganise the country. Of the details of his administration, and of the splendid results which he achieved, we need not speak here; enough to say that he restored order and remodelled the government of the province, and by his firm and judicious proceedings reconciled the whole of the population to the change of rulers, and gained their goodwill as well as their reverence.

Sir Charles remained at the head of the government of Sinde till July, 1847. In the meantime, in addition to taking command of a successful expedition against certain troublesome tribes dwelling beyond the borders of the newly-acquired province,

J

his services had been called for in another direction; and though a severe disappointment had come to him in consequence, yet his promptitude in responding to the call was not the less striking.

The Sikhs, the name given to the warlike people of the Punjab, in the north-west of India, had for some time cherished hostile feelings against their neighbours, the British, and, in December, 1845, their forces, numbering 60,000 men, suddenly crossed the river Sutlej, which divided the two territories, and encamped at a place called Ferozepore. This daring act of war took the British by surprise. They had certainly expected the invasion, but they had not anticipated that it would be effected so soon; and though Sir Hugh (afterwards Lord) Gough, the Commander-in-Chief, had already assembled 50,000 men to be in readiness to repel the Sikhs, his army, when they crossed the Sutlej, was encamped 150 miles away. No time was lost in pushing on to Ferozepore, and this wonderful march—"through heavy sands, the most formidable of all roads, with little time to cook their food, and scarcely an hour for repose"—was accomplished in six days.

It was when the news of the Sikh invasion reached the Governor-General (Sir Henry Hardinge), that he sent urgent orders to Sir Charles Napier to assemble at Roree, a town in Sinde, an army of 15,000 men; and it can well be understood with what alacrity the old warrior set to work with his preparations. He only heard from Sir Henry Hardinge on the 24th of December, but by the 6th of February he was at Roree with 15,000 fighting men, 86 pieces of cannon, together with all the equipments for a campaign;

and within a little while he had formed all his plans for the operations he believed to be in store for him. But his schemes of conquest were not destined to be carried out. While, with hand upon his sword, he impatiently awaited at Roree further instructions, a great battle had been fought at Ferozeshuhur, about ten miles from Ferozepore. But though the Sikhs had been beaten back, their power had not been destroyed; and the Governor-General, anxious to have his advice at such a crisis, ordered Sir Charles to despatch his force to Bhawulpoor, and to proceed himself to headquarters. His hopes of active service were thus dashed to the ground; nor was this to be his only disappointment. Hastening with all speed to the Governor-General's camp, which he reached on the 3rd of March, it was to find that, after a victory at Aliwal, a decisive battle had been fought at Sobraon; that the Sikh power had been destroyed; and that the campaign was at an end! But Sir Charles Napier was, as well as a great soldier, a true-hearted, chivalrous man, and whatever might be his natural feelings at having lost opportunity of taking part in the war, no murmur was heard from him. On the contrary, when the account of the fighting was related to him, and he learned how gloriously the British had maintained the honour of their arms, he was the first to offer generous praise to Sir Hugh Gough and Sir Henry Hardinge (the latter of whom, though Governor-General, had acted as second in command); and that he should have characteristically remarked, as he did, of the former, "Gough is a glorious old fellow, brave as ten lions, each with two sets of teeth and two tails," was no mean tribute of admiration.

Sir Charles now returned to Sinde to resume his civil duties, and there he remained until the following year. By that time his health and that of his wife had begun to suffer; his relations with the East India Company had become of an unpleasant nature, owing to the Directors and others having roughly assailed him for some of his bold doings in connection with the Ameers; he felt hurt and irritated also, because while others, who had done much less than he, had been rewarded and honoured for their military services during the Sikh War, he was not considered worthy of even a passing notice; and he longed for change and for rest. So in October, 1847, he embarked for Europe.

His arrival in England was signalised by a series of magnificent festivals held in his honour; and whatever he may have felt about his treatment by the Company, and by others in official places, the enthusiastic reception accorded to him wherever he went plainly showed that his heroic deeds had won a place in the hearts of his fellow-countrymen.

Then came the day when India again needed this doughty soldier. It had been hoped that after the crushing blow inflicted on the Sikhs in 1846, all danger was over, and that the terms then arranged would secure a long continuance of peace. But it was not to be. The fiery Punjabees soon began to chafe under the yoke which the conqueror had placed upon them, and, gathering fresh courage, they broke out in revolt in 1848, and brought on a second war. Vigorous measures were at once taken to meet this formidable rebellion, and under the Commander-in-Chief, Lord Gough, the British "Grand Army of the

Punjab," at the end of October, crossed into the enemy's country and commenced operations. Little progress, however, was made at first, and notwithstanding that there were two engagements meanwhile, it was not until the following January that an important action took place. But on the 14th of that month there was fought at the village of Chillianwalla a most desperate battle, and though it ended in the retreat of the Sikhs, it has been described as "the nearest approximation to a defeat of any of our great conflicts in India." The contest was a terrible one, lasting until darkness, and when that night the English army lay down to rest, tired out and dispirited, it had to mourn the loss of 2,466 men killed and wounded, besides the colours of three regiments, and several guns!

It was when the news of this battle reached England, where it was received with indignation and sorrow, that a loud outcry was raised against Lord Gough, on whose shoulders the people made haste to lay the blame of the disaster; and in face of the new danger that was now believed to threaten India, a change in the chief command was imperatively called for. All eyes turned to the Hero of Sinde, and in spite of obstacles raised by the East India Company, the plainly-expressed demand of the public was yielded to; whereupon Sir Charles proceeded with all speed to his destination. At first he had some doubts whether he ought to respond to the call, and "when," he tells us, "the Duke of Wellington first told me of my appointment, I objected that my many enemies in India would mar all my usefulness. He laughed, pressed the matter home, and concluded thus: 'If you do not go I must!'" He then hesitated no longer. It was a call to duty, and he obeyed it.

His services were not, however, needed during the war after all, for, happily, before he reached India, Lord Gough, after a brilliant victory at Goojerat and other successful operations by his army, had finally routed the Sikhs; and when Sir Charles landed it was to find that a proclamation had been issued by the Governor-General, by which the kingdom of the Punjab was declared to be at an end, and all its territories added to the British Empire.* Amidst the general rejoicing at this successful close of the war, probably no one felt more thankful than the man who had been sent out to supersede the Commander-in-Chief. Before leaving England he had been foremost amongst those who deprecated the outcry raised against Lord Gough after the battle of Chillianwalla; and when, on reaching Calcutta, he found that the special work he had journeyed so far to perform was already done, and that Lord Gough had recovered his fame, this was what he wrote: "You will have heard that the war is over in India, and that Lord Gough has come off with flying colours. Both these things rejoice me very much. . . . And, again, let me express my delight with old Gough; he is so good, so honest, so noble-minded."

* It was when this annexation was effected (March 29th, 1849) that the celebrated diamond called the Koh-i-noor (Mountain of Light) was surrendered to the Queen of England. This historic gem, which long adorned the crowns of some of the emperors of India, had, after many vicissitudes of fortune, passed into the possession of Runjeet Sing, the ruler of the Punjab; and when given up again it was in the hands of his son, the Maharajah Duleep Sing, who was, henceforth, to be a pensioner of the British Government.

Sir Charles Napier remained in India about two years, during which, as Commander-in-Chief, he devoted himself to reform abuses which had grown up in the army; and at the end of that period—fifty-seven years after receiving his commission as an ensign—he bade a final "adieu" to the East, and returned to England to live in quiet seclusion.

His splendid career was now nearing its end. Disease, which not even his strong frame could resist, had already seized hold of him; and the day came when he was seen in public for the last time. This was when, at St. Paul's Cathedral, he took his place as one of the pall-bearers of his illustrious chief, the Duke of Wellington. Then he caught a severe chill, from which he never recovered; and on the 29th of August, 1853—fitly enough, beneath the old colours of the 22nd Regiment, which loving hands waved over him as he lay dying—the lion-hearted warrior obeyed the last great Summons.

Soldiers of the Cross.

I.—WILLIAM CAREY.

"I CAN plod, I can persevere in any given pursuit. To this I owe everything."

So said William Carey, as in later life he looked back upon what he had accomplished during his eventful career; and though perhaps they err on the side of modesty, the words accurately describe his character. It was by plodding that, from being a shoemaker, he became a preacher; and it was by plodding that he laid the foundation of English missionary enterprise in India, and became the chief means by which within thirty years the Bible was scattered throughout that Empire.

The early surroundings of William Carey were of a humble kind. His home was in the village of Paulerspury, Northamptonshire, where he was born on the 17th of August, 1761; and though, from his father (formerly a weaver) being the parish clerk and the master of the free school there, he enjoyed advantages over some of the rustic children about him, yet his parents were poor, and his prospects in life far from promising. Fortunately, however, the boy gave signs of being blessed with an inquiring mind and persevering spirit, and, as a child, he showed that obstacles which many would have looked on as insurmountable, were not likely to discourage him.

When only six years old his mother sometimes heard him in the night, when the family was asleep, reckoning up accounts, so as to gain insight into arithmetic; and though books were scarce in those days—nor easily borrowed or begged—he soon contrived to master every one that came in his way, especially those on travel, adventure, or history. He took deep interest, too, in collecting birds, flowers, and insects, with whose names he one by one familiarised himself; indeed, it may be said that whatever branches of knowledge were accessible he sought to study.

Nor did he show less fondness for ordinary boyish amusements and recreations, for we learn that he was a favourite among his companions because of his willingness to take the lead in all their sports, while he gained reputation among them for never giving in after once setting his mind upon accomplishing anything. If, for example, in the course of a ramble the boys came to a tree unusually hard to climb, young Carey was generally the first to make an attempt, and often the only one who succeeded. It is related of him that, when on one occasion while in search of birds' nests, he fell to the ground "bruised and half stunned," he resolved that as soon as he was able he would climb the tree again for the prize; and he did so.

Boyhood's days thus passed on; and the time came for William Carey to choose an occupation by which to earn a living; so when about fourteen he was apprenticed to Mr. Nichols, a shoemaker living in the village of Hackleton, about ten miles from his home. This trade was selected because since his seventh year he had suffered from a skin affection, which caused the sun's rays to be unpleasant to him, and therefore made out-door occupation unsuitable. By this time, though opportunities for gratifying it had been few, his love of study had become more marked than ever; and it must have been with no little rejoicing that on entering on his new vocation he found his master possessed several books, which he was permitted to borrow. As an indication of his determination to learn, it is related that among them there was a Commentary on the New Testament, the pages of which contained a number of Greek words. He was utterly ignorant of the meaning of these, but they seem to have fascinated him; and so, determined to find out what they meant, he copied them as well as he could; and then when he went home he induced Tom Jones, a weaver in the village who had had a classical education, to translate them for him. In other ways, too, he continued to gather in knowledge as best he could; and meanwhile he was learning his trade. It was, however, to be a short apprenticeship; for it ended after two years, owing to his master's death, and he then became a journeyman in the employ of Mr. Old in the same village. That he was skilful at his calling seems doubtful, nor is it much to be wondered at, seeing that his thoughts were anywhere but on his bench; and it has been said that he could never make a pair of shoes to match each other, or to please the customer. Singularly enough, he himself was under the impression that he was "a very good workman," though when on one occasion, many years after, a high official in India asked him whether he had not once been a shoemaker, he retorted, "No, sir; only a cobbler!"

It was when he was working for Mr. Old that Carey began to take serious interest in religious matters, hitherto neglected by him. In the same employ was another young man, son of a Dissenter, and as they sat at work they had frequent discussions on these subjects. Carey, as the son of the parish clerk, had been brought up a strict Churchman, and he tells us "he had always looked upon Dissenters with contempt;" he therefore at first paid little heed to the arguments of his companion, and in their verbal disputes usually insisted on having the last word. But after a while, when he came to reflect on what he had heard, he began to feel that his antagonist was right, and that he was wrong, and this caused him to have a growing uneasiness of mind. "I wanted something," he tells us, "but had no idea that nothing but an entire change of heart could do me good." His fellow-workman noticed the change in him, and seized every opportunity to emphasise his arguments; he also furnished him with religious books; and Carey's opinions having thus almost insensibly undergone a change, he determined to attend Church, as well as religious meetings, very frequently, "not doubting but that this would produce ease of mind and make me acceptable to the Almighty." He also resolved to leave off bad habits, and in every way to lead a changed life.

Without following young Carey through all the perplexities and doubts that now beset him—which for a while left him, as he says, in an "inquisitive and unsatisfied state"—it will suffice to say that by the year 1781, when a small Dissenting body, consisting of nine members, had been formed at Hackleton, his name was third on the list. He had left the Church of England for ever, and we now find him beginning to preach in the surrounding villages. "A sort of conference was also begun, and I was," says he, "sometimes invited to speak my thoughts on a passage of Scripture which, the people being ignorant, they sometimes applauded, to my great injury"—such applause tending to make him vain and conceited. In the same year he married; soon after which he succeeded to Mr. Old's business and settled down in the village.

Five years now passed, during which several events happened in Carey's life. He had, at first, continued his preaching in the places around Hackleton; he had afterwards become the pastor of a little chapel at Earl's Barton, six miles from there; he had been publicly baptised in the river Nen, at Northampton, by Dr. Ryland; and he had meanwhile, through misfortunes in business, changed his abode to the neighbouring village of Piddington.

He was now—in 1786—invited to become pastor of the Baptist chapel at Moulton, in Northamptonshire; and his hope was that in settling in this place he would, while fulfilling his ministerial duties, be able to exchange shoemaking for teaching. In this he was disappointed; for apart from the circumstance that the former schoolmaster soon after returned, Carey seems to have had less faculty for imparting than for acquiring knowledge. He was at this time very poor. The school yielded about seven shillings and sixpence per week; and for his duties as pastor he was paid only

£15 a year! Thus his total income was under £35. So it was a hard matter, especially as his family was increasing, to make both ends meet. After a while he resumed his old trade, and obtained orders for work from Northampton, then, as now, the centre of the shoemaking trade. "Once a fortnight," we are told, "the little man, with a far-away look on his face, might be seen trudging thither with wallet full of shoes for a Government contractor, and then returning home with a burden of leather for the next fortnight. All this time, in poverty that would have crushed the spirit out of an ordinary man in three months—borrowing and occasionally buying a book—he went on with his studies." In particular he devoted himself to Greek, Latin, and Hebrew, and he now continued a habit, formed some time previously, of carefully reading in these languages the portion of Scripture selected for each service in his chapel. He acquired a knowledge of Dutch, too, at this time, mainly from an old folio volume which some one living in the neighbourhood had presented to him.

It was while at Moulton that the great project to which Carey was to devote his life first engaged his thoughts. Among the books that he read while there was Cook's "Voyages," from which he had gathered some idea of the general condition of different countries abroad; and one day, while teaching his pupils geography, the thought was borne in upon him of how large a portion of the world had never yet heard the Message of the Gospel. Drawing his hand over the globe before him—said to have been made of leather, by himself—he pointed to different countries, exclaiming, "These are Pagans! and these are Pagans! and these are Pagans!" and from that moment there grew up in his heart a desire to spread knowledge of the Scriptures in heathen lands. He resolved to investigate the subject, so as to ascertain as far as possible the spiritual condition of every country in the known world, as well as to consider the practicability as well as the prospects of mission work. It is of interest to learn how this task was accomplished. He first made a large map, consisting of several sheets of paper, pasted together by himself; then against each country he jotted down all that he had met with in his reading respecting its condition; and by this means he found that no fewer than 400,000,000 people "lay in the blackest night of Paganism." All this information he embodied in a treatise called "An Enquiry into the Obligations of Christians to use Means for the Conversion of the Heathen."

William Carey's thoughts now centred on the necessity of establishing Foreign Missions; but strongly as he felt on the subject—and it is said that "he could scarcely talk or preach, and he could never pray without referring to it"—he received little encouragement from fellow-workers in the ministry. It was not that they were indifferent; indeed, two years previously the Northamptonshire Association of Baptist Ministers had discussed the subject, and had then expressed fervent hopes that the Gospel might soon be spread in heathen countries. But it was felt that the time had not yet arrived for such an undertaking to be entered upon; it seemed "something too great and too much like grasping at an object utterly beyond reach;" and so it was that about six years passed, after he had written his "Enquiry"—during which it lay beside him in manuscript—before he succeeded in persuading others to co-operate with him.

An incident is related which well illustrates the feeling against active missionary enterprise then existing. On one occasion a meeting of Baptist ministers was held at Northampton, and Dr. Ryland called on some of the young men to suggest a subject for their next gathering. Carey rose and proposed "The Duty of Christians to attempt the Spread of the Gospel among Heathen Nations." No sooner had the suggestion been offered, than Dr. Ryland, "springing to his feet, astonished and shocked," ordered him to sit down, saying, "When God pleases to convert the heathen, He will do it without your aid or mine!"

In the meantime—in 1788—Carey had removed to Leicester, having been invited to become pastor of the Baptist chapel in that town, where his income was rather larger than at Moulton. He continued, however, to work at his trade at first; then by-and-by he opened a school, which was more successful than the previous ones; and he still devoted every leisure moment he could spare to various branches of study.

The time now came when Carey's persistent advocacy of the cause he had so much at heart was to bear fruit. The year 1791 had arrived, and though, so far, nothing had been *done*, signs were not wanting that some who had at one time opposed him were now in sympathy with his aims. At an important meeting of Baptist ministers, held in October, the subject of Foreign Missions was earnestly discussed by those present, with the result that, while refusing to commit themselves to any definite line of action, they so far listened to Carey's proposals as to recommend him to print his "Enquiry;" and as the sum of £10 towards the expense of its production had been already subscribed by a friend, the little book appeared in the following year.

The publication of the "Enquiry" was a great stride forward, and through the widespread interest in the subject of Missions which it aroused was the means of hastening the realisation of Carey's dreams. When the Association of Baptist Ministers met at Nottingham in May of the following year, it was William Carey who preached the sermon; and on this occasion he chose the following words from Isaiah liv. 2, 3: "Enlarge the place of thy tent, and let them stretch forth the curtains of thine habitations: spare not, lengthen thy cords, and strengthen thy stakes; for thou shalt break forth on the right hand and on the left; and thy seed shall inherit the Gentiles, and make the desolate cities to be inhabited." This discourse, which is described by one present as having been most animated and impressive, produced a wonderful effect on his hearers, and though doubt still remained in the minds of some, it resulted in a resolution being that day carried "that a plan be prepared against the next meeting, at Kettering, for the establishment of a Society for Propagating the Gospel among the Heathen."

Six months later—on the 2nd of October, 1792—the Association again met, and after the public services of the day were over, there was a memorable gathering in the "little back parlour" of a member of the Baptist chapel at Kettering. Here, on that evening, twelve Midland preachers assembled; here, after earnest deliberation, they all pledged themselves in a solemn vow "to make at least an attempt to carry the Gospel somewhere in the Heathen World;" and here—with a modest subscription list of £13 2s. 6d., which sum was collected among those present—the Baptist Missionary Society was founded. Nor was this all. Hardly had the Society been started when William Carey, who does not appear to have offered a subscription, "contributed himself," by signifying his readiness to go to any part of the world as its first missionary.

India was the field chosen by the Baptist Missionary Society for the commencement of its operations. It so happened, that about the time when the meeting at Kettering was held, a ship-surgeon named Thomas, who had lived in India, and had already begun to preach to the natives, had returned to England in the hope of getting help from the religious public to enable him to go back and spend the rest of his life as a missionary. He was, of course, in ignorance of the scheme which had been so long in Carey's mind; and at the end of 1792, on his becoming aware of the formation of the Baptist Missionary Society, he put himself in communication with its committee, offering to abandon his idea of establishing a mission on his own account, and to join hands with them. The proposition came at an opportune moment; and when in January, 1793, it was discussed, and the Society was acquainted by Thomas with what had been already done in India, as well as with the pressing spiritual needs of that country, it was regarded favourably. And in the end it was resolved that William Carey,

K

who had again volunteered to go, should proceed to Bengal, in company with Thomas, with as little delay as possible.

Not a few obstacles had to be surmounted before the missionaries could embark, not least of which was lack of funds. This having been met, another difficulty arose. The East India Company, as we have already seen, possessed very great authority in those days, and from their well-known prejudices it was believed that they would refuse to grant permission to Carey and his companion to proceed to the East. Such proved to be the case. They then determined to make the voyage without such leave, and run the risk of being sent back on arrival. But when off the Isle of Wight the captain of their vessel, finding out that they were unlicensed, compelled them to disembark. For the moment it seemed as if all their hopes were to be nipped in the bud; and the little party were full of distress as they returned with their baggage to land. But the cloud soon passed. Within a day or two, while waiting with heavy hearts at Portsmouth, a Danish Indiaman was heard of, bound for Bengal; and on board this ship, which sailed on the 13th of June, 1793, the two missionaries, with their wives and children, were soon speeding towards the East.

After a voyage lasting five months—most of it spent by Carey in study of native languages—the ship sighted Bengal; and, contrary to expectation, the missionaries were allowed to land at Calcutta without opposition—indeed, "without notice, so obscure were they." They had now to face the serious question of means of subsistence, for they were poor, they were in a foreign land, and their labours were to be among people of strange speech. It was evident that the small sum they possessed would not permit them to live in Calcutta; and for a time their prospects were very dark. At length, leaving behind Thomas, who was to endeavour to secure practice as a surgeon, Carey started for Dehatta, a place forty miles from Calcutta, where he hoped to find employment.

It was a terrible journey for him and his family—in an open boat; and so straitened were their means that by the time they reached their destination all they possessed consisted of provisions for one day! Help was, however, at hand. On arriving at Dehatta, they saw a house which they found belonged to an Englishman; and on making their wants known he received them with the kindest hospitality, and, moreover, offered them a home until they should be provided for. Soon afterwards Carey built a rough dwelling in the neighbourhood, intending to support his family by cultivating land; but in the following month his plans were changed. His friend Thomas had by this time renewed acquaintance with a Mr. Udney, by whom he had been invited to undertake the superintendence of an indigo factory at Moypaldiggy, near Malda, and a similar post at Mudnabatty, sixteen miles distant, was offered to Carey. To Carey his appointment was doubly acceptable, for it would not only enable him to provide for his family, but, by having a number of natives under his immediate control, his mission labours would be greatly forwarded.

Carey entered upon his new duties in June

1794, and from the time of his settlement at Mudnabatty the carrying out of the great work of his life may be said to have begun. Already he had written to England stating that he should not require support from the Baptist Missionary Society, as he intended to devote all his salary, beyond that needed for necessaries, to the work of the Mission; and he gave up the whole of his leisure, which was considerable, to learning the vernacular, and then to teaching, preaching, and to the translation of the Bible into Bengali. After a time, he made preparations for printing the latter, a press having been presented by Mr. Udney, and set up in the factory. This press was regarded with great curiosity by the natives, "who looked upon it as a European idol!"

Carey's district was of considerable extent. It comprehended, says Dr. Culross, "about 200 villages, scattered amid jungle patches over the monotonous plain. Among these he was continually going about, that he might publish the Gospel; occasionally extending his journey nearly 100 miles up country, where probably no European, and certainly no herald of salvation, had ever been before. In travelling—which was by river—he used two small boats, the one to sleep in and the other for cooking his food; while he himself mostly travelled on foot from village to village. A day's journey might vary from ten to twenty miles, according to the opportunities he had for speaking with the people. On Lord's Day the gathering sometimes numbered nearly 500 persons. His hopes of winning some were often excited and as often disappointed."

Thus five years went by—years during which, as

one writer observes, " the Mission to India was well cradled "—and at the end of this period a change had become necessary. The indigo factory had not been successful; and Carey, obliged to leave Mudnabatty, established a business of the same kind on his own account at a place ten miles distant. But this, too, failed to prosper; and his prospects were again dismal.

Just at this time there arrived from England a small band of missionaries—of whom William Ward and Joshua Marshman were destined to be Carey's co-workers for many years—who had intended to join the Mission at Mudnabatty. But no sooner had their ship arrived off Calcutta than they were forbidden to land; they therefore sought refuge in the Danish settlement of Serampore, on the river Hooghly, about fourteen miles from Calcutta, where the Governor gave them a warm welcome. In the new difficulty which now surrounded him Carey resolved to give up the idea of founding a mission in the Company's territories, and to join Ward and Marshman. He did so; and henceforth the seat of the Mission was at Serampore.

Having secured a suitable dwelling, the little band lost no time in proceeding with their work; and, in order to provide for the support of their families, one of the first steps taken was to establish two boarding-schools, which, under the charge of Mr. and Mrs. Marshman, produced before long an income of between £200 and £300 a year. Preaching among the natives was then commenced; the study of native languages was continued; and at the same time the great work of printing Carey's Bengali version of the

Bible, begun at Mudnabatty, was resumed. Ward, who had formerly been a printer, had charge of this branch of the work; and so rapid was the progress made, that within three months the first sheet of the New Testament was placed in Carey's hands. It is of interest to learn that in these printing-works the missionaries some years later introduced the first steam-engine ever seen in India, which is still preserved at Serampore.

Month by month they thus laboured on, surmounting one by one the many difficulties of their gigantic task; and before the end of their first year in Serampore they succeeded in printing the whole of the New Testament, and Carey was able to write in his diary, "Yesterday was a day of great joy. I had the happiness to desecrate the Ganges by baptising the first Hindoo;" and other conversions followed.

Rather more than twelve months after settling in Serampore, Carey found his success in the study of native languages had brought him into prominent notice in an unlooked-for quarter. The Governor-General, Lord Wellesley, had recently founded the Fort William College, Calcutta, an institution in which junior civilians were to be trained for the Company's service; and a competent Professor of Bengali was needed. Carey's abilities as an Orientalist having by this time become well known, the choice fell on him, though not without opposition on the part of some of the Company's officials. He was appointed teacher of Bengali, and afterwards of Mahratta and Sanskrit, with a salary of £600 a year, which was later on increased to £1,500.

Through his association with Fort William College,

and the welcome increase in his income, which was put into the common fund of the Mission, the work of the latter was much helped. The labours in Biblical translation were now considerably extended, help being received from men of learning connected with the college, and others; and instead of being content to merely publish the Scriptures in Bengali, Carey and his coadjutors determined to issue them in the various other languages of India. Not a little discouragement, of course, continued to attend them at every forward step—discouragement in the form of hostility on the part of many of the Company's officials, of ridicule by certain people in England, of trouble in their own domestic circles. But the three missionaries, who were ere long joined by others, never faltered in their great purpose, and the outward results at the end of about ten years were thus summed up:—" They had established mission stations in several parts of Bengal, at Patna, in Burmah, and on the borders of Bhotan and Orissa —each a city set on a hill, a fortress held for God in the empire of darkness. The number of church members exceeded 200. They had a place of worship in Calcutta erected at a cost of thousands of pounds, with a large church and congregation occupying it, The Scriptures, in whole or part, had been translated into six languages, and six more were in progress. Numerous tracts and books tending to the advancement of the Gospel were being thrown off from the press. All this was visible result; while still more important was the invisible and spiritual, which could not be tabulated."

The years 1812 and 1813 were eventful for

the Serampore Mission. The one began with a calamity, the other closed with a triumph. In March of the former year a terrible fire broke out in the printing-office, by which all the property, except the presses, including types for fourteen Eastern languages, more than a thousand reams of paper, many copies of the Scriptures, and numerous valuable manuscripts, were consumed; and thus a part of the work of the Mission was most seriously retarded. Carey and his companions, however, bore the trial with great fortitude; and when, through the kindly sympathy evinced towards them, the whole of the loss was made good, their work was resumed with redoubled energy.

The other event was a most important one. In 1812, two missionaries, recently arrived from England, who had joined Carey at Serampore, were suddenly summoned to Calcutta by the Government of India, and on their appearance there were ordered to quit the country without delay.* This summary action on the part of the authorities—who thus showed that they were determined that no more missionaries should be allowed to enter India—caused a storm of protest to be raised against the power which the East India Company possessed of preventing even their own countrymen from coming there; and it was resolved that such intolerance should no longer remain unchallenged. It so happened that in the following year the Charter of the Company was

* Serampore was now in the hands of the British, who had occupied it in 1807. They retained it till 1815. In 1801, when hostilities broke out with Denmark, they had also taken possession of the town, and held it for fourteen months. Serampore was finally ceded by purchase to them in 1845.

to come before the British Parliament for renewal; so fitting opportunity was afforded for dealing with the question. And the end of it all was, that after very heated debates the Company was compelled to alter the objectionable clause in the charter; and so "the door of India was set open to the Gospel."

Of the multifarious labours in which, during the rest of his life, William Carey was engaged, it will suffice to mention the founding of the Serampore College, established at a cost of £15,000, for the instruction of native Christians, who were thus to be enabled to qualify themselves to act as missionaries; the numerous native churches and schools that were formed; his efforts to improve the social condition of the peasantry; his valuable philological works, such as Mahratta, Sanskrit, and Punjabi grammars, Bengali and Mahratta dictionaries. And when, in 1834, at the age of seventy-one, he passed from earth, this "hero among heroes" had been the principal instrument by which the first great triumphs of the Cross were won in India; and by that time over 200,000 Bibles, or portions thereof, in forty different languages or dialects, had been issued from the Serampore Mission House.

II.—HENRY MARTYN.

How often it happens that a friendship formed in youth exercises influence which lasts a lifetime! It was so with Henry Martyn, whose whole career was affected by the companionship of a fellow-pupil, which sprang up while he was at his first school.

The father of Henry Martyn was originally a miner, but by industry and steady conduct he worked his way upward until he became chief clerk in a merchant's office in Truro; and he was thus enabled to provide his children with a good education. Like his brothers and sisters, Henry—who was born on the 18th of February, 1781—was a delicate child, and when, between the age of seven and eight, he was placed at the Truro Grammar School under Dr. Cardew, he gave little promise for the future. He was a shy, sensitive lad, and neither took interest in the sports of the playground, nor was he remarkable for studiousness.

To such a boy the associations of a large school are the reverse of pleasant; nor did "little Harry Martyn," as he was called, find them otherwise. Shunning the society of other boys, and somewhat petulant in manner, it was not long before those older and stronger than himself took delight in provoking as well as bullying him; and for a time it seemed likely that school-life would prove intolerable to the lad. Fortunately, however, among his companions there was one boy bigger than himself— near whom he had been placed in the schoolroom in order to receive assistance in his lessons—who conceived a strong liking for him; and from that time "little Harry" found in him not only a staunch champion, but a kindly adviser. To the influence exercised by this friend Martyn owed everything. By him he was often rescued from the grasp of juvenile oppression; by him his battles were fought; by him he was so encouraged in his studies that, by the time he was between fourteen and fifteen, he had made such progress that his father determined that he should offer himself as a candidate for a vacant scholarship at Corpus Christi College, Oxford. He was not, however, successful there, though he acquitted himself so well that some of the examiners said that he ought to have been elected; and he therefore returned to Truro, where he resumed his attendance at the Grammar School. At the end of two more years his thoughts turned to the University of Cambridge, where his old protector and guide was already gaining distinction; and in October, 1797, he began his residence in St. John's College.

The companionship between the two young men was now renewed; and happily for Martyn the friend of his early days became the counsellor of his riper years; nor, we are told, was the influence now again exercised by the elder student lost upon him at the time or obliterated from his memory in after life. "During the first term," says Martyn in his journal, "I was kept a good deal in idleness by some of my new acquaintances, but the kind attention of K—— was a principal means of my preservation from excess;" and from the advance he made in his studies and his successes at examinations, it is evident that he was now making the best use of his time. His old irritability, however—which it is said had been increased in his younger days by the tyranny and cruelty of his schoolfellows—still remained, and, at times, his temper was uncontrollable. One day this nearly proved fatal to a friend who had in some way annoyed him; for seizing a knife, Martyn hurled it at him with all his might! Happily it missed its mark, and only pierced the wall.

The shock of horror which this occurrence produced was never forgotten by Martyn; indeed, it seems to have contributed, in some degree, towards the new direction which, ere long, was given to his life. Up to this period he had been "living the ignoble life of a man whose thoughts and aspirations centred round self, and whose desires were bounded by the world;" but under the guidance of his friend K—— a great change was being imperceptibly wrought in him, and he was beginning to feel that academic honours were not, after all, everything, and that religion had claims upon him too. So we find him directing his thoughts to those higher matters about which he had scarcely troubled himself; and the turning-point seems to have been reached amidst a great grief which suddenly came upon him at the beginning of 1800. This was the death of his father, to whom he was tenderly attached; and there seems little doubt that it was owing to the serious reflections to which this sorrow gave rise that Henry Martyn grew an altered man. About this time also he came under the ministrations of the Rev. Charles Simeon, vicar of Trinity Church, Cambridge; and it was through the teachings of this good clergyman that, as he says, he "gradually acquired more knowledge in divine things," and was led to dedicate himself to the ministry.

Meanwhile, by hard studying—he was known in his college as "the man who had not lost an hour"—he had gained the supreme object of his academic ambition, having come out as Senior Wrangler in January, 1801; but in the condition of mind in which he now found himself, this honour gave him little satisfaction. "I obtained my highest wishes," he said, "but was surprised to find that I had grasped a shadow!"

Henry Martyn was chosen Fellow of St. John's College in 1802; and having determined to devote himself to the ministry, he prepared himself, during the early part of the following year, for holy orders. He had now the privilege of enjoying not only the preaching, but the intimate friendship of Mr. Simeon; and it was at the end of 1803, soon after he had been ordained deacon of the Church of England, that, through hearing a remark by that gentleman, he was led to make the great resolve of his life—to become a missionary. While Martyn was one day in the company of Mr. Simeon, whom he was now assisting in the duties of his parish, the latter happened to speak of the immensity of good that had been already wrought by a single labourer in the mission field in India—referring to William Carey. Martyn's attention was at once arrested; his enthusiasm was fired; and from that moment his thoughts were occupied with the vast importance of the subject. Soon after this the "Life" of David Brainerd—who had preached with self-denying zeal to the North American Indians, and died at the early age of thirty-two—came into his hands; and we are told that he "was so much struck by the career of Brainerd that his soul was filled with a holy emulation of that extraordinary man, and after deep consideration and fervent prayer, he was at length fixed in a determination to imitate his example." And thus it was that he made choice of his career.

At first Martyn hoped to have gone forth under the auspices of the recently formed "Society for

Missions to Africa and the East," now known as the "Church Missionary Society"—he had, indeed, offered himself to that Society—but soon afterwards a misfortune came to him. He lost the whole of the little property left to him by his father, a loss made the heavier by the fact that his younger sister was involved in the calamity; and he began to feel that he would not be doing his duty by leaving the latter in distress when his presence in England might be the means of removing it. Amidst these doubts an unexpected opportunity of attaining his great object presented itself. His friends, knowing how bent he was on going abroad, felt that it was advisable that he should seek one of the chaplaincies founded by the East India Company—for though the Company, as we have seen, were not favourably inclined towards missionary work in their territories, they needed chaplains to minister to their servants — believing that he would thus have peculiar facilities for carrying on his labours in the East. To the young minister this plan of solving the difficulty was most acceptable. Accordingly, the aid of certain influential Directors of the Company was sought; and, after he had been ordained priest, Henry Martyn received the welcome intelligence that a chaplaincy had been bestowed on him, and that he was to sail for India in the following year.

He now took up his abode in London in order to study Hindustani, so as to fit himself for his new sphere of work; and in the month of July, 1805, he embarked from Portsmouth in a ship called *The Union*, which, as usual in those days, was accompanied by a large fleet. About a month later—the vessel having been delayed three weeks at Falmouth—Henry Martyn left England, never to return.

Eager though he had been to begin his Indian labours, and bravely though he had gone forth, animated by true apostolic spirit, yet it was in utter sadness that he had bidden " farewell " to his native land. Nor were the reasons for this far to seek. Just as at the Grammar School at Truro his constitution had been delicate, so was it now; though he had long since conquered his old fits of uncontrollable anger, he was still of a most sensitive and excitable disposition; and it is evident that the thought of relinquishing his friends and severing old ties was hard to bear. Almost as soon as it had been settled that he should go—during his residence in London—" the emotional parts of his nature appear to have been in a state of continual activity. He was one day elevated, another depressed. Any trifling circumstance caused him to burst into sudden tears. He was moved by a divine compassion for the souls of men to go forth to preach the Gospel in a heathen land; but there was something ever tugging at his heart-strings, and bidding him to remain at home." " Shed tears to-night," he wrote in his journal, " at the thought of my departure. I thought of the roaring seas that would soon be rolling between me and all that is dear to me on earth." His depression had increased as the day approached for him to leave Portsmouth, but it was still further added to before he lost sight of England; and no sketch of his life would be complete without a reference to the cause of this fresh sadness, especially as it was one that pursued him to the day of his death.

At Marazion, in Cornwall, there was living a family named Grenfell, with whom he had for some time been acquainted; and to Miss Lydia Grenfell he was deeply attached. When, to his surprise, he had found that his ship was to stay at Falmouth for a few weeks, he had not been able to resist the temptation to once more visit scenes that were so dear to him; so he had made his way to Marazion, about twenty miles distant, where some days were passed in the companionship of his friends. But they had been days of mingled pleasure and pain, for, devoted as he was to Miss Grenfell, his love was not returned. "She had," we are told by Sir John Kaye, "a lingering affection for another man, who appears to have deserted her; and the result of her last meeting with Henry Martyn was that they parted without a betrothal." So, to all his other sorrows, had been added the pain of being refused by the woman to whom he had given his heart; and well might he feel dejected as he returned to his ship to enter on the solitary life in a strange country which lay before him.

After a very long voyage—during which, in spite of the ridicule with which his addresses were received by the majority of the passengers, he frequently preached on board *The Union*—Henry Martyn arrived at Calcutta in May, 1806; and for a time he resided in a disused pagoda, which had been fitted up as a dwelling-place for him, at Aldeen, not far from Serampore. His stipend as chaplain was about £1,000 a year, and as he was now under the orders of the military authorities, he was of course subject to not a few restrictions. He does not appear to have chafed under them so much as might have been expected; and though during the time he was at Aldeen he was longing for the day to come when he might go further afield, to preach the Gospel to idolaters in places where it had never been heard, yet he contentedly remained there for some months. Meanwhile, he preached in the New Church at Calcutta, and pursued with unwearied assiduity his study of Hindustani, in which he was assisted by a Brahmin.

It was during his residence at Aldeen that he first witnessed some of the cruel rites and debasing idolatries of heathenism, and these scenes of horror must have made him more than ever feel pity for those who were then "perishing for lack of knowledge." "In a dark wood at no great distance from Serampore," says one of his biographers, "he heard the sound of the cymbals and drums, summoning the poor natives to the worship of devils—sounds which pierced his heart. And before a black image, placed in a pagoda, with lights burning around it, he beheld his fellow-creatures prostrating themselves, with their foreheads to the earth; a sight which he contemplated with an overwhelming compassion, whilst 'he shivered,' he says, 'as if standing as it were in the neighbourhood of hell.'"

After a residence at Aldeen of six months, Henry Martyn was gladdened by receiving an appointment to the important military station of Dinapore; and in October, 1806, he started thither with three English friends. It was a long journey, and had to be taken in a "budgerow"—a travelling-boat constructed like a pleasure barge, and towed along—and as they proceeded up the Ganges they met with

L

tempestuous weather. To make the position more trying, Martyn's comrades had to leave him on the second day; and he was thus left alone with only natives as his companions.

During this monotonous voyage the young missionary's time was fully occupied. He vigorously studied Hindustani, Sanskrit, and other native languages; he translated the Parables, and seized every opportunity to land from time to time in order to get into conversation with the people of the villages through which he passed, venturing now and then also to point out the errors of their religion. On one occasion, when he had spoken to some natives about their worship, he tells us that they said that they "only did as others did; and that if they were wrong then all Bengal was wrong. I felt love for their souls, and longed for utterance to declare unto those poor simple people the Holy Gospel. I think that when my mouth is opened, I shall preach to them day and night. I feel that they are my brethren in the flesh—precisely on a level with myself."

In this manner six weeks were occupied, and then, when Dinapore was reached, Henry Martyn's missionary labours commenced. He had three objects in view—namely, to acquire such facility in speaking Hindustani that he might be able to preach in that language; to establish native schools; and to prepare translations of the Bible and religious tracts for distribution. The difficulties of his task were enormous; for though he had studied hard already, and had his moonshee (teacher of native languages) now at hand to help him, yet it was necessary for him to master a great number of different dialects, owing to the language of one district being unintelligible to the people of a neighbouring one. He did not despair, however, though he was somewhat low-spirited at first; and with what energy he entered into his work may be seen in his record of a single day's doings:—"Morning . . . . . occupied in Sanskrit. In the afternoon, hearing a Parable in the Behar dialect. Continued till late at night writing on the Parables. My soul much impressed with the immeasurable importance of my work, and the wickedness and cruelty of wasting a moment, when so many nations are, as it were, waiting while I do my work. Felt eager for the morning to come again, that I might resume my work."

By the end of February, 1807, he had translated the Book of Common Prayer—"a work that," as one writer says, "would have been worth living for if he had lived for nothing else;" and later on he was able to commence Divine Worship in the vernacular tongue, at which about two hundred persons —Portuguese, Roman Catholics, and Mahrattas— crowded to attend the service of the Church of England. Before long, too, he had erected schools for the education of native children; and all this was in addition to his ministrations to his countrymen and the soldiers at Dinapore.

A fresh task was proposed to him by his friends in Calcutta, in 1808. It was known by them that he had devoted much time to the translation of the Scriptures into Hindustani; and it was not only suggested that that important work should be hurried on, but he was asked if he could superintend a Persian version. The proposal was eagerly accepted, and he writes in his journal at this time, that "the time fled imperceptibly while so delightfully engaged in the translations." It was now that two fresh trials came to him. The first was the news of the death of his sister, which was a terrible blow; and the next was a severe disappointment brought in a letter from Miss Grenfell. In spite of her refusal of his offer when he was at Marazion, Martyn had again proposed marriage to her, his affection having increased rather than diminished; but the reply was an unqualified refusal. The letter is said to have cut him to the heart; but after a while he strove to feel that the trial was intended to be a blessing in disguise, and he sought solace by devoting himself more than ever to his labours. Two learned natives—the one Mirza of Benares, the other Sabat, an Arabian—arrived just at this time from Calcutta, to assist him in the translations; and thus, fortunately for his comfort, his thoughts were additionally occupied.

And so the months went by—"Martyn always engaged in his Master's business"—until, in 1809, his residence at Dinapore came to an end. In April of that year he was removed to Cawnpore, a military station much farther distant from Calcutta.

Hitherto, as we have seen, Martyn had been mainly occupied in translating, rather than in preaching to the heathen. He now hoped that the time had come when he could engage in more active missionary work. His longing was to be gratified, but only in a limited degree.

We are told that the heat at Cawnpore was so intense that as soon as he reached there he fainted;

and from that time forward he was frequently subject to attacks of fever and to other complaints. Though suffering in this way, he insisted on performing his duties as chaplain; besides which he continued the translation of the Scriptures, including the Persian version, in which Sabat the Arabian assisted him; and by the end of the first year he had begun also to preach to a congregation of natives, who assembled at stated times on the lawn before his house. The latter, sometimes numbering 800, many of whom were mendicants, formed a motley gathering; and the attraction to many of them was not perhaps so much Martyn's preaching as the alms which he distributed among them. To him, however, their presence constituted true happiness, and doubtless, if he had been permitted to remain at Cawnpore his labours would have borne richest fruit.*

But this was not to be. By the year 1810 symptoms of consumption—hereditary in his family—had shown themselves in so marked a form that the conviction was borne in upon him that he must seek rest; and before long the state of his health was such that it was considered advisable that he should visit England, in the hope of a sea voyage arresting the progress of the disease. But though the advice was accepted it was not carried out; for what this Christian hero conceived to be a new call to duty caused all his plans to be changed.

To his great disappointment it was now that he learned from Calcutta, that though his own

---

* It may be of interest to mention that Abdul Messeeh, who was converted here through Martyn's instrumentality, afterwards became the first native clergyman of the Church Missionary Society.

Hindustani version of the Scriptures was pronounced to be completely successful, the Persian version of the New Testament, in which he had been largely helped by Sabat, had been considered "to require too many amendments to admit of its immediate publication." Competent judges had indeed deemed it unfit for general circulation, and not adapted to the capacities of the people for whom it was intended. It was a bitter blow to Martyn; but his mind was instantly made up. He would not return to England, but would go into Persia and collect opinions of the learned and re-translate the New Testament among the people of that country. He would also visit Arabia to complete an Arabic version then unfinished.

Henry Martyn, having obtained sanction of the military authorities, set out on his journey in all cheerfulness at the beginning of January, 1811; "not knowing," as he said, "the things that should befall me there, but assured that an ever-faithful God and Saviour shall be with me in all places whithersoever I go .... and bring me back again to my delightful work in India."

Of what Martyn endured after he left the shores of India only a brief account can be given. Arriving at the seaport town of Bushire at the end of May, and having attired himself in Persian costume, he started for Shiraz, the famous seat of Persian learning. The heat, during some portions of the journey, was so intolerable that he could not travel without a wet towel round his face and neck; at other times the air in the mountains was so cold that he shivered, though covered with all the clothes he could collect. He was, too, often obliged to pass so near to the edges of tremendous precipices that a false step of his horse would have plunged him into inevitable destruction. And in this manner the weary journey was continued until Shiraz was reached.

Undeterred by the state of his health, Henry Martyn lost no time in proceeding with the work on which he was bent; and, as though he felt within himself that his days were numbered, he immediately, with the assistance of natives, commenced a new version of the Testament; and this task having been accomplished, he began to translate the Psalms into Persian. Meanwhile he discussed the claims of Christianity with learned Mahometans and others; and, though exposed to insults of all kinds from the populace—being on several occasions even stoned—he lost no opportunity of proclaiming the Gospel message.

So twelve months went by; and then it was that, his work finished, it become plain to him that the physical sufferings he was enduring were exhausting all his strength; and he resolved to return to England. But one desire remained ungratified. He wished to present his translation of the New Testament to the King of Persia. He failed, however, to do this in person, for while visiting the English Ambassador (Sir Gore Ouseley), at the city of Tabriz, to obtain the requisite letter of introduction to his Majesty, he was stricken with a violent fever, and had to be content with a promise from Sir Gore that he would present the precious manuscript at the royal court.*

---

* We are told that when the promise was afterwards carried out the king publicly expressed his approbation of the work; and that subsequently Sir Gore Ouseley conveyed the manuscript to St. Peters-

For two months Henry Martyn lay ill with fever, fortunately tended during this time by Sir Gore and Lady Ouseley; and then he turned his steps towards his native land, intending to travel thither by way of Constantinople, the latter distant about 1,300 miles. It was, perhaps, natural that at such a time his thoughts should once more be fixed on the spot in Cornwall which, through all his lonely days in India, he had still loved so well. Thus we find him, on the eve of leaving Persia, again writing to Miss Grenfell; and it is evident, from his letter to her—the last one he ever wrote—that he was even yet living in the hope not only of meeting her, but of persuading her to return with him to the mission field as wife and helper.

He set out on his journey on the 2nd of September, 1812, accompanied by two Armenians, carrying letters from the English Ambassador to the Governors of the chief places on the way. But ere many days it was plain that his earthly race would soon be run. The fatigues and hardships which the half-dying man was now called upon to endure more than equalled those he had suffered the year before while making his way to Shiraz; his feeble frame unable to withstand them, he became weaker and weaker; and on the 6th of October he wrote for the last time in his journal. Ten days later, having reached Tokat, in Asia Minor, in safety, and either falling a victim to the plague which then raged there, or sinking beneath the fever by which he had been seized in Persia, his spirit took its flight.

burg, where, under his superintendence, it was printed and put into circulation.

Henry Martyn was only thirty-two years old when his painful career ended; but young though he was, he will long be remembered alike for his mission labours, his preachings, his translations of Holy Writ, made accessible to many millions of strange-tongued men and women, and for the example of Christian heroism presented by his whole life.

Upon his lonely tomb at Tokat these lines, written by Lord Macaulay, are inscribed:—

> "Here Martyn lies! In manhood's early bloom
> The Christian hero found a Pagan tomb;
> Religion, sorrowing o'er her favourite son,
> Points to the glorious trophies which he won—
> Eternal trophies, not with slaughter red,
> Not stained with tears of hopeless captives shed,
> But trophies of the Cross; for that dear Name
> Thro' every form of danger, death, and shame,
> Onward he journeyed to a happier shore,
> Where danger, death, and shame are known no more."

III.—ALEXANDER DUFF.

As a little boy lay musing on the banks of a burn which flowed near his Highland home, "he dreamed that there shone in the distance a brightness surpassing that of the sun. By-and-by from the great light there seemed to approach him a magnificent chariot of gold studded with gems, drawn by fiery horses. The glory overawed him. At last the heavenly chariot reached his side, and from its open window the Almighty God looked out and addressed to him in mildest tones the words 'Come up hither; I have work for thee to do.' In the effort to rise, he awoke with astonishment."*

The little boy who saw the solemn vision was Alexander Duff, then about eight years old; and in the light of his later career we can hardly help feeling that this was the call to his life-work.

It was amidst the grand scenery of the Grampians that the early days of this remarkable Scotsman were spent. He had been born on the 25th of April, 1806, at a place called Auchnahyle; but when he was very young his parents had left there and fixed their abode in a picturesque cottage on the estate of Balnakeilly, near the village of Moulin, Perthshire, where they tenanted a small farm. They both had to work hard upon their little holding; but, in common with so many of the Scottish peasantry, their industry and thrift enabled them to live in comparative comfort. In other respects, too, the home was a very happy one. Both parents were devout Christians; and while he was yet a mere child they had the joy of feeling that little Alexander willingly yielded to the religious influences which they strove to exercise on his mind and character. In later years, Dr. Duff recorded that "my father inspired me in earliest boyhood with sentiments of profoundest reverence and love towards himself as a man of God," and spoke with loving admiration of "how mighty he was in prayer," and with what winning and affectionate tenderness he was accustomed to offer advice and counsel. Nor did the good old Highlander content himself with guiding the lad's footsteps heavenward. "Into a general know-

* "Life of Alexander Duff, D.D., LL.D.," by Dr. George Smith, C.S.I.

ledge of the objects and progress of modern missions," wrote Dr. Duff, "I was initiated from my earliest youth by my revered father, whose catholic spirit rejoiced in tracing the triumphs of the Gospel in different lands, in connection with the different branches of the Christian Church. Pictures of Juggernaut and other heathen idols he was wont to exhibit, accompanying the exhibition with copious explanations, well fitted to create a feeling of horror towards idolatry and of compassion towards the poor blinded idolaters, and intermixing the whole with statements of the love of Jesus."

In addition to such teachings, the imagination of the lad was fired by listening to weird Highland legends and poems which his father and others would recite to him in Gaelic. Some of these were most impressive; and one poem on "The Day of Judgment" so excited the boy that he soon after dreamed he saw the signs of the approaching doom. Then in vision he beheld great multitudes summoned before the Heavenly Throne; after which he heard sentence pronounced—some condemned to eternal punishment, others rewarded with everlasting bliss. "He was seized with an indescribable terror, uncertain what his own fate would be. The doubt became so terrible as to convulse his very frame. When his turn for sentence drew near, the dreamer awoke, shivering very violently. The experience left an indelible impression on his mind." This was when he was between seven and eight years old; and it was not long afterwards that a second experience of a similar kind came to him. Then it was that he saw the remarkable vision described at the beginning of this chapter.

The home training came to an end about this time; and he was now sent to a school between Dunkeld and Perth—his previous instruction having been given by the parish "dominie" of Moulin. Then after three years of rapid progress he was placed at the parish school of Kirkmichael, where he boarded with the teacher; and following this came a course of twelve months' education at the grammar school of Perth. By this time he had made such advance with his studies—especially in Latin and Greek—that he outdid, apparently without effort, all his companions; and when he left, at the age of fifteen, he was dux of the school.

Soon after leaving Perth he entered the University of St. Andrews—his father presenting him with £20 to pay his expenses; and having in the following winter session gained one of the highest bursaries —which enabled him to be independent of help from home—he began to make his mark among his fellow-students. The celebrated Dr. Chalmers, then at the height of his popularity, became Professor of Moral Philosophy while Duff was there; and by his teaching none probably was more influenced than Alexander. And it was not alone by his eloquent lectures that Duff benefited, but, more important still, under Dr. Chalmers's guidance, his religious feelings were quickened, and his interest in the work of Missions increased. It was now that, in company with certain like-minded students, he devoted most of his leisure time to work in Sunday-schools, to visiting the poor of the town, and preaching or distributing tracts to them; he also joined with others in forming a Students' Missionary

Society. Thus about seven years passed, during which he had gained the highest honours in nearly every branch of study; and then the day came when the solemn choice of his life was made.

A staunch friend of his, John Urquhart, had already dedicated himself to missionary work, intending to proceed to India; and his example, together with the teaching of Dr. Chalmers, had created in Duff's heart a similar longing to preach to the heathen. Session after session, when he had returned home for a holiday, he had delighted his father and mother by telling them about his friend and his prospects, though he had never hinted at the aim which he himself was cherishing. But in 1827, when he visited them, his parents observed that the loved name of his friend was not once mentioned. "But what of your friend Urquhart?" at last exclaimed the father. "Urquhart is no more," said Duff, with sorrowful self-restraint. Then he slowly and determinedly added, "But what if your son should take up his cloak? You approved the motive that directed the choice of Urquhart; you commended his high purpose ——the cloak is taken up!"

In this manner he first made known in his home the vow which he had already made, and of which he had told no one till that moment. Nor could his parents, overwhelmed though they were when they realised the full import of his words, withhold their consent; and acquiescing in his deliberate choice as the will of God, they lived to rejoice in his decision.

The Church of Scotland had not yet undertaken any missions to the heathen; but in the same year in which Duff had given himself up to the sacred cause it was considered that the time had arrived when a beginning ought to be made. The endeavour to procure a suitable minister or preacher for Calcutta was, however, at first unsuccessful; and so it came about that when the Committee learnt that the young Highlander was desirous of offering himself they made application to him. And in 1829—after attending college until he had been ordained—he at length accepted the call of the Kirk, and was appointed its first missionary to India. He declined, however, to be bound by any conditions which might fetter his action with the natives, and the only stipulation made was that he was not to commence his ministrations in Calcutta itself—an injunction which, as soon as he saw the country and the people with his own eyes, he felt it his duty to ignore.

On the 19th of September, 1829, Alexander Duff and his wife — for he had recently married — left Leith for London; and in the following month they embarked at Portsmouth in the ship *Lady Holland*.

An eventful journey lay before them. Hardly had they set sail ere contrary winds detained them a week off the Isle of Wight; for three weeks the passengers, who had landed at Madeira, were obliged to remain there, owing to the vessel having been driven out to sea by a gale; and then, after narrowly escaping attack by a pirate ship, the luckless *Lady Holland* met with her crowning disaster. One night —on the 13th of February, 1830—when about forty miles from the Cape of Good Hope, where the captain had intended to call, the ship suddenly bumped with alarming violence upon rocks. The concussion was tremendous, and from the first it seemed wholly uncertain whether any one would be saved; and then the waves dashed with such fury over the vessel that she sank down between the reefs. Duff and others rushed on deck in their night-clothes, but only to hear the captain exclaim in agony, "Oh, she's gone! she's gone!" and the scene during the time of suspense that followed is described as having been awful. After some hours, however, the long-boat was launched; and on a small island called Dassen, inhabited only by myriads of penguins, the passengers and crew were safely landed. From this place they were able to communicate with the Cape, and during the interval of four days while they remained on the island they lived on the eggs of the penguins, which were cooked by fires made of seaweed.

A striking incident occurred when at Dassen. One day a sailor caught sight of an object cast ashore. It was found to be Duff's quarto Bible and Scottish Psalm Book, presented to him by friends before leaving St. Andrews. We are told that when the sailor took them to the hovel where the passengers had sought shelter, all were most deeply affected by what they regarded as a message from God, and that, led by Duff, they kneeled down on the beach, and then, with the precious books spread out on the white sand, they returned thanks to heaven. Duff had had with him on board the *Lady Holland* more than 800 volumes, representing nearly every branch of knowledge. All had been swallowed up save forty, and of these the only ones not reduced to pulp were the Bible and Psalm Book. He had lost, too, his journals, and many other belongings.

The perils of the missionary and his fellow-passengers were not yet at an end. Rescued from Dassen Island by a brig of war, and landed at Cape Town, where they were detained some weeks, they eventually secured a passage by the *Moira*, the last Indiaman of the season, and proceeded on the voyage. The ship meeting with contrary winds was, however, ere long beaten out of her course, and when off Mauritius a hurricane was encountered by which her safety was threatened. Weathering this, she sailed on; and then came a further disaster. As she was about to sail up the river Hooghly "the clouds hid the sun, and gave birth to a storm which soon changed into the dreaded cyclone," and this coming upon the *Moira* with tremendous fury, she was finally left high and dry upon a sandbank of Saugar Island! Here, amidst the perils of the raging storm, the passengers, up to their waists in water, had to be hurriedly landed; and refuge was taken by them in a heathen temple, where they had to remain twenty-four hours. And then they made their way, drenched with mud and utterly exhausted, to Calcutta, which they reached on the 27th of May, 1830.

Thus did the first missionary of the Church of Scotland land on the shores of Bengal; and we can little wonder that when the newspapers told the story of his remarkable voyage and his repeated shipwrecks, the natives should have said, "Surely this man is a favourite of the gods, who must have some notable work for him to do in India!"

In entering upon his labours, Duff employed the first six weeks, during the hottest and wettest period in the year, in making himself acquainted with all that was being done by missionaries and preachers in and around Calcutta, and in studying the vernacular. And he then arrived at two conclusions. These were, "that Calcutta itself must be the scene of his earliest and principal efforts, from which he could best operate on the interior; and that the method of his operations must be different from that of all his predecessors in India." His work was then begun; and how great his aim was may be judged from the plan which he had formed. Knowing that at that time a very large number of natives were desirous of learning English in order to fit themselves for official and mercantile appointments, he resolved to teach every sort of useful knowledge, beginning at the beginning, so to speak, and proceeding, as the pupils progressed, to the higher branches, including natural history and the sciences. "In short, the design of the first of Scottish missionaries was to lay the foundation of a system of education which might ultimately embrace all the branches ordinarily taught in the higher schools and colleges of Christian Europe, but in inseparable combination with the Christian faith and its doctrines, precepts, and evidences, with a view to the practical regulation of life and conduct." It was hoped, also, that not a few of the Hindoo students would become so deeply imbued with the truths of the Christian religion that they might become native teachers and preachers to the heathen population. It was a noble aim, and right bravely the enthusiastic young Scotsman, despite many disheartening influences, set himself to his task.

From nearly all those to whom he naturally looked for sympathy Alexander Duff received discouragement at the very outset. One missionary only—William Carey, then in the evening of his life, who, on meeting Duff, with outstretched hands solemnly blessed him—expressed hearty approval of his plans; the others either kept aloof, or expostulated with him, while from not a few quarters he had to endure opposition and insult. On a certain occasion, for instance, just after he had commenced teaching English, one of the missionaries came to his house to remonstrate with him at the "eleventh hour." Finding he could make no impression, Dr. George Smith tells us that he rose, and, shaking Duff by the hand, looked imploringly in his face, saying that he sorely grieved that his coming to India might, by the course he intended to pursue, prove a curse rather than a blessing; and as he departed he exclaimed, as a "parting shot," "You will deluge Calcutta with rogues and villains!"

Nothing daunted by such obstacles, Duff proceeded with his work, and having secured the friendship and co-operation of one Raja Rammohun Roy — a Hindoo, but leader of the educated natives—his school, which he had opened with five pupils, began to increase in a surprising manner; and before long, its fame having been noised abroad, the applications for admission were so numerous that scores had to be refused, while the missionary himself came "to be loved with that mixture of affection and awe which his lofty enthusiasm and scorn of inefficiency ever excited in the Oriental." In after years Dr. Duff wrote, "The natives craved for 'English reading,' 'English knowledge.' They constantly appealed to the compassion of an 'Ingraji,' or

Englishman, addressing us in the style of Oriental hyperbole, as 'the greatest and fathomless ocean of all imaginable excellences,' for having come so far to teach poor ignorant Bengalis. And then, in broken English, some would say, 'Me, good boy; oh, take me!' others, 'Me poor boy; oh, take me!' Some, 'Me want read you good books; oh, take me!' others, 'Me know your commandments—Thou shalt have no other gods before Me; oh, take me!' And many, by way of final appeal, 'Oh, take me, and I pray for you!'"

The following picture which Dr. George Smith gives of the good missionary and his strange young pupils will convey some idea of how he carried on his teaching :—

"The Lord's Prayer (with which the work of each day began) was succeeded by the master parable of the Prodigal Son, and then came the apostolic teaching to the Corinthians on what our fathers called charity. Throughout all were attentive; and the minds of a few became intensely riveted, which the glistening eye and changeful countenance, reflecting, as in a mirror, the inward thought and varying emotion, most clearly indicated. At last, when to the picture of charity, the concluding stroke was given by the pencil of inspiration in the emphatic words, 'endureth all things,' one of the young men, the very Brahmin who, a few days before, had risen up to oppose the reading of the Bible, now started from his seat, exclaiming aloud, 'Oh, sir, that is too good for us. Who can act up to that? Who can act up to that?' A finer exemplification, taking into view all the circumstances of the case, could not well be imagined of the self-evidencing light of God's Holy Word. . . . Then followed the Sermon on the Mount, which drove home to a people more enslaved by the letter that killeth than even those to whom it was originally addressed, the lesson of the Spirit. . . . Nor was this all. From the simple reading of the words that promise blessedness to him who loves and prays for his enemy, one youth was turned to the feet of the divine speaker, and became the fourth convert of the Mission. For days and weeks the young Hindoo could not help crying out, 'Love your enemies, bless them that curse you! How beautiful! How divine! Surely this is the truth!'"

In this manner the studies of the school were carried on; and the value of Duff's labours was soon felt in distant parts of the Empire as well as in Calcutta. But the very fact of their being so successful created, ere long, a fresh difficulty. When the young natives began in their homes to speak with admiration and enthusiasm of the new Gospel whose truths they were being taught by Duff, their relatives—followers of the Hindoo faith—became alarmed; and not only was a general ferment thereby created, but the cry of "Hindooism in danger" was raised. This opposition did not disturb the good missionary; it only tended to make him more resolute in his purpose; and before long the classes became more crowded than ever. He then fitted up a lecture-room, and discourses on Christianity were delivered, which his own students as well as some belonging to the Hindoo College—an institution established by natives some years previously—attended.

In consequence of these lectures the whole city was

one morning in an uproar. "The Hindoo College that day was almost deserted. Continuing to rage for days, the orthodox leader accused the Government itself of breach of faith. Had it not promised not to interfere with their religion? and now insidiously it had brought out a wild Padre (missionary), and planted him just opposite the college like a battery to break down the bulwarks of the Hindoo faith and put Christianity in its place!" Then for a while the lectures were discontinued; but after the excitement had abated they were resumed. Duff also attended meetings of debating societies, formed by some of the students, and addressed them through the press; and one immediate result was the conversion and baptism of three or four of the most intelligent of their number.

It was after five years of never-ceasing labour of this kind—by which time his institution had become well established—that Duff was stricken by a pestilence which followed a great cyclone that visited India; and, utterly broken in health, he, with his wife and son, returned to England, his work being carried on for him by his friend, Dr. W. S. Mackay, who had recently joined him in Calcutta. Reinvigorated by the homeward voyage, he began soon after his arrival to advocate the cause of missions in his own country, making a tour over the whole of Scotland; and his "flaming enthusiasm and fiery eloquence" were the means of awakening wide interest, as well as of creating new zeal in the cause which he had at heart.

Returning to India in 1840, he resumed his work, which had progressed steadily during his absence;

and, now much extended, still greater blessings attended it through the numbers of natives who were embracing Christianity. But many serious difficulties had still to be encountered, and among these was the loss of the Mission premises, caused by the disruption of the Church of Scotland in 1843. When this event took place, Duff and his fellow-missionaries cast in their lot with the Free Church party, and the consequence was that the Established Church having claimed the buildings and their contents, it was necessary to start afresh. By the liberality of the Church at home, and with help from sympathisers in India and the United States, they were enabled, however, after a time, to erect and equip a new institution quite equal to the old one. Fresh hostility was also at this time directed towards the missionaries by the native community; and not only were public meetings held to denounce their work, but reports were circulated as to plots having been formed to assassinate or injure Duff as the ringleader of the Christians. But, notwithstanding, the work went on unchecked.

In the year 1849 it was thought that the interests of the Mission would be furthered by Duff again visiting England, so he resolved to return thither. But before doing so, he felt that the cause, for which he was going to plead at home, would be much advanced if he could bear personal testimony to the work going on outside Calcutta; and with this object he now made an extensive tour through India before embarking.

Reaching his native land, he laboured hard to arouse the people to yet greater exertions in behalf of the heathen; and, not content with this, he determined, in 1854, to visit the United States on a like errand. His reception, both in Great Britain and America, was most enthusiastic, and his journeyings were attended with great results; and when, in 1855, he again left for Calcutta, he had the gratification of finding that a vastly increasing interest in Indian Missions had grown up among all classes of the Christian world.

For nearly eight years more Alexander Duff toiled on with self-sacrificing ardour; and while his missionary and educational work still prospered more and more, the confidence which he found reposed in him by both Europeans and natives was such that he acquired a commanding influence among rulers and ruled. Whenever any movement for good was to be impelled forward his advocacy was enlisted; and in the settlement of questions relating to education, taxation, land laws, and many other subjects, his opinion and judgment were continually sought by those in power.

Then the day came when, in broken health, he bade "farewell" to India; and what he considered to be some of the results of his thirty-three years of labour he thus epitomises in a journal kept on board the ship which carried him back to England:—" To-day [Monday, December 21, 1863], about noon, had the last glimpse of Saugar Island— *i.e.*, in reality, of India. I remember my first glimpse of it in May, 1830. How strangely different my feelings then and now! I was then entering, in total ignorance, on a new and untried enterprise; but strong in faith, and buoyant with hope, I never wished, if the Lord willed, to leave India at all; but by a succession of Providential dealings, I had to leave it twice before, and now for the third and last time. . . . .

"I began my labours in 1830 literally with nothing. I leave behind me the largest, and, in a Christian point of view, the most successful Christian institution in India: a native Church nearly self-sustaining, with a native pastor, three ordained missionaries, besides—with catechists and native teachers—flourishing branch missions at Chinsurah, Bansbaria, Culna, Mahanad, &c. . . . . Some periods of my career were very stormy ones, especially the first and second. During the first I was in perpetual hostile collision with the natives, who abused and insulted me beyond measure in private and in the newspapers; and also with Europeans such as the ultra-Orientalists. . . . .

"During the second period I was still in violent conflict with all classes of natives on a vast variety of subjects. At one time some of 'the lewd fellows of the baser sort,' beaten down in argument, and confounded in their attempts to confute Christianity and destroy the Christian cause, entered into a conspiracy against my life. Lateeals, or club men, were hired to waylay and beat me in the streets. With the Governor-General, Lord Auckland, I came into violent collision on the subject of education, and all the hosts of officials, secular journalists, and worldlings, joined in a universal shout against me of derision, scorn, contempt, and indignation. . . . .

"The third period of my sojourn has been less stormy, and, praised be God! I now leave India in the happy assurance that in ways unspeakably gracious, and on my part undeserved, He has 'made even my enemies to be at peace with me.'"

After his return from India, Alexander Duff lived for nearly fourteen years in Scotland, where, unwilling to relinquish work, he undertook the chief direction of the Free Church Foreign Missions, and also became Professor of Evangelistic Theology in the Edinburgh New College, besides devoting his energies in other ways to the furtherance of missionary enterprise.

And when in the fulness of time—on the 12th of February, 1878—this soldier of Christ found rest from his labours, it was with the knowledge that the precious seed he had spent his life in sowing was yielding fruit which year by year was becoming richer and more abundant.

Men of the Mutiny.

I.—THE LAWRENCES.

EIGHTEEN hundred and fifty seven will always be memorable in the annals of the East. In that year the great Sepoy Mutiny broke out, and over India swept the fiercest storm by which that land was ever shaken. For months and months the flag of rebellion was flaunted; for months and months fire and sword vied in deadly work; and at no period of its history had the Empire known darker days.

Without attempting to sketch more than a brief outline of this awful crisis, it is proposed to tell here of some of its more striking events, and particularly to speak of a few of the illustrious leaders who at this time of peril defended India from its foes.

First let us see how it was that in the midst of apparent content, and after nearly a century of British rule, the safety of the Empire came to be suddenly endangered. The real causes of the outbreak are not easy to state; but various reasons are assigned. To begin with, there can be no doubt that the rapid extension of British dominion—which in 1856 had culminated in the annexation of the great province of Oude—caused the natives to fear that ere long the Hindoo and Mahometan religion would be eventually abolished, and Christianity forcibly instituted; indeed, so deep did the conviction become, that they lent a willing ear to every rumour that appeared to confirm it. Then, evil-minded men took advantage of this credulity to spread abroad all kinds of false statements as to the intentions of the English. Among these was one to the effect that with the new Enfield rifles, about to be distributed to the army, cartridges greased with the fat of cows and pigs were to be used. It being necessary for the cartridge tops to be bitten off before they could be fired, the express object of their introduction, it was declared, was to cause the Sepoys to lose caste—the cow being sacred to the Hindoo* and the flesh of the swine forbidden to the Mahometan. As early as January, 1857, this report had gained currency. In that month, it is said that while a Sepoy of Brahmin (or the highest) caste, who was one of the rank and file of a Bengal infantry regiment, was at his meals, a Hindoo of low caste, passing by, asked him for a drink of water out of the vessel he had been using.

"I have just scoured it," was his reply, adding, "and you would defile it by your touch."

"You think much of your caste," was the rejoinder, "but wait a little. The 'Sahib logue' (that is, the gentleman strangers, meaning the Indian officials) will make you bite cartridges steeped in cow and pork fat; *then* where will your caste be?"

About the same time a prediction made by

---

* According to their religious laws, the Hindoos are divided into castes or classes. By breaking such laws they lose caste; and, thus forfeiting the privileges of their respective orders, they become pariahs, or persons of no caste.

astrologers was fully believed in, that in 1857 the Company's *raj*, or rule, in India was to end. "The English had been the conquerors at the battle of Plassy a century before; but their doom was sealed by fate, and now there was no chance for them—they must lick the dust!" The Sepoys, too, had now realised their worth, and having begun to believe that to their valour the British owed their victories and conquests, and knowing, too, that the European forces in India had become much smaller, they thought that they held the destiny of the Empire in their own hands. Besides all this, discontent of another kind reigned in the newly-annexed province of Oude, owing to the unpopularity of Mr. Jackson, the British Chief Commissioner; while in Delhi, where the descendant of the old Mogul sovereigns was still permitted to reside, a strong feeling of animosity had been aroused by the threat of the Government to remove the so-called king to another part of India.

Such were a few of the causes of the revolt; and such was the condition of affairs at the beginning of 1857. Nor was it long before the blow was struck. Commencing with incendiary fires at Barrackpore in January—in spite of official assurances that there was no ground for alarm, that the stories about the greased cartridges, the designs on the native religion, and other rumours were utterly false—regiment after regiment of Sepoys in different parts of India speedily became disaffected; and by May the mutiny burst into furious flame. On the evening of Sunday, the 10th of that month, the first serious outbreak occurred at Meerut, where the Sepoys rose, shot their officers, and then after attacking

every defenceless European they could find—
irrespective of sex or of age—marched off to Delhi,
forty miles distant. On their arrival there, all the
Sepoys belonging to the garrison joined them, and
then the terrible work of destruction and murder
went on there too. Save a few who made their
escape, the Europeans, including many ladies and
children, were ruthlessly shot down; and the mutineers having taken possession of the city, proceeded
to proclaim Bahadur Shah, the descendant of the
Moguls, Sovereign of India. Meanwhile the insurrection, accompanied by similar atrocities, spread in every
direction; and ere long thousands and thousands of
Sepoys had deserted their colours and turned their
arms against the British.

It was soon evident that Delhi would be the focus
of the rebellion, and thither all eyes were now turned.
The recovery of that city was vital to the safety of the
Empire, for so long as such an important post remained in the possession of the mutineers no confidence in the British power could be restored, and
India would be at the mercy of the enemy.

But how was the task to be accomplished? Even
with many thousands of men the recapture of this
most formidable stronghold—whose walled defences
measured seven miles in circumference—would be a
gigantic undertaking; but at this juncture there were
comparatively few European troops in India, and for
these every day was bringing fresh calls from different
parts of the Empire.

Undaunted, however, by the strength of the enemy
—now daily increasing through the arrival of fresh

bands of rebels—it was determined that as many troops as were available should be despatched with all speed to Delhi; and by the 8th of June a little army, consisting at first of only three regiments, which were subsequently joined by another detachment, had fought its way there, and after defeating a division of the enemy, had entrenched itself on the Ridge, a rising ground about two miles from the city. By this time there were some thousands of Sepoys in Delhi, and, although on the first appearance at the city gates of the mutineers from Meerut the great powder magazine had, at the sacrifice of nearly all their lives, been blown up by Lieutenant Willoughby, the officer in charge, and eight of his companions, their supply of arms and military stores from the British arsenal was boundless; and so all that this brave little body of "besiegers" could do was to defend their entrenchments, and await either reinforcements from Calcutta, or fitting opportunity for dealing a blow at the enemy.

It was while they were thus stubbornly holding their ground that aid was being actively prepared in a quarter from which they could hardly have expected it. Governing the Punjab—the great province which it will be remembered had been annexed in 1849—was a man of commanding genius, Sir John Lawrence; and from the time that the news was flashed to him that Delhi had been captured, he had not only realised the full gravity of the situation, but had felt himself called upon to work with all his might to help in recovering the city. How Sir John was enabled to carry out his purpose—how he caused the Sikhs (or Punjabees), formerly the danger of

India, to be the means of saving it, we shall more clearly understand by briefly glancing at his previous career.

The son of an officer, who had himself fought in the wars against Tippoo Sahib, John Lawrence—whose own wish to become a soldier like his three elder brothers had been overruled—at the age of eighteen entered the Company's service as a "writer" (in 1829). His early years in India were spent in magisterial and revenue duties in the North-West Provinces, where he laid the foundation of that deep insight into the character and condition of the native peoples which was to stand him in such good stead in later years. Working on steadily in different parts of the Empire, he rapidly gained both the praise of superiors, and the admiration of subordinates; and it was at the close of the first Sikh war in 1846 that, as a reward for the masterly manner in which he had sent up supplies from Delhi, which enabled Sir Hugh Gough to win the decisive battle of Sobraon, that he was selected by the Governor-General as the Commissioner for the newly-acquired Sikh district of Jullundur. So well did he then discharge his duties—introducing reforms of every kind, including a new system of justice, and constructing roads, bridges, and other public works—that ere long the conquered tribes were reduced to content, while the name of "'Jan Larans Sahib' became a household word among the people whom he had been so opportunely sent to govern."

Then came a change. The second Sikh war broke out, and at first there was doubt lest the work he had begun would be destroyed; but in the end, when the whole of the Punjab was annexed, enlarged scope was afforded to his abilities. The province was now to be ruled by a Board of Administration, of which he and his brother, Sir Henry (who was to be the President of it), were two of the three members. Within a little over three years, mainly through the energies of the two brothers, the condition of the Punjab was entirely changed; and in place of chaos, order reigned throughout the province. In 1852 the brothers disagreed on certain points of policy; and it was then, on both resigning, that the Board was dissolved; and the Governor-General, having determined that henceforth there should be one Chief Commissioner of the Punjab instead of three joint administrators, appointed John Lawrence to the post. From this time John Lawrence devoted himself with greater ardour than ever to organising the newly-acquired territory, and under his sway, says Captain Trotter, "the Punjab became, in truth, a model province. Crimes of violence grew rarer and rarer. The native officials in each district proved most useful and trustworthy helpmates to their English chiefs. The trade of the country flourished more and more.... The public at large were prosperous and contented." In other words, by the year in which the mutiny broke out, Sir John Lawrence—who had been made a Knight Commander of the Bath in 1856—had, by his personal influence and ascendency, aided, be it said, by the able civil and military officers, by whom he had surrounded himself,* so gained the respect

* As showing the high regard in which those who worked under him held their chief, the following extract from a letter, written by an

and affections of the Sikh chiefs and people, that these very men, who only a few years previously had fought the British so desperately, were now their faithful friends.

And what did Sir John Lawrence do when the news of the outbreak reached the Punjab? At the time when the telegram arrived he was at some distance from Lahore, the capital, recruiting his health; and the first measures necessary to be taken, namely, those which provided for the security of the Punjab itself, were carried out by the officer whom he had left at the head of affairs, Mr. (afterwards Sir) Robert Montgomery. In the province there were no fewer than 36,000 Sepoys "all ripe for revolt," while the number of European troops was only about 11,000, and of Irregular Sikhs, 14,000; and in Lahore itself " there were three regiments of native infantry and one of cavalry waiting only for a post to bring them information of the hostile movements at Meerut to follow the example." So there was no time to be lost if the atrocities at Meerut and Delhi were not to be imitated. As a first step, it was resolved to immediately disband the native regiments in the capital. Accordingly, on the next morning a general parade was ordered; all the Sepoys there, 3,000 in number, were drawn up as usual; and then, quietly surrounded by 600 British troops, whose twelve cannon were suddenly fixed in a commanding position, they were ordered to lay down their arms. Nor dared they refuse,

old comrade of Sir John Lawrence, is of interest:—" He had nothing mean in his nature; no spite or malice. . . . He was the biggest man I have ever known. We used to call him 'King John' on the frontier, and it is as such that I still love to think of him."

seeing that the artillery and infantry were ready to open fire. And thus Lahore was saved. Then followed the disarming of other regiments in the Punjab, though all were not so successfully dealt with as those just referred to; and his own province being, by these prompt measures, rendered secure for the time, Sir John Lawrence was enabled to turn his attention to the pressing needs of Delhi.

Relying on their loyalty—the loyalty which, as we have seen, was solely the result of his strong, just, and merciful government—he now boldly called upon the Sikh chiefs for aid; and not only did they respond to the call with alacrity, but ere long, in addition to the 14,000 Punjabees already bearing arms, who remained staunch, a force of many thousand others was raised. Then as fast as these could be organised and drilled they were despatched to Delhi, a few being also sent to other places.

As illustrating Sir John's method of procedure, as well as the foresight he showed in thus seeking help from the Sikhs, it is related that on one occasion "he sent for a former Sikh aide-de-camp of his own, and with him made out lists of the leading chiefs who had suffered from the rebellion of 1848. Then he wrote to each urging them to show their loyalty by coming to him with a picked force of retainers. The chieftains came in with their followers, and were promptly despatched to Delhi. The measure had a double effect. The beleaguering force was most sensibly strengthened; while the Punjab was denuded of so many rallying points for disaffection. Envoys from the mutineers came to tamper with these very men, only to find they had left their territories to serve under the English."

Thus some weeks passed by; and now nearer and nearer came the day when Sir John Lawrence's exertions were to bear fruit. On the Ridge outside Delhi, the British had been gallantly holding their own, in spite of being furiously assailed both by the guns of the city and by attacks made by the enemy in their sorties; and though, thus far, the capture of Delhi had not been accomplished, yet by the continued relays of men, horses, guns, and other necessaries, which Sir John had sent to the camp, their position had been most effectually strengthened.

And now arrived from the Punjab the "grandest contribution" of all. Among the distinguished officers by whom Sir John Lawrence was served was Brigadier Nicholson; and at the time when the disbanding of the Sepoy regiments had been carried out in the Punjab, he had been put in command of a Movable Column, 2,000 strong, which had been organised so as to be always available for immediate service, if required. When, towards the end of July, he found that Delhi was still in the hands of the mutineers, and that each week was adding to the numbers of his garrison, owing to the fresh bands who poured in from various quarters, Sir John, feeling that the Column could be dispensed with in the Punjab, determined that Nicholson should march down to Delhi with it, and then and there urge the general in command not to wait any longer, but to attack the city at once.

This course was taken, and we are told that when, on the 8th of August, the Brigadier, who rode into the camp a week ahead of his men, to consult with the General, appeared, "the mere sight of his tall, stately figure and sternly handsome face gave new heart to the war-worn defenders of the Ridge; and the subsequent arrival of his column, headed by the noble leader himself, was hailed by all men as a sure precursor of the victory yet to come."

At length, after the arrival of the great siege-train, and the last detachment of men, from the Punjab, the assault on Delhi, before which the British force had held their position for three and a half months, was begun.

It was on the 13th of September, after an incessant stream of shot and shell had been poured into the city for nearly a week, that a breach in the formidable walls was reported; and then came a most deadly struggle.

Early on the morning of the 14th, the storming columns—the leading one of which was headed by the gallant Nicholson, who, alas! was one of the first to fall—dashed through the breaches; and then, the famous Cashmere Gate having been blown up—a feat performed by a noble band of sixteen Engineers, of whom, save four, all perished in accomplishing the task,—the city was entered by the whole force. For six days after this the fighting was carried on in the streets, during which both the besiegers and the rebels fought with terrible fury; nor was quarter given on either side.

It was on the 20th that the city was captured, though after a loss in killed and wounded of no fewer than 3,537; and by this brilliant triumph, which, be it remembered, was achieved before the arrival of reinforcements from other parts of the Empire or from home, the rebellion received a blow from which it never recovered. "With the fall of Delhi," says Mr. Bosworth Smith, the biographer of Lord Lawrence, "fell the hopes of the mutineers. The extremity of the peril was over, for the rebellion was crushed at its centre, at its heart. The fortifications which we had ourselves erected or repaired, the arms and ammunition which we had ourselves collected, the historic prestige and the inherent strength of the resuscitated capital of the Moguls, had all failed to withstand our onslaught; and how could any other city, or any other force, hope to be more successful? The struggle, indeed, was to be protracted, for many a long month to come, in the North-west and in the Central Provinces; but on the part of the mutineers it was no longer a struggle for empire, but for bare life. Instead of boldly taking the offensive—with the one exception of the force at Lucknow—they appeared before us only to vanish away; and our chief difficulty henceforward was to hunt them down, not to beat them when we had found them."

And now followed a memorable episode. On the day after the capture of the city, Captain Hodson, the daring leader of some irregular cavalry known as Hodson's Horse, whose exploits brought him into much prominence during the siege, went forth with fifty troopers to arrest Bahadur Shah, who, as we have seen, had been proclaimed Sovereign of India. He had escaped to the tomb of Humayoon, a huge building a few miles from the city; and it was from this place that, after two hours' bargaining for his own life and that of his queen and favourite son, he was dragged out, and, having been taken back in a bullock-cart, handed over to the authorities. On the next morning Hodson captured two of Bahadur Shah's sons; and it was while they were on their way to Delhi that—fearing, as he afterwards said, lest a rescue would be attempted by the crowd—he shot them dead with his own hand.

In the following January, in the palace of his own capital city, Bahadur Shah was tried as a traitor to the State for proclaiming himself Sovereign of India, for encouraging and aiding the mutineers, and for the murder of forty-nine British officers, women, and children, at Delhi. He was found guilty, but his life was spared; and it was with the sentence of banishment for life to Rangoon, in Burmah, which was soon after passed upon this its last representative, that the dynasty of the Great Moguls was finally extinguished.

To one man—to John Lawrence*—belongs the undying glory of having been mainly instrumental in causing the splendid victory at Delhi to be achieved. But for his unwearying exertions in pouring in aid from the Punjab, it seems probable that not only would the mutineers, gathering new courage day by day, have overwhelmed the little force on the Ridge, not only would the rebellion have spread more and

---

* For his services Sir John Lawrence received the Grand Cross of the Bath in 1857, followed, in 1859, by a baronetcy and a pension of £2,000 a year; and when, in 1864, Lord Elgin died, he was appointed to succeed him as Viceroy and Governor-General of India. On his return to England in 1869—ten years before his death—he was created a peer with the title of Baron Lawrence of the Punjab and Grately.

more, but that even the Empire itself would have been lost.

Truly the name of "The Saviour of India" was not unearned by him!

Turning to another quarter of the Empire, let us now see what part in this gigantic struggle had meanwhile been played by Sir Henry Lawrence.

At the moment when the Mutiny was on the point of breaking out—in March—Sir Henry had been appointed to succeed Mr. Jackson as Chief Commissioner of Oude. The Governor-General had come to realise that affairs in that province were rapidly drifting from bad to worse; and for the task of removing the discontent and difficulties which were accumulating there, he selected a man peculiarly fitted to undertake it. For Sir Henry Lawrence, an elder brother of Sir John, was one of the most distinguished officers in the Indian service. As a boy of sixteen, when, in 1823, he became an artillery cadet in the Company's army, he won golden opinions from those in authority over him; as he grew older he rapidly acquired reputation alike for ability, intelligence, and high-mindedness; and after serving his country in various ways, first in Burmah, afterwards in Afghanistan, and next in a civil capacity in the Sikh War, he was appointed to the important position of British Resident at Lahore. This post he filled for two years with great distinction, when ill health compelled him to visit England. Returning in 1849 he again resumed his duties in Lahore, though not as Resident, for the Punjab had recently become British territory, and its affairs were to be administered by a new Board, of which he was to be the President. We have already seen what wonders were performed in the newly annexed province during the few years that Sir Henry and his brother John laboured together there; and it was at the end of this period, when the latter was made Chief Commissioner, that Sir Henry parted from him to become the British representative in the States of Rajpootana. Here he laboured for four years more; and he was on the point of again embarking for Europe on account of his health, when, at the pressing request of the Governor-General, he proceeded to Lucknow, the capital, to assume the Chief Commissionership of Oude.

As events soon proved, however, this appointment was made too late. Sir Henry's predecessor, instead of having conciliated the people of Oude, had alienated them; when the new Commissioner reached Lucknow he found, says Sir John Kaye, "that almost everything that ought not to have been done had been done, and that what ought to have been first done had not been done at all, and that the seeds of rebellion had been sown broadcast over the land;" while to crown all, the city was filled with thousands of starving soldiers and retainers of the deposed king.

Sir Henry at once perceived that a crisis was at hand; and he lost no time in coping with the difficulty. Directly after his arrival he set to work to repair the errors of the past, by redressing grievances, by paying delayed pensions, and by showing every courtesy to the native princes and nobles.

But as day by day passed, signs of coming revolt grew more ominous; and it was soon plain that all his efforts to restore confidence would be unavailing. While keeping up an appearance of unconcern, Sir Henry therefore began to make preparations for the siege which seemed to be inevitable; and having turned the Residency into an extemporised fort, well stored with provisions and ammunition, he awaited the storm.

Nor had he long to wait. When on the 3rd of May the first attempt at mutiny occurred, he suppressed it in a masterly manner; but by the 30th five of the Sepoy regiments in the garrison had broken out, and the firing by them of the cantonments, accompanied by the murder of the officers, was the signal for a general rising. Then followed scenes of bloodshed and massacre in different parts of Oude; and before the end of June, not only the capital, but the whole province, was in open rebellion.

Up to this time Sir Henry had maintained his hold on Lucknow and the neighbourhood; but the 30th of June was the last day on which he was able to do so. For on that morning, in attempting to carry out a bold venture, most disastrous consequences ensued. But to better understand the situation, and so that light may be thrown upon other events, to be referred to hereafter, let us glance for a moment at Cawnpore—a military station between Lucknow and Allahabad, and regarded as the "key of Oude"—which had just been the scene of terrible doings.

On the breaking out of the Mutiny, Cawnpore was garrisoned by 3,800 men, consisting of four regiments of Sepoys and a battery of British artillery; but, in all, General Sir Hugh Wheeler, the commandant, had only 200 European soldiers with him; while under his charge were both the European residents, and the families of the 32nd Regiment, then stationed at Lucknow. When in the month of May Sir Hugh perceived a rebellious spirit growing up around him he entrenched a spot about 200 yards square; and having stored this with provisions for a month, he prepared to withdraw into it, if necessary, with the Europeans who were about him. On the 5th of June the rising took place, when one after another the native regiments mutinied; and after plundering £170,000 from the treasury, taking with them horses, arms, and ammunition, opening the gaols, and firing the bungalows, they prepared to march to Delhi. But they did not proceed thither. Instead, they were induced to put themselves under the leadership of Nana Sahib, a miscreant who had been foremost among the conspirators against the British. This man, the son of a Brahmin, had been adopted by Bajee Rao, the Ex-Peshwa, or nominal head of the Mahrattas; and the chief reason of his hatred of the British was the refusal of the Indian Government to continue to him the pension of eight lacs of rupees (£80,000), which had been paid to Bajee Rao; though he was permitted to have a retinue of 200 soldiers, and a fortified palace at Bithoor, ten miles from Cawnpore. He had recently been journeying from station to station in the North-west Provinces, fomenting the spirit of rebellion among the Sepoy regiments; and it was when the mutinous troops were marching off to Delhi that he, for the first time, took open command. Then it was that he persuaded the Sepoys to return to Cawnpore, in order to attack the small British garrison there;

and on their consenting he raised the Mahratta standard and hastened to the deadly work.

Sir Hugh Wheeler had by this time taken refuge in his fortified enclosure, and with him were about 900 Europeans, of whom more than two-thirds were women, children, and other non-combatants. Around this slender entrenchment the wild rebels now closed, and Nana Sahib's force, increased hourly by the arrival of mutineers from Allahabad and other places, was soon at least ten times stronger than the garrison. The siege began on the 7th of June; and for three weeks, while shot and shell were incessantly poured into the fortification, and the hapless defenders suffered untold horrors and privations, it went on in all its fury.

But gallant though the defence, and nobly though all—not only men, but even gently nurtured ladies—laboured, it was of no avail; and when, on the 26th, Nana Sahib offered to allow Sir Hugh and his companions to proceed by the river to Allahabad, if they would surrender, the General, for the sake of the women and children, felt compelled to agree to the terms.

So on the faith of an oath taken by Nana Sahib upon the Ganges—the most solemn oath of a Hindoo—the capitulation was effected.

For the first time for twenty-one days the din of cannon, and of mortars, and of musketry now ceased; but little dreamed Sir Hugh and his noble comrades that the monster in whom they were trusting had three weeks before murdered in cold blood no fewer than 130 fugitives—men, women, and children—who had escaped from the mutineers at Futtygurh, and landed at Cawnpore; little, too, dreamed the brave women and the helpless children of what the morrow was to bring forth! On that terrible morning there was perpetrated one of the foulest deeds of treachery ever known.

The surviving Europeans—many of them wounded and exhausted—had reached the riverside at about eight o'clock, and were permitted without molestation to enter the boats which they believed were to convey them to Allahabad. But no sooner had they embarked, than at a pre-arranged signal two cannon, which had been hidden, were immediately opened upon them; and then a murderous fire was showered down by the ferocious Sepoys, who lined both banks of the river. Thereupon we are told "the native boatmen deserted them at once, but a few of the boats escaped to the opposite bank. They were met there by Sepoys and by Oude cavalry, and all except one boat-load were seized. The men were either drowned, or shot in the river, or carried back before Nana Sahib, and massacred by these savages in his presence; while the women and the children (about 200 in number) were shut up for the present in one building. The boat that escaped struck upon a sandbank on the 28th. Sepoys, who had followed its course, constantly fired upon the passengers. Fourteen officers and soldiers fought them desperately, and got clean away; but they lost their road, and were obliged to take refuge in a temple. From their shelter they were smoked out. They then again fought the Sepoys, and five of them escaped to the Ganges. By hard swimming with the current four left their pursuers behind them, and at a distance of seven miles from the spot where they had taken the water they were rescued by the servants of a friendly rajah, and finally saved." On the day after this ghastly massacre Nana Sahib caused himself, amid great ceremony, to be proclaimed Peshwa; and thus terminated the first—though alas! not the greatest— of the diabolical crimes with which the villain's name is inseparably linked.

Leaving Nana Sahib for a brief time in triumphant possession of Cawnpore—holding in captivity the women and children whom he had carried off from the boats—let us return to Lucknow; after which we shall see how the infamies of which their countrymen had been the victims were avenged at the hands of Havelock, Outram, and Colin Campbell.

By their successes at Cawnpore, the mutineers were not only much encouraged, but numbers of them had now moved off in the direction of Lucknow; and it was on receiving news that bodies of rebels were marching upon the city that Sir Henry Lawrence determined, on the 30th of June, to present a bold front. He therefore led out a force to attack them; but unfortunately he did so without having accurate knowledge of their numbers. These proved to be several thousands, while his own men mustered only about 700, of whom half were Europeans, the rest faithful natives; and to add to his difficulties the native artillerymen, in whose loyalty he had trusted, having proved treacherous, cut the traces of their horses, threw the guns in a ditch, and rode away to join the mutineers. The gallant leader was therefore obliged to retreat, and it was with the loss of one-sixth of his men, as well as of "the reputation which had hitherto held the city in awe," that he and his followers returned to Lucknow.

The rebels now advanced in thousands towards the city, to which they immediately laid siege; and it was on the same afternoon that Sir Henry and his garrison, numbering 1,692 (Europeans and loyal natives), besides about 350 Europeans, including women and children, shut themselves within the Residency, to begin a defence lasting four long months, which forms one of the most striking episodes of the Mutiny.

Sad to say, however, though it was solely to Sir Henry's foresight that every preparation had been made to meet the worst emergencies—though it was by following his plan of operations that the besiegers, who scarcely ceased their assaults day or night, were kept at bay—it was not ordained that he should share in the triumph in which the defence at length culminated—the deliverance of the garrison at the hands of Havelock, Outram, and Colin Campbell. For on the second morning after the siege began, while in an exposed room of the Residency, where he was giving some instructions to a subordinate, a shell burst beside him, which shattered his thigh.

From this he never rallied, and after two days of intense suffering, during which he tried to forget his pain, so as to give directions for securing the safety of those who were around him, the gallant soldier breathed his last.

"Here lies Henry Lawrence, who tried to do his duty," was the simple inscription which he himself wrote for his tomb. How he more than acted up to it during the whole of his career, his life and his death alike abundantly testify.

While the beleaguered garrison—mourning their dead chief, and keeping in remembrance one of his last injunctions, "Never give in!"—were repelling with unflinching courage the fearful storm of fire that now raged round them from day to day, and were cheerfully enduring inconceivable hardships, an Army of Relief was already marching towards Cawnpore and Lucknow; and to the story of its famous leaders and their achievements we will now turn.

II.—SIR HENRY HAVELOCK AND SIR JAMES OUTRAM.

"No, I had too much else to do to be frightened; I was afraid all the pretty birds' eggs would be smashed; so I hadn't time to think of myself falling."

Young Havelock, a boy of seven, climbing a tall tree in search of a nest, had tumbled from the topmost branch; and this was his reply when asked whether he was not terrified as he crashed headlong through the branches. So was it always with him. He never thought of himself; and whatever the task he took in hand he performed it regardless of his own safety.

Havelock often said, in later life, that he attributed his stern notions of duty—his own ready obedience and his rigid exaction of it from others—to the discipline of the Charterhouse. And we can have no doubt that not only was such the case, but that there his whole character was formed and fixed. Born on the 5th of April, 1795, at Bishopwearmouth, near Sunderland, where his father had been a shipbuilder, Henry was sent to this famous London school (afterwards removed to Godalming) at the age of nine; and during the seven years he attended he gave every promise of a bright future. He studied hard, even gaining from his schoolmates the nickname of "Old Phloss" (a corruption of philosopher), because of his grave and thoughtful disposition; he won the love of those about him by his open-hearted, manly disposition; and he ever stood forward as champion of the weak against the strong.

It was in those days, too, that marked indications were given of the two strong characteristics by which his life was distinguished—his interest in religion, and his fondness for everything pertaining to military matters. And while on the one hand we find him with Napoleon Bonaparte as his favourite hero, eagerly reading every book he could obtain about great battles, so on the other we find the religious impressions received at his mother's knee becoming more and more deepened. Not that he made a parade of his convictions: they were a source of happiness to him, and as such he clung to them; nor could any taunt from this or that companion deter him from putting into everyday practice that in which he truly believed.

It was his mother's wish that young Havelock should be trained to the law, and, contrary to his own inclination, he, after leaving the Charterhouse, entered at the Middle Temple. But owing to some misunderstanding with his father, means of support were withdrawn from him; and at the end of six months he was thrown on his own resources. His brother William had just then come home from Waterloo—a circumstance which again directed Henry's thoughts to the army; so seeking his advice and influence, he was enabled to obtain a commission as second lieutenant in the 95th Rifles.

His profession thus definitely fixed, he now gave his whole thoughts to the mastery of it. "He read," says his brother-in-law, Mr. Marshman, "every military memoir within his reach. He laid in a rich store for his future guidance. He became familiar with every memorable battle and siege of ancient and modern times, and examined the detail and the result of every movement in the field with the eye of a soldier." And in thus fitting himself for the work that lay before him, eight years passed—most of them spent in different parts of the United Kingdom. Then it was that in the hope of seeing active service he exchanged into an infantry regiment bound to the East; and having studied Hindostani and Persian in London, he embarked for Calcutta in January, 1823.

On landing in India Havelock, amid all his military duties, took practical interest in every kind of religious work. He associated himself with the missionaries at Serampore; he sought the acquaintance of ministers and others in Calcutta; and it was now that he began to devote himself to the spiritual and moral welfare of his regiment. He would assemble the men together when there was leisure, that they might hold religious converse or join together in prayer or worship; and in this way he gained over them a strong influence for good. It was no easy task—especially at first—surrounded as he was by many only too ready to scoff at his efforts; but he never faltered, and all through his life he kept up the practice of holding such services.

In the year after his arrival in India, he was serving in Burmah, where there was war; and after the capture of Rangoon, there was fear of excesses on the part of the victorious troops. Havelock was not content to go about imploring the soldiers to keep within bounds, but he was accustomed to assemble his men for worship in the grand Buddhist pagoda of the city. An officer relates that as he was wandering round this place one day, "he heard the sound of distant psalmody, and threading his way through the passages to the spot whence it proceeded, he found himself in a small side chapel with little images of Buddha arranged round the room. A little oil lamp had been placed in the lap of each figure, and the pious soldiers of the 13th were standing up, with Havelock in their midst, singing a Christian hymn." And, as showing the practical results of his teaching, the following incident in the same campaign is recorded. One night the army was suddenly apprised of the near approach of the enemy; and a certain corps was directed to take a post of danger. But so many men of that regiment were intoxicated that they would not obey the order.

"Then call out Havelock's saints," exclaimed the General; "they are always sober, and can be depended upon; and Havelock himself is always ready!"

And the bugle sounded, and by these "saints" the enemy were promptly repulsed.

Nor was Havelock's desire to do good to those around him confined to teaching and preaching. Though only a subaltern, he cheerfully sacrificed one-tenth of his slender pay to objects of benevolence; and even in later years, although family claims increased, he continued to devote that proportion of his income to similar purposes.

But while he thus exhibited the religious side of his character, he gave abundant proof of splendid soldierly qualities; and his coolness, courage, and knowledge of military science won the regard and admiration of all. Some have said that he was too rigid a disciplinarian; but though he expected strictest obedience from those under him, he never exacted more than he was willing to submit to himself. No man could have recognised the claims of duty more fully than he did. A characteristic illustration of this was given on his wedding day. He had returned to India from Burmah in 1829, and he was to be married at Serampore to a daughter of Dr. Marshman, one of the Baptist missionaries there. But it happened that he was summoned to attend a court-martial in Calcutta at noon the same day. What was he to do? His friends urged him to absent himself from it, on the ground that so important an event would be considered to form sufficient excuse. But their entreaties were in vain. "He maintained that, as a soldier, he was bound to obey orders, regardless of his own convenience. The marriage was therefore solemnised at an earlier hour, after which he proceeded to Calcutta by a swift boat, attended the court, and returned to Serampore in time for the nuptial banquet."

Havelock's regiment—the 13th—now moved from place to place in India; but having by this time made himself proficient in Oriental languages, he left it temporarily in 1834 to become interpreter to the 16th Regiment, then stationed at Cawnpore. In the following year he rejoined the 13th, having been appointed adjutant. When he was proposed for this, some of the officers wrote to Lord William Bentinck, the Governor-General, to protest, on account of his religious habits.

"But," said Lord William, who had found out on inquiry that Havelock's men were the best-behaved in the regiment, "there is no reflection on his courage, or his loyalty, or his moral character?"

"Not the least; but he is a Baptist!"

"I only wish the whole regiment were Baptists, too!" was his lordship's reply; and Havelock received the appointment.

Notwithstanding all his merits, promotion came very slowly to Havelock, while, not being a rich man, he was prevented from rising to higher rank by purchase; and he had been twenty-three years in the army before he was made captain. This rank was attained in 1838, shortly after which he was ordered to Afghanistan, to accompany the expedition to Cabul to reinstate Shah Soojah. He exhibited his wonted bravery during this campaign, being always found where the fire was fiercest and the enemy most obstinate; and when, in 1841, he took part in the prolonged defence of Jellalabad, under General Sale, it was in a large measure due to his bold measures that the besiegers were unsuccessful. Great though they were, however, for these services he was only promoted to a majority, and made a Companion of the Bath.

Next we find him acting as interpreter to Sir Hugh Gough, the Commander-in-Chief; and when the first Sikh war was raging, he had two horses shot under him at Moodkee; while at the battle of Sobraon a cannon ball entered his charger through the saddle-cloth, and passed within an inch of his thigh.

Soon after these events—like so many of the great heroes of India—Havelock found his health fail; and reluctant though he was to do so at first, he embarked for his native land in 1849, in search of rest and strength. Then after a pleasant stay of two years, first in England, afterwards at Bonn—where he left his wife and children—he returned to the East as brevet-colonel; and not long afterwards he became Quartermaster-General and Adjutant-General of the Queen's troops in India. His duties during the next five years called him to various parts of the Empire; and it was at the end of that time that he was eagerly looking forward to being rejoined at Bombay by Mrs. Havelock and one or two of the children. But it was not to be. Just before the time arranged for the happy meeting, a sudden and unexpected call to duty came, which caused its postponement, and the brave soldier was never to see his wife again.

At the beginning of 1857 war broke out against Persia, and when, on the recommendation of Sir James Outram, Havelock was appointed to the command of a division, he accepted it. "When the post of honour and danger was offered me by telegraph," he wrote, "old as I am, I did not hesitate a moment;" and he immediately started for Bombay, whence he sailed in the month of January. During this campaign—in which his eldest son, Henry, who had now joined him, also took part—Havelock won high praise from Sir James Outram for the skill and courage which he again displayed; and in no small degree he contributed to the success of the British operations, which came to a close within two months, when the Persians were beaten, and a treaty of peace signed. Another instance of Havelock's courage was given during this expedition. As the steamer, conveying his men to Persia, was nearing the coast, he saw that they must be exposed to a heavy cannonade from a fort that was bristling with guns. Thereupon he ordered his men to lie down flat on the deck, and then took his own station on the paddle-box, to act as emergency might require. The danger to himself, we are told, was imminent, for there came around him a perfect shower of bullets; but he escaped unhurt.

The campaign in Persia was scarcely at an end when the Mutiny broke out: and when Havelock returned to Bombay at the end of May he was greeted with the intelligence that the Sepoys had risen in revolt at Meerut, that Delhi was in possession of the insurgents, and that disaffection was everywhere spreading in the Upper Provinces. He resolved, therefore, to lose no time in placing his services at the disposal of the Commander-in-Chief; so he took passage to Galle, where he would get an early steamer to Calcutta. It was during this voyage that

Havelock had a narrow escape from drowning. As the vessel neared Ceylon she struck upon a reef and became a total wreck. Every moment it was expected that she would go down head foremost; while, to make matters worse, the captain lost his nerve, and the crew became first helpless and then insubordinate. It was when the vessel struck again, and confusion grew worse confounded, that Havelock sought to reassure the sailors. "Now, my men," cried he, "if you will but obey me, and keep from the spirit cask, we shall all be saved!" And such was the effect of his words that the affrighted crew recovered their calmness, and no lives were lost.

It was on reaching Calcutta, about the middle of June, that Havelock heard that Cawnpore was threatened, and that Lucknow was pressed hard; and he was at once appointed, with the rank of Brigadier-General, to the command of the Flying Column for the relief of those places. Hastening to Allahabad, where on his arrival he heard of the surrender of General Wheeler, and of the terrible massacre that followed, he marched from there, within a few days, at the head of only 1,000 European troops, 130 loyal Sikhs, and six guns. It was with such a force, and through a country "which was one sea of mutiny," that Havelock was expected to do his work; and after joining hands within a day or two with a small detachment, numbering a few hundreds, under Major Renaud, which had already gone forward a short distance, he arrived at Futtehpore. It had been a terrible journey, for it was now the rainy season, and, in addition to having to bear the scorching sun, the troops had been often delayed on the march, owing to the rivers being full, and the country in many places quite under water.

Scarcely had the column encamped at Futtehpore when spies brought in news that the enemy was advancing, some thousands strong, and at the same moment a shot fell close to the General. Every man flew to his post, and soon a heavy fire was opened; but the rebels, though there were 4,000 of them, were no match for the British, and before long they had fled, leaving behind eleven guns.

The march to Cawnpore was now resumed, and three days later another battle was fought, and the enemy utterly routed. The heat during this time was so intense that already twelve men had died from exposure to it, while the fatigue which the troops endured was indescribable.

They were now nearing their goal; but on approaching the bridge of the Pandoo River, which they would have to cross to reach Cawnpore, they found it defended by heavy guns, and the enemy entrenched on the opposite bank. Again Havelock's men rushed forward, and eventually the enemy gave in at all points, and made for Cawnpore. The gallant little army now crossed the bridge, and on the following day stood face to face with Nana Sahib's forces, numbering 5,000, strongly entrenched, and so sheltered that it seemed hopeless to attack them. Havelock showed no hesitation, and soon "the admirable strategy of the commander, and the indomitable courage of the British soldiers, especially the 78th Highlanders, gave him a brilliant victory." The battle commenced at two o'clock in the afternoon, and when evening came, and darkness was approaching, Havelock saw that there was no time to be lost. Pointing to some of the enemy's artillery, he then rode up to his Highlanders and exclaimed: "Those guns must be taken by the bayonet; and, men, remember I am with you." And on hearing this command the brave fellows, "like a pack of greyhounds," dashed forward with a ringing cheer; and so effectual was this movement, that without waiting for the bayonets the rebels had lost all heart, and retreated—hopelessly beaten.

It was on the next morning, July 17th, that Havelock and his army, in full belief that, after their terrible march of 126 miles, the rescue of the 200 women and children whom Nana Sahib had made prisoners was to be accomplished, entered Cawnpore. But what an awful sight met their view! On hearing that Havelock had carried the Pandoo bridge, and was advancing on the town, Nana Sahib had crowned his previous atrocities by a deed even more hideous. He had seized his prisoners, butchered them in cold blood, hacked their bodies to pieces, and thrown them all into a deep well! And when Havelock and his troops entered the building in which these helpless women and children had been confined, it was not to free them, but to behold a scene never surpassed in horror. The three narrow rooms in which the captives had been kept were swimming in blood two inches deep; and lying around were scores of mournful relics—little shoes belonging to the children, portions of dresses, leaves of Bibles, locks of hair, and many others—while not far off was the ghastly well into which, some only half dead, the poor creatures had been ruthlessly cast. Well might the soldiers shed tears as they gazed on the scene; well might they, with clenched teeth, swear to avenge the awful massacre!

Too late to rescue the prisoners of Cawnpore, Havelock could now only prepare to press on to Lucknow, from which the sad news of the death of Sir Henry Lawrence had arrived; and having burned to the ground the palace at Bithoor, belonging to Nana Sahib—who had by this time fled with his army—the British marched forward on the 25th of July. Cawnpore was meanwhile left under the command of Colonel Neill, who had just come in with a small force.

But difficulties greater than any Havelock had yet experienced now began to arise. On the 29th of July, having crossed the Ganges, he had beaten the enemy, some thousands in number, at Aong, capturing fifteen guns; and then another victory was won at Busseerut-gunge. But by this time, besides having lost eighty-eight officers and men in these actions, his troops were being decimated by sickness, and there seemed likely to be many more obstacles to their advance as they neared Lucknow—thirty-eight miles distant. So the general resolved to return to Munglewar to await reinforcements, which he had begged to be sent from Calcutta. But these did not come; and he made a second attempt to advance. Again reaching Busseerut-gunge, he defeated 20,000 mutineers with great slaughter; but the cholera then arrested his march. He therefore returned to Cawnpore. And for more than one reason it was fortunate that he thus turned back; for by this time Nana

Sahib had reappeared with a large force at Bithoor, and was threatening Colonel Neill. As soon as Havelock arrived he therefore marched out to Bithoor; and at that place he defeated 4,000 of the rebels, and again put them to flight.

It was after this victory, when his men in spite of their fatigue cheered Havelock, that he said to them, "Don't cheer me, my men; you did it all yourselves!" and it was on the morning afterwards that he issued his famous Order of the Day, in which the following passages occur: "If," said he, "conquest can now be achieved under the most trying circumstances, what will be the triumph and retribution of the time when the armies from China, from the Cape, and from England, shall sweep through the land? Soldiers, in that moment your labours, your privations, your sufferings and your valour will not be forgotten by a grateful country. You will be acknowledged to have been the stay and prop of British India in the time of her severest trial."

Havelock's army, now sadly reduced by battle and disease, was doomed to enforced inactivity at Cawnpore for five weeks, by which time the reinforcements of which he stood in need arrived. But meanwhile unexpected and startling news reached Havelock. He was to be superseded! Though he had won battle after battle, surmounted the greatest difficulties by which a general could be beset, the Government of India had thought fit to deprive him of his command, and had appointed Sir James Outram in his stead. Sir James was also to resume his duties as Chief Commissioner of Oude—a post he had a few years before given up through ill-health—in succession to Sir Henry Lawrence. It was a cruel blow, and why such a step should have been taken is incomprehensible, but such was the official decision; and whether it had been arrived at thoughtlessly or otherwise, Havelock could only bow to it manfully.

It was, however, by no ordinary man that Havelock had been thus superseded; and even if Sir James's generous and chivalrous act, of which we shall learn more presently, had never been dreamed of, it must have been some consolation to him to feel that such a true hero had been placed over him. This distinguished soldier and statesman —born in 1803—had served his country in various posts, in all of which he had gained high repute not only for military and administrative capacity, but especially also for splendid personal qualities. Eighteen years before this time he had distinguished himself in Cabul, when the ill-fated expedition had been despatched thither; then he had been appointed Political Agent at Goojerat, and subsequently British Resident in Sinde. It was while in the latter province that he had adopted views at variance with those of Sir Charles Napier, for he had disapproved of the policy of invading the country. But he had never allowed personal feelings to come before duty; and in spite of their disagreements, not only had Sir Charles acknowledged that Outram's services had been of the most brilliant character, but in recognition of his courage and high sense of honour, he had bestowed on him the title of " The Bayard of India." And, as showing Outram's consistent conduct, when after the war in Sinde the spoils lay at the conquerors' feet and the prize money came to be distributed, he had refused his share of it, and paid the whole amount—about £3,000—to public charities in Bombay. Subsequently he had filled other high offices in India; and, as we have seen, he had been in command of the expedition to Persia, in which Havelock bore a part.

And what did "The Bayard of India" do when, on his return from Persia, he was appointed to take Havelock's place as Commander of the Lucknow Relief force? Let his own words speak. Just before he reached Cawnpore, and every preparation had been made for facilitating the success of the expedition, Sir James wrote to Havelock: "I shall join you with the reinforcements. But to you shall be left the glory of relieving Lucknow, for which you have already struggled so much. I shall accompany you only in my civil capacity as Commissioner of Oude, placing my military service at your disposal, and, should you please, serving under you as a volunteer." And on his arrival he officially announced this resolution in a Divisional Order issued to the troops.

Such was Outram's noble conduct towards Havelock; and in the grim annals of war which this act of self-sacrifice illumines, it would be difficult to find its parallel. Nor need it be said how gratefully Havelock acknowledged Sir James's generosity.

All preparations having been completed, the new Army of Relief—numbering rather over 3,000 men, nearly all British—left Cawnpore on the 19th of September, and commenced the famous "march of fire" which was to complete the great deeds linked with the name of Havelock. Forward the little force pushed, and having crossed the Ganges, they came upon the rebels strongly posted at Munglewar; but a well-directed attack soon repulsed them; and then, amidst torrents of rain, the wearisome journey was resumed. Every hour was precious, for none knew how the beleaguered garrison at Lucknow might be faring by this time; so, regardless of privations and sufferings, all speed was made; and by the 23rd of the month the booming of guns around the Residency was distinctly heard, and a salute was fired by Havelock in the hope that the sound of the approach of his army might be made known to the garrison. It was on this day, too, that the troops were cheered by the news of the recapture of Delhi, which had been finally accomplished, as we have seen, a few days before. They had now reached the Alum-baugh, formerly the summer palace of the princes of Oude, some few miles from the Residency, where the foe was found to have taken up a strong position to interrupt their progress. But Havelock's heavy guns soon cleared this obstruction, while Sir James Outram, at the head of some cavalry, bravely pursued the enemy, notwithstanding their numbers; and now, after a day devoted to much needed rest, came the final struggle—the attack on the city itself. Before this could be attempted, however, it was necessary that the sick and wounded should be cared for; it was determined, therefore, to leave them at the Alum-baugh, under a guard of 300 men—the strongest force that could be spared.

From the Alum-baugh there were three ways of reaching the Residency, and it was decided to choose the route over a bridge which crossed the canal. At the head of this bridge stood six of the enemy's guns, while numbers of temporary fortresses with loopholed walls had also been erected to sweep the road. The order was given; and then the advance was made amidst a terrible stream of fire, which poured down and created sad havoc amongst the troops. But nothing could stay their progress; "there was a shout, a rush, and a brief struggle, and the battery was theirs," after which, while the Highlanders kept the now captured bridge, the rest of the brave warriors—save those who had fallen—dashed across it. And "then Lucknow rose before them with all its gilded minarets, its rich domes, its splendid mosques, and many palaces—its regular and thickly crowded streets of houses, but all relieved by beautiful gardens, stately parks, and foliaged trees."

Proceeding onwards the troops ere long found themselves at the Kaiser-baugh, a fortified palace, where the whole strength of the enemy was concentrated for a final effort; but again, in face of "an iron deluge of grape, canister, and round shot," British valour prevailed; and they were now within 500 yards of the Residency. It was nearing evening, and the troops, fighting all day, had not rested, and had scarcely tasted food; so it was thought by some that it would be wise to halt for the night. But Havelock felt there was danger in such a course, for before morning the rebels, said to be 50,000 strong, might hem in the relieving force, or even annihilate it; besides which the garrison was now believed to be in great extremity. And so the column pushed on through fire and death. Then "from every wall, from every house top, from every corner, streamed incessant storms of shot. The infuriated enemy, secure behind their walls and in their numbers, showed their heads over their parapets or from their casements, and poured forth hideous curses as they fired from their many thousand rifles on the handful below. The path was marked by the slain and the dying; the brave Neill (who had accompanied the force) fell dead; but nothing could stop our men—every obstacle was overcome; and at last the gates of the Residency appeared before the heroic remnant. It was full time. Another day, and the horrors of Cawnpore would have been repeated, for the enemy had driven their mines under the fortifications, and further resistance would have been impossible."

The barricades of the Residency were now broken down; through the gates the deliverers fought their way; and then, says an eye-witness, "the garrison's long pent-up feelings of anxiety and suspense burst forth in a succession of deafening cheers. From every pit, trench, and battery—from behind the sand-bags piled on shattered houses—from every post still held by a few gallant spirits—rose cheer on cheer; even from the hospital many of the wounded crawled forth to join in that glad shout of welcome to those who had so bravely come to our assistance. It was a moment never to be forgotten. The delight of the ever gallant Highlanders, who had fought twelve battles to enjoy that moment of ecstasy, and in the last four days had lost a third of their number, seemed to know no bounds. . . . . They rushed forward, the rough-bearded warriors, and shook the ladies by the hand with loud and repeated gratulations. They took the children up in their arms and, fondly caressing

"THEY TOOK THE CHILDREN UP IN THEIR ARMS" (*p.* 240).

them, passed them from one to another in turn. Then, when the first burst of enthusiasm was over, they mournfully turned to speak among themselves of the heavy losses they had sustained, and to inquire the names of the comrades who had fallen in the way."

And so, with loss of over 460 killed and wounded, was Lucknow relieved, and its garrison and refugees, numbering about 1,600 in all, rescued, after a captivity of twelve weeks, from the dreadful fate which had threatened to overtake them at any moment.

On the day after entering the Residency, Havelock gave over to General Outram the chief command of the forces; and Sir James's first thought was for the women and children, as well as for the sick and wounded, whom he hoped to convey to Cawnpore. But it was soon evident that this would not be possible; for around the captured Residency the enemy were swarming in greater numbers than ever; and the relievers were now to be themselves besieged. Nor until Sir Colin Campbell came to their rescue, six weeks later, were they able to stir out of the city.

It was just after this second relief of Lucknow had been effected that illness seized Sir Henry Havelock (who had by this time been made a Knight Commander of the Bath, while subsequently, though too late for him to be aware of it, he was created a Baronet, with a pension of £1,000 a year); and to the inexpressible grief of all it was plain that his course was nearly run. The tremendous exertions and privations of the march to Lucknow had done their work on a frame already enfeebled; and, attacked by dysentery, on the 20th of November he lay down to die.

P

Just before the end—which came on the morning of the 24th—he said to his comrade in arms, Sir James Outram, whose own illustrious career was to close, full of honours, within six short years: "For more than forty years I have so ruled my life that when death came I might face it without fear." And it was with the parting words, "Come and see how a Christian can die," addressed to his eldest son, who had himself played a prominent part in the campaign, that this "happy warrior" fell asleep.

"Every inch a soldier, but every inch a Christian." So had one of his chiefs, many years before, summed up Havelock's character; and, than this, we should seek in vain for epitaph more fitting.

III.—COLIN CAMPBELL, LORD CLYDE.

"How soon could you start for India?" was the question put to Sir Colin Campbell by Lord Panmure, the Secretary at War, on Saturday afternoon, July 11th, 1857. For the startling news had just been received from the East that not only was the Mutiny spreading, but that the Commander-in-Chief, General Anson, had fallen a victim to cholera.

"This evening, if necessary," was the prompt reply. And on the next day Sir Colin, appointed General Anson's successor, was speeding towards Calcutta.

A right gallant old soldier was he, who, responding to duty's call, thus went forth to serve his Queen and country in the hour of need. Sixty-five years of age, his life for close on half a century had been nearly all spent amid the din of arms. Born in Glasgow on the 20th of October, 1792, he entered the army in 1808, and within three months was promoted to a lieutenancy, and saw active service in the Peninsula. This was at Vimiera, where the Duke of Wellington, then Sir Arthur Wellesley, defeated the French. It was here, we are told, that just as the battle began, Colin's captain suddenly called him to his side, and, taking his hand, led him to the front, in view of the enemy's fire, where he walked him up and down for several minutes to try his nerve and inspire him with confidence. He then let him go, and, his object attained, bade him rejoin his regiment.

Later on the young officer served under Sir John Moore, and, along with Sir Charles Napier, was present at the retreat on Corunna; and it was his regiment that had the sorrowful honour of preparing the grave on the ramparts, where, "at dead of night," their brave chief was silently laid to rest. Among other places in the Peninsula at which he played a distinguished part was San Sebastian, where he led the storming party. Here he was first shot through the hip, in consequence of which he fell down the breach; and next, on rushing forward again, he received a dangerous wound in the thigh. He gained high commendation for his courage during this campaign, and by the time he was twenty-one he was made captain. Nova Scotia saw him next; after which he served in the West Indies; then in England; until in 1841, then lieutenant-colonel, he saw service in China, and was made a Companion of the Bath. Six years later he drew sword for the first time on Indian soil; and at Chillianwalla and Goojerat, during the Sikh war, he so distinguished himself that in recognition of his services he was made a Knight Commander of the Bath.

Then a few years later, after other important services, came an eventful period in his career. In 1854, in command of the Highland Brigade, Major-General Sir Colin Campbell was called to the Crimea. At the battle of the Alma he took a most prominent part; and he and his gallant Highlanders not only routed the enemy, but created terror by their very presence. Then came Balaclava, where Sir Colin's duty was to defend the British landing-place; and here it was that, contrary to the usual custom, instead of meeting the rush of the enemy's cavalry by forming a square, he arranged his force in an unbroken even line. Just before the battle, addressing the men as they stood all in readiness, he said, "Remember, now, there is no retreat for you; you must die where you stand." And then came the answer, with a cheer, "Ay, ay, Sir Colin, we'll do that!" But they did not fall; for as the Russian hordes swept down on them, the immortal "Thin Red Line" (so called from the colour of their coats) greeted the enemy with such a deluge of fire that those who were not shot down were glad to fly. When, later on, he found that an officer, General Sir William Codrington, who was his junior, was appointed Commander-in Chief, Sir Colin felt so indignant at the slight put upon him that his resignation followed, and he returned to England. He was, however, asked by the Queen to return to the Crimea, and he did so; it is said, indeed, that when he went to Windsor her Majesty was so gracious to him that he told her he was ready to go back and serve under a corporal if she wished it! For his many services in this campaign, Sir Colin received the Grand Cross of the Bath; and, on his coming back to England, on the conclusion of peace, he found himself lionised by his admiring countrymen. Nor could this be wondered at. He had in every way proved himself a real hero, and his achievements had been such as appealed directly to the hearts of the people. "He was," says one writer, "a man who, like Sir Charles Napier, could not help loving war for its own sake, even while he knew its horrors; a man whose heart beat stronger on the day of battle; a general who could inspire his soldiers with his own spirit, because while he harangued them the glow on his cheek and the tremour of his voice told how strongly his own nature was stirred."

Such was the soldier who, in the serious emergency caused by the Sepoy Revolt, was regarded as the one of all others capable of stemming the tide of disaster; nor, as events proved, could more fitting choice have been made.

Arriving in India, unencumbered with baggage, on the 13th of August, Sir Colin Campbell, having fully acquainted himself with the condition of affairs, made immediate preparations for crushing the rebellion; and it was when the news arrived that Havelock and Outram, after relieving Lucknow, had themselves been in turn besieged there with the old garrison, that he resolved to put himself at the head of a large force, and go to the rescue. Fortunately, about this time reinforcements reached India; and not a moment having been lost by him in organising his forces, he began his march from Cawnpore on the 9th of November. His army, which included, among others, the 93rd Highlanders who were with him in the Crimea, numbered 5,000 men; and this force was well equipped in every respect, and though there was urgent need to reach Lucknow, all care had been taken that every plan should be carefully prepared, so as to ensure success.

With utmost speed Sir Colin now pushed on; and, as showing the eagerness with which he and his gallant men were longing to reach their goal, within three days they reached the Alum-baugh, where, it will be remembered, the enemy had tried hard to prevent the approach of Havelock and Outram, and where the latter had left the sick and wounded with a guard of 300 men. And it was from the summit of this place, which, though communication between it and the city had been cut off by the rebels, had providentially been left unmolested by them, that Sir Colin was able to signal his arrival to the British Residency.

It was just after the joyful news of the approach of the relieving army had come to the garrison that a heroic feat was undertaken by an Irish civilian, Mr. James Kavanagh, who was one of those who had been so long shut up in the Residency. At this juncture it was most important that, if possible, Sir Colin Campbell should have accurate information as to the condition of the blockaded garrison, and particularly, also, about the route to be taken by him in his advance. But Lucknow was crowded with thousands of rebel troops; and every outlet was closely guarded by them. How, then, could the communication be effected? The brave Kavanagh volunteered to undertake the task. He well knew the perils attending it; knew that if, as was probable, he fell into the rebels' hands, he would have to endure a death of exquisite torture. He saw, however, that the life or death of the whole garrison depended upon whether Sir Colin could successfully reach the Residency; and so, in the end, though Sir James Outram was reluctant that such terrible danger should be faced, his offer was accepted.

Kavanagh, in his account of the adventure, says: "I was dressed as a budmash, or as an irregular soldier of the city, with sword and shield, native-made shoes, tight trousers, a yellow silk koortah over a tight-fitting white muslin skirt, a yellow-coloured chintz sheet thrown over my shoulders, a cream-coloured turban, and a white waistband or cummerbund. My face down to the shoulders and my hands to the wrists were coloured with lampblack, the cork used being dipped in oil to cause the colour to adhere a little." Thus disguised he started off in the evening, accompanied by a native guide; and having forded the river Goomtee—$4\frac{1}{2}$ feet deep and 100 yards wide—he advanced towards the British camp under cover of the night. Several adventures now befell him, for he was again and again challenged by the enemy's pickets, and narrowly escaped detection; while, as he got nearer and nearer to the Alumbaugh, his guide became so terrified that he begged Kavanagh not to proceed farther. He still pressed on, however, meeting with more and more danger, and not till four o'clock did he near the camp. At this hour, he says, "I stopped at the corner of a tope, or grove of trees, to sleep for an hour, which Kunoujee Lal, the guide, entreated I would not do; but I thought he overrated the danger, and, lying down, I told him to see if there was any one in the grove who would tell him where we then were. We had not gone far when I heard the English challenge, 'Who comes there?' with a native accent. We had reached a British cavalry outpost; my eyes filled with joyful tears, and I shook the Sikh officer in charge of the picket heartily by the hand. The old soldier was as pleased as myself when he heard from whence I had come, and he was good enough to send two of his men to conduct me to the camp of the advanced guard. An officer of her Majesty's 9th Lancers, who was visiting his pickets, met me on the way, and took me into his tent, where I got dry stockings and trousers, and, which I much needed, a glass of brandy—a liquor I had not tasted for nearly two months."

We are told that the excitement in the British camp on the arrival of the plucky Irishman was unbounded. Even Sir Colin Campbell, "grim in his sternness and singularly chary of his praise, waxed enthusiastic as Kavanagh sat at his table and told the startling story of that night's adventure;" and so valuable was the information he was able to impart that the Commander-in-Chief was glad to have Kavanagh by his side to act as guide during the march on Lucknow that soon followed. Eventually, Kavanagh's services on this, as well as on subsequent occasions, were rewarded with a gift of £2,000, the appointment of Assistant-Commissioner of Oude, and, what such a hero would prize more than all, the Victoria Cross.

On the 14th of November the advance on the city was began; and from the tower of the Residency, where several of the besieged garrison had betaken themselves, the progress of Sir Colin and his 5,000 men was watched with breathless interest. A different route was chosen from that adopted by Havelock and Outram; and instead of crossing the canal, Sir Colin made first for a strong position held by the enemy at the Dilkhoosha, a hunting castle of the ancient kings of Oude, about three miles from the Residency. A tough fight took place here, but eventually the rebels were driven back and pursued past the Martinière College, whereupon both that building and the Dilkhoosha fell into the hands of the British. The latter now formed Sir Colin's headquarters; and early on the 16th, leaving every kind of baggage there, the advance on the Secunder-baugh (or "Alexander's garden") was made. This place, the most formidable stronghold of the enemy, was a large square building surrounded by a wall of solid masonry, with loopholes all round; and here it was evident that the rebels, who had mustered in tremendous force, intended to offer desperate resistance. The first move was to dislodge the enemy from a line of barracks which they held outside the Secunder-baugh; and this accomplished, and the barracks turned into a military post, the storming of the main building commenced.

Now began a struggle terrible beyond description;

but full of horrors though it was, yet when we remember the unavenged atrocities committed by Nana Sahib and his followers, it was little wonder that at length the British should have given vent to their righteous fury. After battering at the walls of this place for about an hour and a half with little effect, a small breach, only about two feet square, was at last made; and then the order was given to open the assault, for which work the Highlanders and a body of faithful Sikhs were selected.

Dashing forward to the little hole, each man eager to be first, the stormers dragged themselves through as quickly as its narrow limits would permit; and once inside they tore out the iron bars of the windows and leaped headlong in on the astonished defenders. There was no escape for the foe now, for every exit from the place was covered by the British guns, and to the fierce onslaught by the bayonet commenced by the Highlanders and the Sikhs resistance was in vain. "It was," says one writer, "a horrible struggle. No quarter was asked; except in a few instances, none was given. The grim Highlanders, whenever an appeal was made, hissed in the ear of the suppliant, '*Cawnpore!*' and the next moment buried the bayonet in his heart. . . . The hour of vengeance had come. . . . It was not a sudden rush and the conflict over, but the work of death went on hour after hour for three long hours. Then all was still; and as the crimsoned haggard avengers staggered out of that Aceldama they bore on their persons the testimonials of the terrific work they had accomplished. Few wished to look on the scene the building presented. The floor swam in blood, and in the corners and passage-ways lay the dead—2,000 of them! Thus was Cawnpore avenged—but many a plume that waved proudly in the morning air now dropped mournfully over the cold and pallid face, attesting that the fearful punishment had not been without heavy sacrifice."

The Secunder-baugh was captured; but the Residency was not yet reached; and Sir Colin's progress was next barred by a large fortified mosque. Again, however, British valour triumphed after a stubborn fight; and now came the beginning of the end.

During this time, as Sir Colin advanced nearer and nearer to the Residency, Generals Outram and Havelock had been preparing to co-operate with him as soon as his approach was close enough for them to act with safety; and it is not difficult to imagine with what excitement the pent-up garrison had, from their look-out, watched the relieving force ploughing its way amidst the sea of fire that surrounded it. But nearer and still nearer it had come; and already, on the 16th of November, the garrison had commenced to clear the way from their side. On the next day the junction was effected. Sir Colin had on that morning encountered the rebels at a building known as the Mess House; and it was after this place had been carried with a rush that the enemy, having made a last despairing stand, were finally overcome in an enclosure known as the Motee Mahal.

"And then," says Sir Colin, in his despatch, "I had the inexpressible satisfaction shortly afterwards of greeting Sir James Outram and Sir Henry Havelock, who came out to meet me before the action was at an end. The relief of the besieged garrison had been accomplished."

What words can describe the joy that now filled the hearts of the heroic men, women, and children, who, after their weeks of suffering and suspense, at length heard the welcome sounds of "The Campbells are coming," piped by the gallant Highlanders, as the Army of Deliverance poured into the Residency? What shouts of triumph and of thankfulness rang through Lucknow on that memorable day! And yet with all this gladness was mingled deepest sorrow; for during this march no fewer than 122 officers and men had been killed and 345 wounded; and who could forget that it was at such cost that success had been achieved? And when only a few days later—by which time Sir Colin had succeeded in removing the garrison, the women and children, and about a thousand sick and wounded, from the Residency—it was known that the beloved Havelock had been stricken down, yet fresh gloom was cast over the British camp.

The main portion of Sir Colin Campbell's task was now accomplished; but much work was still to be done. First, there was the conveyance to Cawnpore of the rescued garrison—no easy undertaking even under favourable circumstances; but though when he arrived at Cawnpore he found that place in the hands of the enemy, he succeeded in despatching the sick and wounded to Calcutta, after which he attacked the rebels, numbering 25,000, and defeated them at all points.

Following this came Sir Colin's second campaign in 1858; and during that year not only was Lucknow, which after his departure had, of course, fallen into the hands of the rebels, reconquered by him and Sir James Outram, and British authority firmly re-established in the province of Oude, but by a series of masterly movements—which included the successful operations of Sir Hugh Rose (afterwards Lord Strathnairn) in Central India—the Commander-in-Chief and his able Generals succeeded in reducing one after another of the enemy's strongholds, and finally in stamping out the rebellion.

Sir Colin in the meantime, in recognition of his achievements, had been raised to the peerage under the title of Baron Clyde of Clydesdale, with a pension of £2,000 a year.

Remaining in India until 1860, Lord Clyde then set sail for his native land. He longed for rest; yet even after arrival in England, though almost worn out, he said—referring to the possibility of being required in Canada—that "if asked to go I am quite ready." But his services were not needed; and so, his trusty sword returned to its scabbard for ever, he settled down in London; and there—until the 14th of August, 1863—the great hero spent his remaining days.

In the sketches given in the foregoing pages it has been shown, first, how the British obtained foothold in India; next, how, after subduing province after province, they established their authority there; and, finally, how, when the vast fabric of Empire which they had built up and consolidated was threatened by foes from within, the same valour which had aforetime led them to victory enabled them to hold their own. With a brief reference to three important episodes which subsequently took place this volume may appropriately close.

Before the last spark of the Sepoy Rebellion had been extinguished a Proclamation was issued by the Governor-General, who then became the first Viceroy, that the East India Company had been abolished, and that henceforth the direct sovereignty of their possessions would be assumed by the British Crown. A strong feeling of hostility against the Company's rule had grown up in England during the progress of the Mutiny, and eventually it had been felt that, especially as order and authority had been restored by the armies sent by the Queen, it was desirable that India should form an integral part of the British Empire. And so the great Company, whose first charter had been granted by Queen Elizabeth more than 250 years before, ceased to exist; and on the 1st of November, 1858, the sceptre of India passed into the hands of Queen Victoria.

Following this came a graceful act performed by her Majesty. This was the institution of a new Order of Knighthood, entitled "The Most Exalted Order of the Star of India," with the express object of recognising both the services rendered to the Indian Empire by Englishmen, and the loyal support given to the ruling power by native princes and chiefs. It was exactly three years after the Queen had proclaimed herself ruler of India that she held the first investiture of this Order; and on that day—the 1st of November, 1861—a notable assemblage of those who had deserved well of their Sovereign was gathered in the throne room at Windsor to receive the decoration, of which "Heaven's Light Our Guide" is the motto. More than one of the heroes of whose deeds these pages have told was present. Prominent among them was the veteran Colin Campbell, Lord Clyde; by his side stood the gallant Lord Gough; and General Sir George Pollock, avenger of the Cabul massacre, and he who won the name of "The Saviour of India," Sir John (afterwards Lord) Lawrence, were also among the illustrious knights. Others, too, not perhaps so well known, but none the less worthy of their honours, were there; and in far-off Calcutta the Viceroy had, by the Queen's command, already conferred the Order on those native magnates who had faithfully stood by the British during the Mutiny, as well as on distinguished Englishmen then on active duty in India, who had likewise been selected for decoration. Since that historic gathering was held at Windsor, the muster-roll of the "Star of India" has received not a few additions, while a second and kindred Order—"The Order of the Indian Empire" —has also been instituted (December 31st, 1877) to reward services rendered to her Majesty in her Eastern Dominions; and the achievements of some of the later recipients of the royal favour — for example, those of Sir Frederick Roberts, the Commander-in-Chief of the Indian Army, whose famous March from Cabul to Candahar in 1880 can never be forgotten—bear ample testimony that the splendid qualities which distinguished India's past heroes are not lacking in those of the present.

Then came the third great event, which took place on the 1st of January, 1877. On that day, in the famous city of Delhi, amidst a pageant of unexampled splendour, proclamation was made by the Viceroy to a vast assemblage numbering over 100,000 persons, including many of the principal native princes and chiefs, that Queen Victoria had assumed the title of Empress of India. And thus was it made known to the two hundred and fifty millions of Asiatics, who then became our fellow-subjects, that the destinies of India were linked with those of Great Britain; and thus was crowned the great work of which, more than a century before, the foundations had been laid by Robert Clive.

PRINTED BY CASSELL & COMPANY, LIMITED, LA BELLE SAUVAGE, LONDON, E.C.

Selections from Cassell & Company's Publications.

Bibles and Religious Works.

Bible, The Crown Illustrated. With about 1,000 Original Illustrations. With References, &c. 1,248 pages, crown 4to, cloth, 7s. 6d.
Bible, Cassell's Illustrated Family. With 900 Illustrations. **Leather,** gilt edges, £2 10s.
Bible Dictionary, Cassell's. With nearly 600 Illustrations. 7s. 6d.
Bible Educator, The. Edited by the Very Rev. Dean PLUMPTRE, D.D., Wells. With Illustrations, Maps, &c. Four Vols., cloth, 6s. each.
Bible Work at Home and Abroad. Volume. Illustrated. 3s.
Bunyan's Pilgrim's Progress (Cassell's Illustrated). Demy 4to. Illustrated throughout. 7s. 6d.
Bunyan's Pilgrim's Progress. With Illustrations. Cloth, 3s. 6d.
Child's Life of Christ, The. With 200 Illustrations. 21s.
Child's Bible, The. With 200 Illustrations. 143rd Thousand. 7s. 6d.
Church at Home, The. A Series of Short Sermons. By the Rt. Rev. ROWLEY HILL, D.D., Bishop of Sodor and Man. 5s.
Day-Dawn in Dark Places; or, Wanderings and Work in Bechwanaland. By the Rev. JOHN MACKENZIE. Illustrated. 3s. 6d.
Difficulties of Belief, Some. By the **Rev. T. TEIGNMOUTH SHORE, M.A.** *New and Cheap Edition.* 2s. 6d.
Doré Bible. With 230 Illustrations by GUSTAVE DORÉ. Cloth, £2 10s.
Early Days of Christianity, The. By the Ven. Archdeacon FARRAR, D.D., F.R.S.
    LIBRARY EDITION. Two Vols., 24s.; morocco, £2 2s.
    POPULAR EDITION. Complete in One Volume, cloth, 6s.; cloth, gilt edges, 7s. 6d.; Persian morocco, 10s. 6d.; tree-calf, 15s.
Family Prayer-Book, The. Edited by Rev. Canon GARBETT, M.A., and Rev. S. MARTIN. Extra crown 4to, cloth, 5s.; morocco, 18s.
Geikie, Cunningham, D.D., Works by:—
    HOURS WITH THE BIBLE. Six Vols., 6s. each.
    ENTERING ON LIFE. 3s. 6d.
    THE PRECIOUS PROMISES. 2s. 6d.
    THE ENGLISH REFORMATION. 5s.
    OLD TESTAMENT CHARACTERS. 6s.
    THE LIFE AND WORDS OF CHRIST. Two Vols., cloth, 30s. *Students' Edition.* Two Vols., 16s.
Glories of the Man of Sorrows, The. By Rev. H. G. BONAVIA HUNT, F.R.S., Ed.: Evening preacher at St. James's, Piccadilly. 2s. 6d.
Gospel of Grace, The. By a LINDESIE. Cloth, 3s. 6d.
"Heart Chords." A Series of Works by Eminent Divines. **Bound in** cloth, red edges, One Shilling each.

My Father.	My Aspirations.	My Hereafter.
My Bible.	My Emotional Life.	My Walk with God.
My Work for God.	My Body.	My Aids to the Divine Life.
My Object in Life.	My Soul.	My Sources of Strength.
	My Growth in Divine Life.	

Helps to Belief. A Series of Helpful Manuals on the Religious Difficulties of the Day. Edited by the Rev. TEIGNMOUTH SHORE, M.A., Chaplain-in-Ordinary to the Queen. Cloth, 1s. each.

CREATION. By the Lord Bishop of Carlisle.
THE DIVINITY OF OUR LORD. By the Lord Bishop of Derry.
THE MORALITY OF THE OLD TESTAMENT. By the Rev. Newman Smyth, D.D.
MIRACLES. By the Rev. Brownlow Maitland, M.A.
PRAYER. By the Rev. T. Teignmouth Shore, M.A.
THE RESURRECTION. By the Lord Archbishop of York.
THE ATONEMENT. By the Lord Bishop of Peterborough.

Selections from Cassell & Company's Publications.

Life of Christ, The. By the Ven. Archdeacon FARRAR, D.D., F.R.S.
    ILLUSTRATED EDITION, with about 300 Original Illustrations. Extra crown 4to, cloth, gilt edges, 21s.; morocco antique, 42s.
    LIBRARY EDITION. Two Vols. Cloth, 24s.; morocco, 42s.
    BIJOU EDITION. Five Volumes, in box, 10s. 6d. the set.
    POPULAR EDITION, in One Vol. 8vo, cloth, 6s.; cloth, gilt edges, 7s. 6d.; Persian morocco, gilt edges, 10s. 6d.; tree-calf, 15s.

Marriage Ring, The. By WILLIAM LANDELS, D.D. Bound in white leatherette, gilt edges, in box, 6s.; morocco, 8s. 6d.

Moses and Geology; or, The Harmony of the Bible with Science. By SAMUEL KINNS, Ph.D., F.R.A.S. Illustrated. *Cheap Edition*, 6s.

Music of the Bible, The. By J. STAINER, M.A., Mus. Doc. 2s. 6d.

New Testament Commentary for English Readers, The. Edited by the Rt. Rev. C. J. ELLICOTT, D.D., Lord Bishop of Gloucester and Bristol. In Three Volumes, 21s. each.
    Vol. I.—The Four Gospels.
    Vol. II.—The Acts, Romans, Corinthians, Galatians.
    Vol. III.—The remaining Books of the New Testament.

Old Testament Commentary for English Readers, The. Edited by the Right Rev. C. J. ELLICOTT, D.D., Lord Bishop of Gloucester and Bristol. Complete in 5 Vols., 21s. each.
    Vol. I.—Genesis to Numbers.
    Vol. II.—Deuteronomy to Samuel II.
    Vol. III.—Kings I. to Esther.
    Vol. IV.—Job to Isaiah.
    Vol. V.—Jeremiah to Malachi.

Patriarchs, The. By the late Rev. W. HANNA, D.D., and the Ven. Archdeacon NORRIS, B.D. 2s. 6d.

Protestantism, The History of. By the Rev. J. A. WYLIE, LL.D. Containing upwards of 600 Original Illustrations. Three Vols., 27s.

Quiver Yearly Volume, The. 250 high-class Illustrations. 7s. 6d.

Revised Version—Commentary on the Revised Version of the New Testament. By the Rev. W. G. HUMPHRY, B.D. 7s. 6d.

Sacred Poems, The Book of. Edited by the Rev. Canon BAYNES, **M.A.** With Illustrations. Cloth, gilt edges, 1s.

St. George for England; and other Sermons preached to Children. By the Rev. T. TEIGNMOUTH SHORE, M.A. 5s.

St. Paul, The Life and Work of. By the Ven. Archdeacon FARRAR, D.D., F.R.S., Chaplain-in-Ordinary to the Queen.
    LIBRARY EDITION. Two Vols., cloth, 24s.; morocco, 42s.
    ILLUSTRATED EDITION, complete in One Volume, with about 300 Illustrations, £1 1s.; morocco, £2 2s.
    POPULAR EDITION. One Volume, 8vo, cloth, 6s.; cloth, gilt edges, 7s. 6d.; Persian morocco, 10s. 6d.; tree-calf, 15s.

Secular Life, The Gospel of the. Sermons preached at Oxford. By the Hon. W. H. FREMANTLE, Canon of Canterbury. 5s.

Sermons Preached at Westminster Abbey. By ALFRED BARRY, D.D., D.C.L., Primate of Australia. 5s.

Shall We Know One Another? By the Rt. Rev. J. C. RYLE, D.D. Bishop of Liverpool. *New and Enlarged Edition*. Cloth limp, 1s.

Simon Peter: His Life, Times, and Friends. By E. HODDER. 5s.

Twilight of Life, The. Words of Counsel and Comfort for the Aged. By the Rev. JOHN ELLERTON, M.A. 1s. 6d.

Voice of Time, The. By JOHN STROUD. Cloth gilt, **1s.**

Educational Works and Students' Manuals.

Alphabet, Cassell's Pictorial. 3s. 6d.
Algebra, The Elements of. By Prof. WALLACE, M.A. 1s.
Arithmetics, The Modern School. By GEORGE RICKS, B.Sc. Lond. With Test Cards. (*List on application.*)
Book-Keeping. By THEODORE JONES. For Schools, 2s.; cloth, 3s. For the Million, 2s.; cloth, 3s. Books for Jones's System. 2s.
Chemistry, The Public School. By J. H. ANDERSON, M.A. 2s. 6d.
Commentary, The New Testament. Edited by the Lord Bishop of GLOUCESTER and BRISTOL. Handy Volume Edition. St. Matthew, 3s. 6d. St. Mark, 3s. St. Luke, 3s. 6d. St. John, 3s. 6d. The Acts of the Apostles, 3s. 6d. Romans, 2s. 6d. Corinthians I. and II., 3s. Galatians, Ephesians, and Philippians, 3s. Colossians, Thessalonians, and Timothy, 3s. Titus, Philemon, Hebrews, and James, 3s. Peter, Jude, and John, 3s. The Revelation, 3s. An Introduction to the New Testament, 3s. 6d.
Commentary, Old Testament. Edited by Bishop ELLICOTT. Handy Volume Edition. Genesis, 3s. 6d. Exodus, 3s. Leviticus, 3s. Numbers, 2s. 6d. Deuteronomy, 2s. 6d.
Copy-Books, Cassell's Graduated. *Eighteen Books.* 2d. each.
Copy-Books, The Modern School. *Twelve Books.* 2d. each.
Drawing Books, Cassell's New Standard. 7 Books. 2d. each.
Drawing Books, Superior. 4 Books. Price 5s. each.
Drawing Copies, Cassell's Modern School Freehand. First Grade, 1s.; Second Grade, 2s.
Drawing Copies, Cassell's New Standard. Seven Books. 2d. each.
Electricity, Practical. By Prof. W. E. AYRTON. Illustrated. 5s.
Energy and Motion: A Text-Book of Elementary Mechanics. By WILLIAM PAICE, M.A. Illustrated. 1s. 6d.
English Literature, First Sketch of. *New and Enlarged Edition.* By Prof. MORLEY. 7s. 6d.
Euclid, Cassell's. Edited by Prof. WALLACE, M.A. 1s.
Euclid, The First Four Books of. In paper, 6d.; cloth, 9d.
French Reader, Cassell's Public School. By GUILLAUME S. CONRAD. 2s. 6d.
French, Cassell's Lessons in. *New and Revised Edition.* Parts I. and II., each 2s. 6d.; complete, 4s. 6d. Key, 1s. 6d.
French-English and English-French Dictionary. *Entirely New and Enlarged Edition.* 1,150 pages, 8vo, cloth, 3s. 6d.
Galbraith and Haughton's Scientific Manuals. By the Rev. Prof. GALBRAITH, M.A., and the Rev. Prof. HAUGHTON, M.D., D.C.L. Arithmetic, 3s. 6d.—Plane Trigonometry, 2s. 6d.—Euclid, Books I., II., III., 2s. 6d.—Books IV., V., VI., 2s. 6d.—Mathematical Tables, 3s. 6d.—Mechanics, 3s. 6d.—Optics, 2s. 6d.—Hydrostatics, 3s. 6d.—Astronomy, 5s.—Steam Engine, 3s. 6d.—Algebra, Part I., cloth, 2s. 6d.; Complete, 7s. 6d.—Tides and Tidal Currents, with Tidal Cards, 3s.
German-English and English-German Dictionary. *Entirely New and Revised Edition.* 3s. 6d.
German Reading, Modern. By Prof. HEINEMANN. 1s. 6d.
German Reading, First Lessons in. By A. JAGST. Illustrated. 1s.
German of To-day. By Dr. HEINEMANN. 1s. 6d.
Handbook of New Code of Regulations. By JOHN F. MOSS. 1s.
Historical Course for Schools, Cassell's. Illustrated throughout. I.—Stories from English History, 1s. II.—The Simple Outline of English History, 1s. 3d. III.—The Class History of England, 2s. 6d.

Selections from Cassell & Company's Publications.

Latin-English and English-Latin Dictionary. By J. R. BEARD, D.D., and C. BEARD, B.A. Crown 8vo, 914 pp., 3s. 6d.

Little Folks' History of England. By ISA CRAIG-KNOX. With 30 Illustrations. 1s. 6d.

Making of the Home, The: A Book of Domestic Economy for School and Home Use. By Mrs. SAMUEL A. BARNETT. 1s. 6d.

Marlborough Books:—Arithmetic Examples, 3s. Arithmetic Rules, 1s. 6d. French Exercises, 3s. 6d. French Grammar, 2s. 6d. German Grammar, 3s. 6d.

Music, An Elementary Manual of. By HENRY LESLIE. 1s.

Natural Philosophy. By Prof. HAUGHTON, F.R.S. Illustrated. 3s. 6d.

Popular Educator, Cassell's. *New and Thoroughly Revised Edition.* Illustrated throughout. Complete in Six Vols., 5s. each.

Physical Science, Intermediate Text-Book of. By F. H. BOWMAN, D.Sc., F.R.A.S., F.L.S. Illustrated. 3s. 6d.

Readers, Cassell's Readable. Carefully graduated, extremely interesting, and illustrated throughout. (*List on application.*)

Readers, Cassell's Historical. Illustrated throughout, printed on superior paper, and strongly bound in cloth. (*List on application.*)

Readers for Infant Schools, Coloured. Three Books. Each containing 48 pages, including 8 pages in colours. 4d. each.

Reader, The Citizen. By H. O. ARNOLD FORSTER, with Preface by the late Right Hon. W. E. FORSTER, M.P. 1s. 6d.

Readers, The Modern Geographical, illustrated throughout, and strongly bound in cloth. (*List on application.*)

Readers, The Modern School. Illustrated. (*List on application.*)

Reading and Spelling Book, Cassell's Illustrated. 1s.

Right Lines; or, Form and Colour. With Illustrations. 1s.

School Manager's Manual. By F. C. MILLS, M.A. 1s.

Shakspere's Plays for School Use. 5 Books. Illustrated, 6d. each.

Shakspere Reading Book, The. By H. COURTHOPE BOWEN, M.A. Illustrated. 3s. 6d. Also issued in Three Books, 1s. each.

Spelling, A Complete Manual of. By J. D. MORELL, LL.D. 1s.

Technical Manuals, Cassell's. Illustrated throughout:—
Handrailing and Staircasing, 3s. 6d.—Bricklayers, Drawing for, 3s.—Building Construction, 2s.—Cabinet-Makers, Drawing for, 3s.—Carpenters and Joiners, Drawing for, 3s. 6d.—Gothic Stonework, 3s.—Linear Drawing and Practical Geometry, 2s.—Linear Drawing and Projection. The Two Vols. in One, 3s. 6d.—Machinists and Engineers, Drawing for, 4s. 6d.—Metal-Plate Workers, Drawing for, 3s.—Model Drawing, 3s.—Orthographical and Isometrical Projection, 2s.—Practical Perspective, 3s.—Stonemasons, Drawing for, 3s.—Applied Mechanics, by Sir R. S. Ball, LL.D., 2s.—Systematic Drawing and Shading, 2s.

Technical Educator, Cassell's. Four Vols. 6s. each. *New and Cheap Edition,* in Four Vols., 5s. each.

Technology, Manuals of. Edited by Prof. AYRTON, F.R.S., and RICHARD WORMELL, D.Sc., M.A. Illustrated throughout:—
The Dyeing of Textile Fabrics, by Prof. Hummel, 5s.—Watch and Clock Making, by D. Glasgow, 4s. 6d.—Steel and Iron, by W. H. Greenwood, F.C.S., Assoc. M.I.C.E., &c., 5s.—Spinning Woollen and Worsted, by W. S. Bright McLaren, 4s. 6d.—Design in Textile Fabrics, by T. R. Ashenhurst, 4s. 6d.—Practical Mechanics, by Prof. Perry, M.E., 3s. 6d.—Cutting Tools Worked by Hand and Machine, by Prof. Smith, 3s. 6d.—Practical Electricity, by Prof. W. E. Ayrton, 5s. *Other Volumes in preparation. A Prospectus sent post free on application.*

CASSELL & COMPANY, LIMITED, *Ludgate Hill, London.*

Selections from Cassell & Company's Publications.

Books for Young People.

Under Bayard's Banner. By HENRY FRITH. Illustrated. 5s.
The King's Command. A Story for Girls. By MAGGIE SYMINGTON. Illustrated. 5s.
The Romance of Invention. By JAMES BURNLEY. Illustrated. 5s.
The Tales of the Sixty Mandarins. By P. V. RAMASWAMI RAJU. With an Introduction by Prof. HENRY MORLEY. Illustrated. 5s.
A World of Girls: The Story of a School. By L. T. MEADE. Illustrated. 3s. 6d.
Lost among White Africans; A Boy's Adventures on the Upper Congo. By DAVID KER. Illustrated. 3s. 6d.
Perils Afloat and Brigands Ashore. By ALFRED ELWES. Illustrated. 3s. 6d.
Freedom's Sword: A Story of the Days of Wallace and Bruce. By ANNIE S. SWAN. Illustrated. 3s. 6d.
Strong to Suffer: A Story of the Jews. By E. WYNNE. Illustrated. 2s. 6d.
The Merry-go-Round. Original Poems for Children. Illustrated throughout. 5s.
Heroes of the Indian Empire; or, Stories of Valour and Victory. By ERNEST FOSTER. Illustrated. 2s. 6d.
In Letters of Flame: A Story of the Waldenses. By C. L. MATÉAUX. Illustrated. 2s. 6d.
Through Trial to Triumph. By MADELINE B. HUNT. Illustrated. 2s. 6d.
Sunday School Reward Books. By Popular Authors. With Four Original Illustrations in each. Cloth gilt, 1s. 6d. each.

- Rhoda's Reward; or, "If Wishes were Horses."
- Jack Marston's Anchor.
- Frank's Life-Battle; or, The Three Friends.
- Rags and Rainbows: a Story of Thanksgiving.
- Uncle William's Charge; or, The Broken Trust.
- Pretty Pink's Purpose; or, The Little Street Merchants.

"Golden Mottoes" Series, The. Each Book containing 208 pages, with Four full-page Original Illustrations. Crown 8vo, cloth gilt, 2s. each.

- "Nil Desperandum." By the Rev. F. Langbridge.
- "Bear and Forbear." By Sarah Pitt.
- "Foremost if I Can." By Helen Atteridge.
- "Honour is my Guide." By Jeanie Hering (Mrs. Adams-Acton).
- "Aim at the Sure End." By Emilie Searchfield.
- "He Conquers who Endures." By the Author of "May Cunningham's Trial," &c.

The New Children's Album. Fcap. 4to, 320 pages. Illustrated throughout. 3s. 6d.
The History Scrap Book. With nearly 1,000 Engravings. 5s.; cloth, 7s. 6d.
"Little Folks" Half-Yearly Volume. With 200 Illustrations and several Pictures in Colour. 3s. 6d.; or cloth gilt, 5s.
Bo-Peep. A Book for the Little Ones. With Original Stories and Verses, Illustrated throughout. Boards, 2s. 6d.; cloth gilt, 3s. 6d.
The World's Lumber Room. By SELINA GAYE. Illustrated. 3s. 6d.
The "Proverbs" Series. Original Stories by Popular Authors, founded on and illustrating well-known Proverbs. With Four Illustrations in each Book, printed on a tint. 1s. 6d. each.

- Fritters. By Sarah Pitt.
- Trixy. By Maggie Symington.
- The Two Hardcastles. By Madeline Bonavia Hunt.
- Major Monk's Motto. By the Rev. F. Langbridge.
- Tim Thomson's Trial. By George Weatherly.
- Ursula's Stumbling-Block. By Julia Goddard.
- Ruth's Life-Work. By the Rev. Joseph Johnson.

Selections from Cassell & Company's *Publications.*

The "Cross and Crown" Series. Consisting of Stories founded on incidents which occurred during Religious Persecutions of Past Days. With Illustrations in each Book, printed on a tint. 2s. 6d. each.

By Fire and Sword: A Story of the Huguenots. By Thomas Archer.
Adam Hepburn's Vow: A Tale of Kirk and Covenant. By Annie S. Swan.
No. XIII.; or, The Story of the Lost Vestal. A Tale of Early Christian Days. By Emma Marshall.

The World's Workers. A Series of New and Original Volumes. With Portraits printed on a tint as Frontispiece. 1s. each.

General Gordon. By the Rev. S. A. Swaine.
Charles Dickens. By his Eldest Daughter.
Sir Titus Salt and George Moore. By J. Burnley.
Florence Nightingale, Catherine Marsh, Frances Ridley Havergal, Mrs. Ranyard ("L.N.R."). By Lizzie Aldridge.
Dr. Guthrie, Father Mathew, Elihu Burritt, George Livesey. By the Rev. J W. Kirton.
David Livingstone. By Robert Smiles.
Sir Henry Havelock and Colin Campbell, Lord Clyde. By E. C. Phillips.
Abraham Lincoln. By Ernest Foster.
George Muller and Andrew Reed. By E. R. Pitman.
Richard Cobden. By R. Gowing.
Benjamin Franklin. By E. M. Tomkinson.
Handel. By Eliza Clarke.
Turner, the Artist. By the Rev. S. A. Swaine.
George and Robert Stephenson. By C. L. Matéaux.

The "Chimes" Series. Each containing 64 pages, with Illustrations on every page, and bound in Japanese morocco, 1s.

Bible Chimes.
Daily Chimes.
Holy Chimes.
Old World Chimes.

Books for Boys. Cloth gilt, 5s. each.

"Follow My Leader;" or, the Boys of Templeton. By Talbot Baines Reed.
For Fortune and Glory: a Story of the Soudan War. By Lewis Hough.
The Champion of Odin; or, Viking Life in the Days of Old. By J. Fred. Hodgetts.
Bound by a Spell; or, the Hunted Witch of the Forest. By the Hon. Mrs. Greene.

Price 3s. 6d. each.

On Board the "Esmeralda;" or, Martin Leigh's Log. By John C. Hutcheson.
In Quest of Gold; or, Under the Whanga Falls. By Alfred St. Johnston.

For Queen and King; or, the Loyal 'Prentice. By Henry Frith.

The "Boy Pioneer" Series. By EDWARD S. ELLIS. With Four Full-page Illustrations in each Book. Crown 8vo, cloth, 2s. 6d. each.

Ned in the Woods. A Tale of Early Days in the West.
Ned on the River. A Tale of Indian River Warfare.
Ned in the Block House. A Story of Pioneer Life in Kentucky.

The "Log Cabin" Series. By EDWARD S. ELLIS. With Four Full-page Illustrations in each. Crown 8vo, cloth, 2s. 6d. each.

The Lost Trail. | Camp-Fire and Wigwam. | Footprints in the Forest.

Sixpenny Story Books. All Illustrated, and containing Interesting Stories by well-known Writers.

Little Content.
The Smuggler's Cave.
Little Lizzie.
Little Bird.
The Boot on the Wrong Foot.
Luke Barnicott.
Little Pickles.
The Boat Club. By Oliver Optic.
Helpful Nellie: and other Stories.
The Elchester College Boys.
My First Cruise.
Lottie's White Frock.
Only Just Once.
The Little Peacemaker.
The Delft Jug. By Silverpen.

The "Baby's Album" Series. Four Books, each containing about 50 Illustrations. Price 6d. each; or cloth gilt, 1s. each.

Baby's Album.
Dolly's Album.
Fairy's Album.
Pussy's Album.

Selections from Cassell & Company's *Publications.*

Illustrated Books for the Little Ones. Containing interesting Stories. All Illustrated. 1s. each.

- Indoors and Out.
- Some Farm Friends.
- Those Golden Sands.
- Little Mothers & their Children.
- Our Pretty Pets.
- Our Schoolday Hours.
- Creatures Tame.
- Creatures Wild.

Shilling Story Books. All Illustrated, and containing Interesting Stories

- Thorns and Tangles.
- The Cuckoo in the Robin's Nest.
- John's Mistake.
- Pearl's Fairy Flower.
- The History of Five Little Pitchers.
- Diamonds in **the Sand.**
- Surly Bob.
- The Giant's Cradle.
- Shag and Doll.
- Aunt Lucia's Locket.
- The Magic Mirror.
- The Cost of Revenge.
- Clever Frank.
- Among the Redskins.
- The Ferryman of Brill.
- Harry Maxwell.
- A Banished Monarch.

"Little Folks" Painting Books. With Text, and Outline Illustrations for Water-Colour Painting. 1s. each.

- Fruits and Blossoms for "Little Folks" to Paint.
- The "Little Folks" Proverb Painting Book.
- The "Little Folks" Illuminating Book.
- Pictures to Paint.
- "Little Folks" Painting Book.
- "Little Folks" Nature Painting Book.
- Another "**Little** Folks" Painting Book.

Eighteenpenny Story Books. All **Illustrated** throughout.

- Three Wee Ulster Lassies.
- Little Queen Mab.
- Up the Ladder.
- Dick's Hero; and other Stories.
- The Chip Boy.
- Raggles, Baggles, and **the** Emperor.
- Roses from Thorns.
- Faith's Father.
- By Land and Sea.
- The Young Berringtons.
- Jeff and Leff.
- Tom Morris's Error.
- Worth more than Gold.
- "Through Flood—Through Fire;" and other Stories.
- The Girl with the Golden Locks.
- Stories of the Olden Time.

The "Cosy Corner" Series. Story Books for Children. Each containing nearly ONE HUNDRED PICTURES. 1s. 6d. each.

- See-Saw Stories.
- Little Chimes for All Times.
- Wee Willie Winkie.
- Pet's Posy of Pictures and Stories.
- Dot's Story Book.
- Story Flowers for Rainy Hours.
- Little Talks with Little People.
- Bright Rays for Dull Days.
- Chats for Small Chatterers.
- Pictures for Happy Hours.
- Ups and Downs of a Donkey's Life.

The "World in Pictures." Illustrated throughout. 2s. 6d. each.

- A Ramble Round France.
- All the Russias.
- Chats about Germany.
- The Land of the Pyramids (Egypt).
- Peeps into China.
- The Eastern Wonderland (Japan).
- Glimpses of South America.
- Round Africa.
- The Land of Temples (India).
- The Isles of the Pacific.

Two-Shilling Story Books. All **Illustrated.**

- Stories of the Tower.
- Mr. Burke's Nieces.
- May Cunningham's Trial.
- The Top of the Ladder: How to Reach it.
- Little Flotsam.
- Madge and her Friends.
- The Children of the Court.
- A Moonbeam Tangle.
- **Maid Marjory.**
- The Four Cats of the Tippertons.
- Marion's Two Homes.
- Little Folks' Sunday Book.
- Two Fourpenny Bits.
- Poor Nelly.
- Tom Heriot.
- Through Peril to Fortune.
- Aunt Tabitha's Waifs.
- In Mischief Again.

Selections from Cassell & Company's Publications.

Half-Crown Story Books.

- Little Hinges.
- Margaret's Enemy.
- Pen's Perplexities.
- Notable Shipwrecks.
- Golden Days.
- Wonders of Common Things.
- Little Empress Joan.
- Truth will Out.
- At the South Pole. *Cheap Edition.*
- Soldier and Patriot (George Washington). [hood.
- Picture of School Life and Boyhood.
- The Young Man in the Battle of Life. By the Rev. Dr. Landels.
- The True Glory of Woman. By the Rev. Dr. Landels.

Library of Wonders. Illustrated Gift-books for Boys. 2s. 6d. each.

- Wonderful Adventures.
- Wonders of Animal Instinct.
- Wonders of Architecture.
- Wonders of Acoustics.
- Wonders of Water.
- Wonderful Escapes.
- Bodily Strength and Skill.
- Wonderful Balloon Ascents.

Gift-Books for Children. With Coloured Illustrations. 2s. 6d. each.

- The Story of Robin Hood.
- Playing Trades.
- Reynard the Fox.
- The Pilgrim's Progress.

Three and Sixpenny Library of Standard Tales, &c. All Illustrated and bound in cloth gilt. Crown 8vo. 3s. 6d. each.

- Jane Austen and her Works.
- Mission Life in Greece and Palestine.
- The Dingy House at Kensington.
- The Romance of Trade.
- The Three Homes.
- My Guardian.
- School Girls.
- Deepdale Vicarage.
- In Duty Bound.
- The Half Sisters.
- Peggy Oglivie's Inheritance.
- The Family Honour.
- Esther West.
- Working to Win.
- Krilof and his Fables. By W. R. S. Ralston, M.A.
- Fairy Tales. By Prof. Morley.

The Home Chat Series. All Illustrated throughout. Fcap. 4to. Boards, 3s. 6d. each. Cloth, gilt edges, 5s. each.

- Half-Hours with Early Explorers.
- Stories about Animals.
- Stories about Birds.
- Paws and Claws.
- Home Chat.
- Sunday Chats with Our Young Folks.
- Peeps Abroad for Folks at Home.
- Around and About Old England.

Books for the Little Ones.

- The Little Doings of some Little Folks. By Chatty Cheerful. Illustrated. 5s.
- The Sunday Scrap Book. With One Thousand Scripture Pictures. Boards, 5s.; cloth, 7s. 6d.
- Daisy Dimple's Scrap Book. Containing about 1,000 Pictures. Boards, 5s.; cloth gilt, 7s. 6d.
- Little Folks' Picture Album. With 168 Large Pictures. 5s.
- Little Folks' Picture Gallery. With 150 Illustrations. 5s.
- The Old Fairy Tales. With Original Illustrations. Boards, 1s.; cloth, 1s. 6d.
- My Diary. With 12 Coloured Plates and 366 Woodcuts. 1s.

Books for Boys.

- Kidnapped. By R. L. Stevenson. 5s.
- King Solomon's Mines. By H. Rider Haggard. 5s.
- The Phantom City. By W. Westall. 5s.
- Famous Sailors of Former Times. By Clements Markham. Illustrated. 2s. 6d.
- Treasure Island. By R. L. Stevenson. Illustrated. 5s.
- Modern Explorers. By Thomas Frost. Illustrated. 5s.
- Cruise in Chinese Waters. By Capt. Lindley. Illustrated. 5s.
- Wild Adventures in Wild Places. By Dr. Gordon Stables, M.D., R.N. Illustrated. 5s.
- Jungle, Peak, and Plain. By Dr. Gordon Stables, R.N. Illustrated. 5s.

CASSELL & COMPANY, Limited, London; Paris, New York and Melbourne.

Selections from **Cassell** *&* Company's **Publications.**

Illustrated, Fine-Art, and other Volumes.

Art, The Magazine of. Yearly Volume. With 500 choice Engravings. 16s.
After London; or, Wild England. By RICHARD JEFFERIES. 3s. 6d.
Along Alaska's Great River. By F. SCHWATKA. Illustrated. 12s. 6d.
Artist, Education of the. By E. CHESNEAU. Translated by CLARA BELL. 5s.
Bimetallism, The Theory of. By D. BARBOUR. 6s.
Bismarck, Prince. By CHARLES LOWE, M.A. Two Vols. 24s.
Bright, John, Life and Times of. By W. ROBERTSON. 7s. 6d.
British Ballads. With 275 Original Illustrations. Two Vols. 7s. 6d. each.
British Battles on Land and Sea. By JAMES GRANT. With about 600 Illustrations. Three Vols., 4to, £1 7s.; Library Edition, £1 10s.
British Battles, Recent. Illustrated. 4to, 9s.; Library Edition, 10s.
Browning, An Introduction to the Study of. By ARTHUR SYMONDS. 2s. 6d.
Butterflies and Moths, European. By W. F. **KIRBY.** With 61 Coloured Plates. Demy 4to, 35s.
Canaries and Cage-Birds, The Illustrated Book of. By W. A. BLAKSTON, W. SWAYSLAND, and A. F. WIENER. With 56 Fac-simile Coloured Plates, 35s. Half-morocco, £2 5s.
Cannibals and Convicts. By JULIAN THOMAS ("The Vagabond"). 10s. 6d.
Cassell's Family Magazine. Yearly Vol. Illustrated. 9s.
Cathedral Churches of England and Wales. Illustrated. 21s.
Choice Poems by H. W. Longfellow. Illustrated from Paintings **by** his Son, ERNEST W. LONGFELLOW. Small 4to, cloth, 6s.
Choice Dishes **at Small** Cost. By A. G. PAYNE. 1s.
Cities of the World: their Origin, Progress, and Present Aspect. Three Vols. Illustrated. 7s. 6d. each.
Civil Service, Guide to Employment in the. 3s. 6d.
Civil Service.—Guide to Female Employment in Government Offices. 1s.
Clinical Manuals for Practitioners and Students of Medicine. A List of Volumes forwarded post free on application to the Publishers.
Clothing, The Influence of, on Health. By FREDERICK TREVES, F.R.C.S. 2s.
Colonies and India, Our, How we Got Them, and Why we Keep Them. By Prof. C. RANSOME. **1s.**
Columbus, Christopher, The Life **and Voyages of.** By WASHINGTON IRVING. Three Vols. 7s. 6d.
Cookery, Cassell's Dictionary of. Containing about **Nine Thousand** Recipes, 7s. 6d.; Roxburgh, 10s. 6d.
Co-operators, Working Men: What they have Done, and What they are Doing. By A. H. DYKE-ACLAND, M.P., and B. JONES. 1s.
Cookery, A Year's. By PHYLLIS BROWNE. 3s. 6d.
Cook Book, Catherine Owen's New. 4s.
Countries **of** the World, The. By ROBERT BROWN, M.A., Ph.D., &c. Complete in Six Vols., with about 750 Illustrations. 4to, 7s. 6d. each.
Cromwell, Oliver: The Man and his Mission. By J. ALLANSON PICTON, M.P. Cloth, 7s. 6d.; morocco, cloth sides, 9s.
Cyclopædia, Cassell's Concise. With 12,000 subjects, brought down to the latest date. With about 600 Illustrations, 15s.; Roxburgh, 18s.

Selections from Cassell & Company's Publications.

Dairy Farming. By Prof. J. P. SHELDON. With 25 Fac-simile Coloured Plates, and numerous Wood Engravings. Cloth, 31s. 6d.; half-morocco, 42s.

Decisive Events in History. By THOMAS ARCHER. With Sixteen Illustrations. Boards, 3s. 6d.; cloth, 5s.

Decorative Design. By CHRISTOPHER DRESSER, Ph.D. Illustrated. 5s.

Deserted Village Series, The. Consisting of *Éditions de luxe* of the most favourite poems of Standard Authors. Illustrated. 2s. 6d. each.

SONGS FROM SHAKESPEARE. | GOLDSMITH'S DESERTED VILLAGE.
MILTON'S L'ALLEGRO AND IL | WORDSWORTH'S ODE ON IMMORTALITY,
PENSEROSO. | AND LINES ON TINTERN ABBEY.

Dickens, Character Sketches from. SECOND and THIRD SERIES. With Six Original Drawings in each, by F. BARNARD. In Portfolio, 21s. each.

Diary of Two Parliaments. By W. H. LUCY. Vol. I.: The Disraeli Parliament. Vol. II.: The Gladstone Parliament. 12s. each.

Dog, The. By IDSTONE. Illustrated. 2s. 6d.

Dog, Illustrated Book of the. By VERO SHAW, B.A. With 28 Coloured Plates. Cloth bevelled, 35s.; half-morocco, 45s.

Domestic Dictionary, The. Cloth, 7s. 6d.

Doré's Adventures of Munchausen. Illustrated by GUSTAVE DORÉ. 5s.

Doré's Dante's Inferno. Illustrated by GUSTAVE DORÉ. 21s.

Doré's Don Quixote. With about 400 Illustrations by DORÉ. 15s.

Doré's Fairy Tales Told Again. With Engravings by DORÉ. 5s.

Doré Gallery, The. With 250 Illustrations by DORÉ. 4to, 42s.

Doré's Milton's Paradise Lost. Illustrated by DORÉ. 4to, 21s.

Edinburgh, Old and New. Three Vols. With 600 Illustrations. 9s. each.

Educational Year-Book, The. 6s.

Egypt: Descriptive, Historical, and Picturesque. By Prof. G. EBERS. Translated by CLARA BELL, with Notes by SAMUEL BIRCH, LL.D., &c. Two Vols. With 800 Original Engravings. Vol. I., £2 5s.; Vol. II., £2 12s. 6d. Complete in box, £4 17s. 6d.

Electricity in the Service of Man. With nearly 850 Illustrations. 21s.

Electrician's Pocket-Book, The. By GORDON WIGAN, M.A. 5s.

Encyclopædic Dictionary, The. A New and Original Work of Reference to all the Words in the English Language. Ten Divisional Vols. now ready, 10s. 6d. each; or the Double Divisional Vols., half-morocco, 21s. each.

Energy in Nature. By WM. LANT CARPENTER, B.A., B.Sc. 80 Illustrations. 3s. 6d.

England, Cassell's Illustrated History of. With 2,000 Illustrations. Ten Vols., 4to, 9s. each.

English History, The Dictionary of. Cloth, 21s.; Roxburgh, 25s.

English Literature, Library of. By Prof. HENRY MORLEY. Five Vols., 7s. 6d. each.
    VOL. I.—SHORTER ENGLISH POEMS.
    VOL. II.—ILLUSTRATIONS OF ENGLISH RELIGION.
    VOL. III.—ENGLISH PLAYS.
    VOL. IV.—SHORTER WORKS IN ENGLISH PROSE.
    VOL. V.—SKETCHES OF LONGER WORKS IN ENGLISH VERSE AND PROSE.
    Five Volumes handsomely bound in half-morocco, £5 5s.

English Literature, The Story of. By ANNA BUCKLAND. 3s. 6d.

English Literature, Morley's First Sketch. Revised Edition, 7s. 6d.

Selections from Cassell & Company's Publications.

English Literature, Dictionary of. By W. DAVENPORT ADAMS. *Cheap Edition*, 7s. 6d.; Roxburgh, 10s. 6d.

English Poetesses. By ERIC S. ROBERTSON, M.A. **5s.**

Æsop's Fables. With about 150 Illustrations by E. GRISET. Cloth, 7s. 6d.; gilt edges, 10s. 6d.

Etching. By S. K. KOEHLER. With 30 Full-Page Plates by Old and Modern Etchers. £4 4s.

Etiquette of Good Society. 1s.; cloth, 1s. 6d.

Eye, Ear, and Throat, The Management of the. 3s. 6d.

False Hopes. By Prof. GOLDWIN SMITH, M.A., LL.D., D.C.L. 6d.

Family Physician, The. By Eminent PHYSICIANS and SURGEONS. Cloth, 21s.; half-morocco, 25s.

Fenn, G. Manville, Works by. Cloth boards, 2s. each.

SWEET MACE.	THE VICAR'S PEOPLE.
DUTCH, THE DIVER.	COBWEB'S FATHER.
MY PATIENTS. Being the Notes of a Navy Surgeon.	THE PARSON O' DUMFORD. POVERTY CORNER.

Ferns, European. By JAMES BRITTEN, F.L.S. With 30 Fac-simile Coloured Plates by D. BLAIR, F.L.S. 21s.

Field Naturalist's Handbook, The. By the Rev. J. G. WOOD and THEODORE WOOD. 5s.

Figuier's Popular Scientific Works. With Several Hundred Illustrations in each. 3s. 6d. each.

THE HUMAN RACE.	THE OCEAN WORLD.
WORLD BEFORE THE DELUGE.	THE VEGETABLE WORLD.
REPTILES AND BIRDS.	THE INSECT WORLD.
MAMMALIA.	

Fine-Art Library, The. Edited by JOHN SPARKES, Principal of the South Kensington Art Schools. Each Book contains about 100 Illustrations. 5s. each.

TAPESTRY. By Eugène Müntz. Translated by Miss L. J. Davis.	THE EDUCATION OF THE ARTIST. By Ernest Chesneau. Translated by Clara Bell. (Not illustrated.)
ENGRAVING. By Le Vicomte Henri Delaborde. Translated by R. A. M. Stevenson.	GREEK ARCHÆOLOGY. By Maxime Collignon. Translated by Dr. J. H. Wright.
THE ENGLISH SCHOOL OF PAINTING. By E. Chesneau. Translated by L. N. Etherington. With an Introduction by Prof. Ruskin.	ARTISTIC ANATOMY. By Prof. Duval. Translated by F. E. Fenton.
THE FLEMISH SCHOOL OF PAINTING. By A. J. Wauters. Translated by Mrs. Henry Rossel.	THE DUTCH SCHOOL OF PAINTING. By Henry Havard. Translated by G. Powell.

Fisheries of the World, The. Illustrated. 4to. 9s.

Five Pound Note, The, and other Stories. By G. S. JEALOUS. **1s.**

Flowers, and How to Paint them. By MAUD NAFTEL. With Coloured Plates. 5s.

Forging of the Anchor, The. A Poem. By Sir SAMUEL FERGUSON. LL.D. With 20 Original Illustrations. Gilt edges, 5s.

Fossil Reptiles, A History of British. By Sir RICHARD OWEN, K.C.B., F.R.S., &c. With 268 Plates. In Four Vols., £12 12s.

Four Years of Irish History (1845-49). By Sir GAVAN DUFFY, K.C.M.G. 21s.

Franco-German War, Cassell's History of the. Two Vols. With 500 Illustrations. 9s. each.

Fresh-Water Fishes of Europe, The. By Prof. H. G. SEELEY, F.R.S. Cloth, 21s.

Selections from Cassell & Company's Publications.

From Gold to Grey. Being Poems and Pictures of Life and Nature. By MARY D. BRINE. Illustrated. 7s. 6d.

Garden Flowers, Familiar. FOUR SERIES. By SHIRLEY HIBBERD. With Coloured Plates by F. E. HULME, F.L.S. 12s. 6d. each.

Gardening, Cassell's Popular. Illustrated. 4 vols., 5s. each.

Gladstone, Life of **W. E.** By BARNETT SMITH. With Portrait, 3s. 6d. *Jubilee Edition,* **1s.**

Gleanings from Popular **Authors.** Two Vols. With Original Illustrations. 4to, **9s.** each. **Two Vols.** in One, 15s.

Great Industries of Great Britain. Three Vols. With about 400 Illustrations. 4to., cloth, 7s. 6d. each.

Great Painters of Christendom, The, from Cimabue to Wilkie. By JOHN FORBES-ROBERTSON. Illustrated throughout. 12s. 6d.

Great Northern Railway, The Official Illustrated Guide to the. 1s.; or in cloth, 2s.

Great Western Railway, The Official Illustrated Guide to the. *New and Revised Edition.* With Illustrations, 1s.; cloth, 2s.

Gulliver's Travels. With 88 Engravings by MORTEN. *Cheap Edition,* 5s.

Gun and its Development, The. By W. W. GREENER. With 500 Illustrations. 10s. 6d.

Health, The Book of. By Eminent Physicians and Surgeons. Cloth, 21s.; half-morocco, 25s.

Health, the Influence of Clothing on. By F. TREVES, F.R.G.S. 2s.

Health in School. By CLEMENT DUKES, M.D.B.S. 6s.

Heavens, The Story of the. By Sir ROBERT STAWELL BALL, F.R.S., F.R.A.S. With Coloured Plates and Wood Engravings. 31s. 6d.

Heroes of Britain in Peace and War. **In Two Vols., with 300** Original Illustrations. Cloth, 5s. **each.**

Horse Keeper, The Practical. By GEORGE FLEMING, LL.D., F.R.C.V.S. With Illustrations. Crown 8vo, cloth, 7s. 6d.

Horse, The Book of the. By SAMUEL SIDNEY. With 25 *fac-simile* Coloured Plates. *Enlarged Edition.* Demy 4to, 35s.; half-morocco, 45s.

Horses, The Simple Ailments of. By W. F. Illustrated. 5s.

Household Guide, Cassell's. With Illustrations and Coloured Plates. *New and Cheap Edition,* in Four Vols., 20s.

How Women may Earn a Living. By MERCY GROGAN. **1s.**

India, The Coming Struggle **for.** By Prof. VAMBÉRY. 5s.

India, Cassell's History of. By JAMES GRANT. With about 400 Illustrations. Library binding. One Vol., 15s.

India: the Land and the People. By Sir J. CAIRD, K.C.B. 10s. 6d.

Indoor Amusements, Card Games, and Fireside Fun, Cassell's Book of. Illustrated. 3s. 6d.

Invisible Life, Vignettes from. By JOHN BADCOCK, F.R.M.S. Illustrated. 3s. 6d.

Irish Parliament, The; **What it Was** and What it Did. **By J. G.** SWIFT MACNEILL, M.A. **1s.**

Italy. By J. W. PROBYN. 7s. 6d.

Kennel Guide, The Practical. By Dr. GORDON STABLES. Illustrated. 2s. 6d.

Khiva, A Ride to. By the late Col FRED. BURNABY. 1s. 6d.

Kidnapped. By R. L. STEVENSON. 5s.

Ladies' Physician, The. A Guide for Women in the Treatment of their Ailments. By a Physician. **6s.**

Selections from Cassell & Company's Publications.

Land Question, The. By. Prof. J. ELLIOT, **M.R.A.C.** 10s. 6d.

Landscape Painting in Oils, A Course of **Lessons** in. By A. F. GRACE. With Nine Reproductions in Colour. *Cheap Edition*, 25s.

Law, About Going to. By A. J. WILLIAMS, M.P. **2s. 6d.**

Letts's Diaries and other Time-saving Publications are now published exclusively by CASSELL & COMPANY. (*A list sent post free on application.*)

Liberal, **Why** I am a. By ANDREW REID. 2s. 6d. *People's Edition*. 1s.

London & North-Western Railway Official Illustrated Guide. 1s.; cloth, 2s.

London, Greater. By EDWARD WALFORD. Two Vols. With about 400 Illustrations. 9s. each.

London, Old and New. Six Vols., each containing about 200 Illustrations and Maps. Cloth, 9s. each.

London's Roll of Fame. With Portraits and Illustrations. 12s. 6d.

Longfellow's Poetical Works. Illustrated throughout, £3 3s.; *Popular Edition*, 16s.

Love's Extremes, At. **By** MAURICE THOMPSON. 5s.

Luther, Martin: the Man and his Work. By Dr. PETER BAYNE. Two Vols. 24s.

Mechanics, The Practical Dictionary of. Containing 15,000 Drawings. Four Vols. 21s. each.

Medicine, Manuals for Students of. (*A List forwarded post free.*)

Midland Railway, Official Illustrated Guide to the. *New and Revised Edition*. 1s.; cloth, 2s.

Modern Artists, Some. With highly-finished Engravings. 12s. 6d.

Modern Europe, A History of. By C. A. FYFFE, M.A. Vol. I., from 1792 to 1814. 12s. Vol. II., from 1814 to 1848. 12s.

Music, Illustrated History of. By EMIL NAUMANN. Edited by the Rev. Sir F. A. GORE OUSELEY, Bart. Illustrated. Two Vols. 31s. 6d.

National Library, Cassell's. In Weekly Volumes, each containing about **192** pages. Paper covers, 3d.; cloth, 6d. (*A List sent post free on application.*)

Natural History, Cassell's Concise. By E. PERCEVAL **WRIGHT,** M.A., M.D., F.L.S. With several Hundred Illustrations. 7s. 6d.

Natural History, Cassell's New. Edited by Prof. P. **MARTIN** DUNCAN, M.B., F.R.S., F.G.S. With Contributions by **Eminent** Scientific Writers. Complete in Six Vols. With about 2,000 high-class Illustrations. Extra crown 4to, cloth, 9s. each.

Nature, Short Studies from. Illustrated. 5s.

Nimrod in the North; or, Hunting and Fishing Adventures in the Arctic Regions. By F. SCHWATKA. Illustrated. 7s. 6d.

Nursing for the Home and for the Hospital, A Handbook of. By CATHERINE J. WOOD. *Cheap Edition*. 1s. 6d.; cloth, 2s.

Oil Painting, A Manual of. By the Hon. JOHN COLLIER. 2s. 6d.

Our Homes, and How to Make them Healthy. By Eminent Authorities. Illustrated. 15s.; half-morocco, 21s.

Our Own Country. Six Vols. With 1,200 Illustrations. 7s. 6d. each.

Painting, Practical Guides to. With Coloured Plates and full instructions:—Animal Painting, 5s.—China Painting, 5s.—Figure Painting, 7s. 6d.—Flower Painting, 2 Books, 5s. each.—Tree Painting, 5s.—Water-Colour Painting, 5s.—Neutral Tint, 5s.—Sepia. in 2 Vols., 3s each.—Flowers, and how to Paint them, 5s.

Selections from Cassell & Company's Publications.

Paris, Cassell's Illustrated Guide to. 1s.; cloth, **2s.**

Parliaments, A Diary of Two. By H. W. Lucy. The Disraeli Parliament, 1874—1880. 12s. The Gladstone Parliament. 12s.

Paxton's Flower Garden. By Sir Joseph Paxton and Prof. Lindley. Three Vols. With 100 Coloured Plates. £1 1s. each.

Peoples of the World, The. In Six Vols. By Dr. Robert Brown. Illustrated. 7s. 6d. each.

Perak and the Malays, "Sarong" and "**Kris.**" By Major Fred McNair. With Illustrations. 10s. 6d.

Phantom City, The. By W. Westall. 5s.

Photography for Amateurs. By T. C. Hepworth. Illustrated. **1s.**; or cloth, 1s. 6d.

Phrase and Fable, Dictionary of. By the Rev. Dr. Brewer. *Cheap Edition, Enlarged,* cloth, 3s. 6d.; or with leather back, 4s. 6d.

Picturesque America. Complete in Four Vols., with 48 Exquisite Steel Plates and about 800 Original Wood Engravings. £2 2s. each.

Picturesque Canada. With 600 Original Illustrations. Two Vols. £3 3s. each.

Picturesque Europe. Complete in Five Vols. Each containing 13 Exquisite Steel Plates, from Original Drawings, and nearly 200 Original Illustrations. £10 10s. The Popular Edition is published in Five Vols., 18s. each.

Pigeon Keeper, The Practical. By Lewis Wright. Illustrated. 3s. 6d.

Pigeons, The Book of. By Robert Fulton. Edited and Arranged by L. Wright. With 50 Coloured Plates, 31s. 6d.; half-morocco, £2 2s.

Poems and Pictures. With numerous Illustrations. 5s.

Poets, Cassell's Miniature Library of the:—

Burns. Two Vols. 2s. 6d.	Milton. Two Vols. 2s. 6d.
Byron. Two Vols. 2s. 6d.	Scott. Two Vols. 2s. 6d. [2s. 6d.
Hood. Two Vols. 2s. 6d.	Sheridan and Goldsmith. 2 Vols.
Longfellow. Two Vols. 2s. 6d.	Wordsworth. Two Vols. 2s. 6d.

Shakespeare. Twelve Vols., in Case, 15s.

*** *The above are also publishing in cloth, 1s. each Vol.*

Police Code, and Manual of the Criminal Law. By C. E. Howard Vincent, M.P. 2s.

Popular Library, Cassell's. Cloth, 1s. each.

The Russian Empire.	The Story of the English Jacobins.
The Religious Revolution **in the** 16th Century.	Domestic Folk Lore.
	The Rev. Rowland Hill: **Preacher** and Wit.
English Journalism.	Boswell and Johnson: their Companions and Contemporaries.
The Huguenots.	
Our Colonial Empire.	The Scottish Covenanters.
John Wesley.	History of the Free-Trade Movement in England.
The Young Man **in the Battle** of Life.	

Poultry Keeper, The Practical. By L. Wright. With Coloured Plates and Illustrations. 3s. 6d.

Poultry, The Illustrated Book of. By L. Wright. With Fifty Coloured Plates. Cloth, 31s. 6d.; half-morocco, £2 2s.

Poultry, The Book of. By Lewis Wright. *Popular Edition.* 10s. 6d.

Quiver Yearly Volume, The. With about 300 Original Contributions by Eminent Divines and Popular Authors, and upwards of 250 high-class Illustrations. 7s. 6d.

Rabbit-Keeper, The Practical. By Cuniculus. Illustrated. 3s. 6d.

Rainbow Series, Cassell's, of New and Original Novels. Price 1s. each.

As it was Written. By S. Luska.	A Crimson Stain. By A. Bradshaw.
Morgan's Horror. By G. Manville Fenn.	

Rays from the Realms of Nature. By the Rev. J. Neil, M.A. 2s. 6d.

Selections from Cassell & Company's Publications.

Red Library, Cassell's. Stiff covers, 1s. each; cloth, 2s. each; or half-calf, marbled edges, 5s. each.

Old Mortality.	Last Days of Palmyra.
The Hour and the **Man**.	Tales of the Borders.
Scarlet Letter.	American Humour.
Poe's Works.	Sketches by Boz.
Pride and Prejudice.	Macaulay's Lays and **Selected** Essays.
Last of the Mohicans.	
Heart of Midlothian.	Harry Lorrequer.
Last Days of Pompeii.	Old Curiosity Shop.
Yellowplush Papers.	Rienzi.
Handy Andy.	The Talisman.
Washington Irving's Sketch-Book.	Pickwick (2 Vols.)

Representative Poems of Living Poets, American and English. Selected by the Poets themselves. 15s.

Royal River, The: The Thames from Source to Sea. With Descriptive Text and a Series of beautiful Engravings. £2 2s.

Russia. By D. MACKENZIE WALLACE, M.A. 5s.

Russo-Turkish War, **Cassell's History of**. With about 500 Illustrations. Two Vols., 9s. each.

Sandwith, Humphry. A Memoir by T. H. WARD. 7s. 6d.

Saturday Journal, Cassell's. Yearly Volume. 6s.

Science for All. Edited by Dr. ROBERT BROWN, M.A., F.L.S., &c. With 1,500 Illustrations. Five Vols. 9s. each.

Sea, The: Its Stirring Story of Adventure, Peril, and Heroism. By F. WHYMPER. With 400 Illustrations. Four Vols., 7s. 6d. each.

Sent Back by the **Angels**. And other Ballads. By FREDERICK LANGBRIDGE, M.A. Cloth, 4s. 6d.

Shaftesbury, The Earl of, **K.G., The Life and Work of**. By EDWIN HODDER. With Portraits. Three Vols., 36s.

Shakspere, The **Leopold**. With 400 Illustrations. Cloth, 6s.

Shakspere, The Royal. With Steel Plates and Wood Engravings. Three Vols. 15s. each.

Shakespeare, Cassell's Quarto Edition. Edited by CHARLES and MARY COWDEN CLARKE, and containing about 600 Illustrations by H. C. SELOUS. Complete in Three Vols., cloth gilt, £3 3s.

Shakespeare's Romeo and Juliet. *Édition de Luxe*. Illustrated with Twelve Superb Photogravures from Original Drawings by F. DICKSEE, A.R.A. £5 5s.

Shakespearean Scenes and Characters. With 30 Steel Plates and 10 Wood Engravings. The Text written by AUSTIN BRERETON. 21s.

Sketching from Nature in Water Colours. By AARON PENLEY. With Illustrations in Chromo-Lithography. 15s.

Skin and Hair, The Management of the. By MALCOLM MORRIS, F.R.C.S. 2s.

Smith, The Adventures and Discourses of Captain John. By JOHN ASHTON. Illustrated. 5s.

Sports and Pastimes, Cassell's Book of. With more than 800 Illustrations and Coloured Frontispiece. 768 pages. 9s. (Can be had separately thus: Outdoor Sports, 7s. 6d.; Indoor Amusements, 3s. 6d.)

Steam Engine, The Theory and Action of the: for Practical Men. By W. H. NORTHCOTT, C.E. 3s. 6d.

Stock Exchange Year-Book, The. By THOMAS SKINNER. 10s. 6d.

Stones of London, The. By E. F. FLOWER. 6d.

"Stories from Cassell's." A Series of Seven Books. 6d. each; cloth lettered, 9d. each.

Sunlight and Shade. With numerous Exquisite Engravings. 7s. 6d.

Surgery, Memorials of the Craft of, in England. With an Introduction by Sir JAMES PAGET. 21s.

Selections from Cassell & Company's Publications.

Telegraph Guide, The. Illustrated. 1s.
Thackeray, Character Sketches from. Six New and Original Drawings by FREDERICK BARNARD, reproduced in Photogravure. 21s.
Trajan. An American Novel. By H. F. KEENAN. 7s. 6d.
Transformations of Insects, The. By Prof. P. MARTIN DUNCAN, M.B., F.R.S. With 240 Illustrations. 6s.
Treasure Island. By R. L. STEVENSON. Illustrated. 5s.
Treatment, The Year-Book of. A Critical Review for Practitioners of Medicine and Surgery. 5s.
Trees, Familiar. First Series. By G. S. BOULGER, F.L.S., F.G.S With 40 full-page Coloured Plates, from Original Paintings by W. H. J. BOOT. 12s. 6d.
Twenty Photogravures of Pictures in the Salon of 1885, by the leading French Artists.
"Unicode": the Universal Telegraphic Phrase Book. 2s. 6d.
United States, Cassell's History of the. By EDMUND OLLIER. With 600 Illustrations. Three Vols. 9s. each.
Universal History, Cassell's Illustrated. Four Vols. 9s. each.
Vicar of Wakefield and other Works by OLIVER GOLDSMITH. Illustrated. 3s. 6d.
Wealth Creation. By AUGUSTUS MONGREDIEN. 5s.
Westall, W., Novels by. *Popular Editions.* Cloth, 2s. each.
                         RALPH NORBRECK'S TRUST.
    THE OLD FACTORY. | RED RYVINGTON.
What Girls Can Do. By PHYLLIS BROWNE. 2s. 6d.
Wild Animals and Birds: their Haunts and Habits. By Dr. ANDREW WILSON. Illustrated. 7s. 6d.
Wild Birds, Familiar. First and Second Series. By W. SWAYSLAND. With 40 Coloured Plates in each. 12s. 6d. each.
Wild Flowers, Familiar. By F. E. HULME, F.L.S., F.S.A. Five Series. With 40 Coloured Plates in each. 12s. 6d. each.
Winter in India, A. By the Rt. Hon. W. E. BAXTER, M.P. 5s.
Wise Woman, The. By GEORGE MACDONALD. 2s. 6d.
Wood Magic: A Fable. By RICHARD JEFFERIES. 6s.
World of the Sea. Translated from the French of MOQUIN TANDON, by the Very Rev. H. MARTYN HART, M.A. Illustrated. Cloth. 6s.
World of Wit and Humour, The. With 400 Illustrations. Cloth, 7s. 6d.; cloth gilt, gilt edges, 10s. 6d.
World of Wonders. Two Vols. With 400 Illustrations. 7s. 6d. each.
Yule Tide. Cassell's Christmas Annual, 1s.

MAGAZINES.

The Quiver, for Sunday Reading. Monthly, **6d.**
Cassell's Family Magazine. Monthly, 7d.
"Little Folks" Magazine. Monthly, 6d.
The Magazine of Art. Monthly, 1s.
Cassell's Saturday Journal. Weekly, 1d.; Monthly, 6d.

Catalogues of CASSELL & COMPANY'S PUBLICATIONS, which may be had at all Booksellers', or will be sent post free on application to the publishers:—
    CASSELL'S COMPLETE CATALOGUE, containing particulars of One Thousand Volumes.
    CASSELL'S CLASSIFIED CATALOGUE, in which their Works are arranged according to price, from *Threepence to Twenty-five Guineas.*
    CASSELL'S EDUCATIONAL CATALOGUE, containing particulars of CASSELL & COMPANY's Educational Works and Students' Manuals.

CASSELL & COMPANY, LIMITED, *Ludgate Hill, London.*